BETWEEN
BLACK AND WHITE

ELECTION DAY IN KINGSTON. Daguerreotype by Duperly entitled A View of the Court House. *Courtesy of the National Library of Jamaica, Institute of Jamaica, Kingston.*

BETWEEN BLACK AND WHITE

Race, Politics, and the
Free Coloreds in Jamaica,
1792–1865

GAD J. HEUMAN

CONTRIBUTIONS IN COMPARATIVE COLONIAL STUDIES, NUMBER 5

GREENWOOD PRESS
WESTPORT, CONNECTICUT

Library of Congress Cataloging in Publication Data

Heuman, Gad J
   Between Black and White.

   (Contributions in comparative colonial
studies ; no. 5 ISSN 0163-3813)
   Includes bibliographical references and index.
    1. Blacks—Jamaica—History. 2. Jamaica—
Politics and government. 3. Jamaica—Race
relations. I. Title. II. Series.
F1896.N4H48   972.92'00496   80–661
ISBN 0–313–20984–7 (lib. bdg.)

Library of Congress Catalog Card Number: 80–661
ISBN: 0–313–20984–7
ISSN: 0163–3813

First published in 1981

Greenwood Press
A division of Congressional Information Service, Inc.
88 Post Road West, Westport, Connecticut 06881

Printed in the United States of America

10 9 8 7 6 5 4 3 2 1

To Ruthie

Contents

Illustrations

Tables

Series Foreword

In the last three decades the old field of imperial history has fragmented into a variety of fields to the point that virtually no one is thought to be an historian of empire any longer. The purpose of this series in comparative colonial and imperial studies is, in part, to show how this fragmentation has both enriched the old field when viewed as a whole and created new fields more relevant to present concerns. Inter-disciplinary area studies, which seek to focus on a geographical or cultural region, have contributed significantly to imperial history, while obscuring the fact that they are asking some of the same questions in different ways that historians of colonialism have always asked.

Four fields in particular have grown rich in insights and dense with data as a result of our reorientation on the imperial revolution—that fundamental change brought to virtually all present nations of the globe by the period of exploration and discovery, of colonialism and imperialism. Three of these fields stand at the heart of traditional imperial issues: studies of the collaborator (that is, of how empires gained power through the indigenous societies, once dismissed simplistically as "divide and rule" as a technique of governance); studies of social engineering (that is, of how the empires administered their colonies and to what ends); and studies of resistance movements and decolonization. The fourth field deals with the infrastructure of imperialism: race relations. This field has been enormously strengthened by the development of studies of slave systems, ancient and modern, and in particular through the use of comparative methods by which the history of the United States has become integrated with the history of Africa and the West Indies.

It is to this fertile and significant field that Gad Heuman has made a major contribution through his close study of the free coloreds in Jamaica. At once black history, imperial history, and West Indian history, this inquiry into how the free coloreds came to play a significant role in the politics of Jamaica to 1865 is also, by implication, a contribution to the comparative history of race relations and of the United States, for Dr. Heuman shows the options that were open as well as those that were closed to the "free browns" in a society still shaping the full nuance of color prejudice. Thus the conclusions so ably and carefully argued here are of great interest well outside the immediate Jamaican context. (They pose fascinating questions, for example, with respect to the continuing role of the planter class in both Jamaica and Barbados after Emancipation.)

The author brings sophisticated use of quantitative data to his analysis of voting patterns in Jamaica without losing sight of the fact that he is writing a work of historical interpretation. He has been thorough in his use of sources, judicious in his judgments, and meticulous in examining all relevant secondary literature, pointing out how his views differ from the interpretations of others. Dr. Heuman's work joins, and in important ways extends, the earlier work of such scholars as Philip Curtin, Elsa Goveia, Douglas Hall, Orlando Patterson, Edward Brathwaite, William Green, Mavis C. Campbell, Michael Craton, and Barry Higman. Jamaica continues to be the most carefully studied of the West Indian sugar and slavery colonies. Heuman's study has carried the general argument concerning political loyalties and race forward in making way for fresh analysis. In conception and execution this work ably represents the type of study this series was designed to make possible.

Robin W. Winks
Series Editor

Preface

The free people of color occupied an important position in nineteenth-century slave and post-emancipation Jamaica. A small and largely inarticulate group of under 10,000 in 1789, their number had more than tripled by 1825. At the same time, they began to be more vocal politically and organized a movement to gain their civil rights. In 1830, their objective—legal equality with the whites—was achieved. Thereafter, the people of color participated in island politics both at the parish level and in the House of Assembly, and were often a significant political force in the colony.

The chief purpose of this book is to examine the coloreds' role in Jamaican politics during slavery and after emancipation. It charts their campaign for full legal rights, initially in the face of strong white opposition and later with the help of British humanitarians and the Colonial Office. This study suggests that after 1830 the coloreds formed an opposition to the white planter class. Unlike many of the whites, the brown politicians did not regard the island simply as a vehicle for producing sugar. Furthermore, they believed that Jamaica would eventually be controlled by blacks and browns rather than by whites. Because of the politics of the people of color as well as their success in winning seats in the House of Assembly, the plantocracy ultimately stifled the coloreds' political development. The book also raises other issues, especially about the aftermath of slavery. In a multiracial society, how did emancipation affect race relations? Who were the brown and black representatives in the Assembly, and how important was race in determining their party unity and their appeals for votes? What were the politics of the planter class? And how did officials in the Colonial Office respond to developments in Jamaica?

It may be useful to note what this book does not do. No attempt has been made to write a definitive work on the Jamaican people of color. Rather, this study concentrates on the most articulate men of color rather than on the group as a whole. While it has not always been easy to identify even the most prominent people of color, this approach makes it possible to explore their ideas and politics during slavery as well as after emancipation.

There have been several studies on nineteenth-century Jamaica, but only one treats the people of color in detail: Mavis Campbell, *The Dynamics of Change in a Slave Society* (Rutherford, N.J., 1976). Since Campbell's treatment of the people of color is very different from the one adopted here, a general critique of her book is given in Appendix A. Other works that touch on the people of color include Douglas Hall's *Free Jamaica* (New Haven, Conn., 1959). This book, however, is primarily an economic history of the post-emancipation era, and Hall himself cites the need for a closer examination of the politics of the period. Like Hall's book, Philip Curtin's *Two Jamaicas* (Cambridge, Mass., 1955) is invaluable. Yet, as is perhaps apparent from the title, Curtin concentrates on black and white Jamaica. He skims over the particular contribution of the coloreds and the political and social differences between whites and browns. He also suggests that one of the major problems of the colonial society was its failure to generate ideas of its own, and that, frequently, ideas imported from Europe were not applicable in a colonial setting. Although Curtin is generally accurate in describing the origin of ideas among the whites in Jamaica, he is on less certain ground with the coloreds. The people of color developed local solutions to Jamaica's problems: their ideas reflected a creole outlook rather than the unthinking adoption of European attitudes. Finally, a more recent study, William Green's *British Slave Emancipation* (Oxford, 1976), fills a vacuum in our knowledge of the British Caribbean after 1830. But Green focuses on imperial policymaking and ranges widely over the region rather than discussing a single colony.

A large number of people and institutions have been helpful in the course of this work. The bibliography at the end of the book provides a list of the principal libraries and archives in Jamaica, England, and the United States that I have visited. I am grateful to all of them, and I would especially like to mention the extraordinary kindness and assistance of the staff at the West India Reference Library (now the National Library of Jamaica) in the Institute of Jamaica, of Clinton Black and his colleagues at the Jamaica Archives, and of the officials in the Island Record Office.

The Council on Comparative and European Studies at Yale University provided generous funding for research in Jamaica and in England. Robin Winks ably guided the formative stages of this study and has continued to do so as an editor. Without him, this book would not have been completed. Sydney Mintz not only explained the intricacies of Caribbean anthropology but also opened many doors in Jamaica.

Brief portions of this book have appeared elsewhere. I am grateful to the University of Surrey and the Royal Institute of Linguistics and Anthropology as well as to Malcolm Cross and Arnaud Marks for permission to use an essay of mine that was published in their *Peasants, Plantations and Rural Communities in the Caribbean* (University of Surrey and Royal Institute of Linguistics and Anthropology, 1979). Parts of Chapters 1 and 6 appeared in *The Journal of Caribbean History*, Volume 14 (1980). In addition, several paragraphs in Appendix A were first printed in *The Journal of Imperial and Commonwealth History*, Volume 6 (1978). I wish to thank the publishers of these journals for allowing me to use this material.

I was particularly fortunate in the help I received during a year spent in Jamaica. Douglas Hall calmed the immigration authorities at a crucial point and offered much sound advice. H. P. Jacobs and the late Ansell Hart pointed me in directions that more standard sources had not revealed. On subsequent visits, Barry Higman provided generous hospitality. He also supplied the map of Jamaica (Figure 1) and commented on an earlier draft of the book.

In England, the members of the imperial history seminar at the Institute of Historical Research, University of London, put up with, and ably criticized, more papers on the free coloreds than they might care to remember. Colin Clarke, Richard Hart, and David Lowenthal all read earlier versions of this study, while Freda Harcourt and Donald Wood commented on parts of the manuscript as it progressed. My colleagues at the University of Warwick, particularly Alistair Hennessy, were especially understanding about the demands of completing a book. Elsewhere, Franklin Knight and Arnold Sio also read drafts of the entire manuscript, and Sio spent a considerable amount of time sharing with me his extensive knowledge of the Jamaican free coloreds. Lewis Weinstock helped to clarify the writing, and Phyllis Woodford and Janet Marks made improvements in the text in addition to typing it. However, I am responsible for any errors that remain.

To my wife, I owe the most. She prepared the figures and helped to compile the statistics in Chapter 9 and also proved to be a stern critic. Even more importantly, she encouraged the project all along the way. The book is dedicated to her.

A Note on Terminology

In dealing with the free coloreds, various problems of definition arise. For the purposes of this book, the term *free people of color* is used as they defined it themselves: that is, to denote persons who were neither white nor black. Its synonyms include browns, coloreds, and men of color. Unless otherwise stated, these terms refer to free persons; the word *free*, however, is not repeated in every case. The term *mulatto* is generally avoided, except in quotations and when specifically referring to a person who was the offspring of a white and a black.

There is a further semantic difficulty in writing about the free coloreds. During the slave period and generally after emancipation, the people of color used *colored* and its synonyms to refer exclusively to browns. But travelers and local officials did not always follow this practice. Sometimes they used these words to mean browns only and at other times to denote blacks and browns. Since the variety of usages has led to some confusion, scholars have recently developed their own terminology to deal with the problem. (For example, see Jerome S. Handler, *The Unappropriated People* [Baltimore, 1974], pp. 5–6.) The term *freedmen* is therefore employed here to refer to persons of both sexes who were either colored or black and born free or manumitted. (*Freedwomen* is used when women in this category are referred to specifically.) In this study, *freedmen* generally serves as a synonym for free coloreds and free blacks, although it is also used when the color composition of a group or an individual is unclear. It is especially important to keep in mind the use of the term *freedmen* in the early chapters of the book, because free blacks and browns enjoyed the same legal rights during slavery and are therefore often treated together.

However, the terms *free colored* and *free black* are used to differentiate the various groups among the freedmen, when appropriate.

Less of a semantic problem is the word *creole*. It refers to anyone born in the British Caribbean, regardless of color. Since the publication of Edward Brathwaite's *The Development of Creole Society in Jamaica* (Oxford, 1971), the term has taken on an additional meaning, implying a local point of view, as opposed to a primarily metropolitan attitude. I have used it in this sense as well.

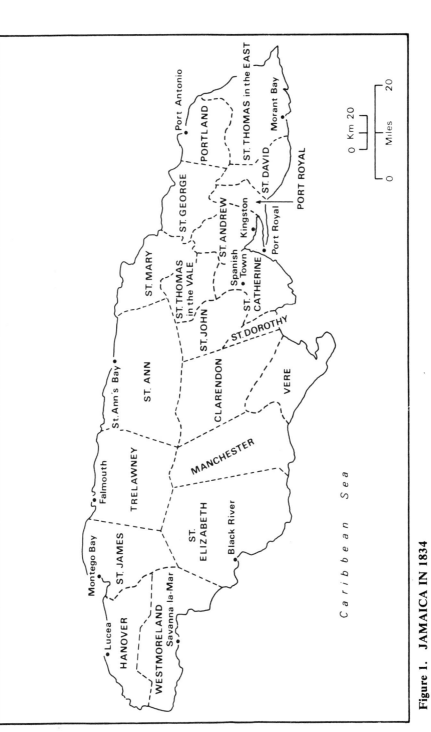

Figure 1. JAMAICA IN 1834

Abbreviations

ASSP	Anti-Slavery Society Papers, Rhodes House, Oxford
CO	Colonial Office Records, Public Record Office, London
IRO	Island Record Office, Spanish Town, Jamaica
JAJ	*Journals of the Assembly of Jamaica*
MMS	Methodist Missionary Society Records, London
PP	*British Parliamentary Papers*
PRO	Public Record Office, London
VAJ	*Votes of the Assembly of Jamaica*

BETWEEN
BLACK AND WHITE

The Free Coloreds in Jamaican Slave Society

Jamaican slave society was dominated numerically by blacks and economically by whites. Africans had little choice about their importation to Jamaica; whites, on the other hand, often came to the island with little intention of settling there permanently. Many whites worked on the sugar plantations, with the hope of returning home as wealthy absentee owners. However, the majority of them never attained their goal. A contemporary observer has estimated that no less than four-fifths of the white settlers died before they had "realized a sufficiency while only a favoured few (perhaps no more than five or six in a hundred) ever returned to their native country with a fortune, or competency."[1]

In the eighteenth century, it seemed worth taking the risk. Jamaica's plantation economy was booming, and the dramatic increase in the number of slaves and in cane production was evidence of this rapid growth. In 1673, there were only 9,504 slaves on the island; this figure jumped to 86,546 by 1734, and within the next thirty years, the slave population almost doubled. Sugar output kept pace. While the island yielded an insignificant amount of cane in 1675, by 1739 there were 429 estates producing 33,000 hogsheads of sugar per annum. During the following two decades, the number of plantations rose to 640.[2]

Since sugar was the mainstay of the economy, planters played an important role in the life of the colony. Those who retired to England often sought to safeguard Jamaican and West Indian interests through the activities of the West India Committee.[3] Because many of them could afford to buy seats in Parliament, they formed a group that was able to influence colonial policymaking. Planters who remained in Jamaica dominated politics there as delegates to the local House of Assembly.[4] But not all whites on the Jamaican plantations were wealthy estate owners. Whites also served as bookkeepers, supervising the slaves in the field and in the boiling house; as overseers, superintending the planting and giving the daily orders; and as skilled artisans. In the absence of a resident proprietor, an attorney acted as the agent of the absentee. Since attorneys frequently had more than one plantation under their supervision, they were among the most important men on the island.[5]

Whites did other work as well. Edward Brathwaite has estimated that between 18,000 and 24,000 whites lived in Jamaica around the turn of the nineteenth century, not including an "upper class" of about 6,000 wealthy planters, merchants, and their families. Those in the towns accounted for a large proportion of this total: some of them were in the professions, while others were involved in a wide range of commercial and skilled activities. Brathwaite's conclusions suggest that the white population was larger and more diverse than previous research has indicated.[6] Nonetheless, many whites expressed a strong urge to return home; adhering to this ideal, the white offspring of planters were often sent to Europe for their education. Few probably ever came back to resettle on the island.[7]

The effect of this absentee mentality was apparent in the social life of the colony.[8] There was a shortage of white women in Jamaica, at least partly because of an unwritten rule that young planters arriving in the island remain single. With an overwhelming slave population and a scarcity of white females, intercourse between white males and black slave women became common.[9] The resulting brown population added another dimension to Jamaican society which was to prove a recurrent problem in the eighteenth and nineteenth centuries.

The offspring of whites and slaves at first merged into the slave population. Since the children of these unions inherited the status of their mothers, they were born slaves. However, colored slaves usually received preferential treatment, in part because whites believed that people of mixed color could not work in the fields as effectively as blacks. Brown slaves had a greater opportunity to learn skills, and many worked as house slaves. White attitudes toward the people of color also meant that they were more likely to gain their freedom than blacks. According to one contemporary estimate, 80 percent of freedmen were colored and 20 percent black.[10] The liberality of many white fathers added to the population of freedmen. Whites often manumitted their black or brown mistresses and their illegitimate children, sometimes at birth. But whatever their parentage, freedmen did not become the legal equals of whites; for them manumission meant only a release from ownership and was not a grant of full civil rights.[11]

In time, freedmen formed a separate group in Jamaican society with their own social hierarchies and a specific nomenclature to account for their varied racial origins.[12] While the law did not recognize these color distinctions, it divided the freedmen on the basis of birth. Blacks and browns born of free mothers were entitled to trial by jury, but those born as slaves and later freed were still subject to slave courts. In addition, manumitted freedmen could not give evidence in court against free-born coloreds and blacks. Despite these differences, the two groups of freedmen shared in common the other disabilities directed against the free nonwhite community.[13]

The restrictions limited the freedmen's political, economic, and social life. Like slaves, free blacks and coloreds could not participate in politics, which meant that they were not eligible to sit in the legislature and, after a law enacted in 1733, that they lost the right to vote. Freedmen were not allowed in court to give evidence against whites and were barred from serving on juries. Moreover, their participation in the economic life of the colony was severely restricted. An act passed in 1711 made it an offense to employ a free black or brown person in a public office. A year later, the Assembly approved a bill prohibiting them from acting as navigators or driving carriages for hire, probably to ensure that they would not encroach on jobs held by whites. More importantly, the deficiency legislation of 1715 served to exclude freedmen from supervisory positions on the plantations. The measure imposed fines on planters who did not retain a certain number of whites on each estate in proportion to the plantation's slave population. Even free colored estate owners had to employ whites in proportion to the slaves they owned, as the coloreds and their families did not qualify to avoid the deficiency fines. In the last half of the eighteenth century, planters increasingly chose to pay the fines rather than maintain the prescribed ratio of whites on their estates. Nonetheless, the general habit of barring freedmen from posts on the plantations continued.[14]

The Assembly also enacted legislation to differentiate free blacks and browns from the rest of society. One act stated that any freedman who did not own land and at least ten slaves had to wear a blue cross on his right shoulder.[15] Freedmen also had to register in a parish and to appear before a magistrate for proper certification of their freedom. Not surprisingly, freedmen regarded these requirements as degrading. They complained that the statutes created "an ignominious distinction, which can answer no purpose but to render them[selves] odious."[16]

The delegates to the House were not averse to making some minor improvements in the status of the freedmen. In 1748, the representatives therefore granted manumitted blacks and browns the same rights in court as those who had been born free.[17] This measure reflected the increasing wealth of at least part of the free black and brown population. Although there were restrictions on the freedmen's economic opportunities, planters on occasion left estates to their colored children or to their mistresses. As this trend increased, whites became alarmed at the amount of land the free coloreds and blacks were inheriting. An inquiry by the House of Assembly in 1761 substantiated these fears when the representatives found that property already bequeathed to freedmen was valued between £200,000 and £300,000. As a result, the assemblymen moved to counteract this development. They approved legislation that prohibited whites from leaving real or personal property worth more than £1,200 (sterling) to any colored or black. Combined with the earlier disabilities against the freedmen, this statute crippled their potential economic growth.[18] The whites had decided that it was more important to keep the land in European hands than to follow parental instincts.

But restrictive legislation against the freedmen did not apply to all of them. Some coloreds and blacks successfully appealed to the Assembly for a remission of the various enactments. The earliest example of this kind occurred in the 1707–1708 session and allowed two manumitted free blacks the right of trial by jury. Another bill which granted a free black similar concessions specified the reasons for the award: it noted that the recipient had discovered a French plot to invade the island and was a Christian as well. The next privilege bill passed in 1733 was more generous, as it accorded a brown man and his family all the rights of Englishmen born of white ancestors. While this was a considerable concession, the acts that followed it usually required the privileged freedmen to marry whites if their children were to inherit the same immunities. According to a later report, some freedwomen complied with this stipulation by marrying white husbands. Certainly most of those who applied for privileges after 1733 were mulatto or quadroon women and their children.[19]

The privileged freedmen presented a serious problem for the whites. Often better educated than the planters, the privileged blacks and coloreds generally adopted European values and rejected any association with slaves or any link with Africa.[20] Many of them were wealthy and owned slaves themselves. Yet, the position of the privileged freedmen upset the racial stereotype that was at the heart of the slave society. For the system to be successful, slaves had to associate the ownership of land and people with whites; slaveholding freedmen were dangerous because their existence suggested that browns and blacks were no different from whites. The situation was complicated because psychological considerations of parentage were involved. Without attempting to analyze these implications, it seems clear that the privileged coloreds and blacks raised the question of the freedman's place in Jamaica to its logical conclusion. In 1761, the delegates to the Assembly were no longer willing to face the issue. When they realized how much wealth was passing into colored and black hands, they not only put a limit on the size of wills but also ceased granting full civil rights to those who applied for them. After 1761, privileges were fewer and less generous. Many petitioners were not allowed to hold public office of any kind, and some privilege acts were limited to the right of testifying against whites in court.[21]

The legislation in 1761 significantly affected the legal status of the privileged blacks and coloreds as well as the economic development of the group as a whole. However, it did little to halt the freedmen's numerical growth. As Table 1 shows, the free brown population increased rapidly during the remainder of the eighteenth and early part of the nineteenth centuries. The growth was particularly evident in the period preceding emancipation. Even though the figures are unreliable, it seems likely that the free colored population more than tripled during the three decades after 1790 and that it surpassed the white population during the 1820s. There was also a considerable expansion of the free black population in this period.

Scattered figures for individual parishes reveal the extent of the free brown population in 1812 (Table 2). By then, they made up nearly half the total free population in St. George and Westmoreland. When the number of free blacks is taken into account, it is apparent that whites were already becoming a minority of the free population in Westmoreland as well as in St. Thomas in the East. More ominous for the whites was the number of free black and colored children. As Table 3 suggests, in two of the four parishes cited, the population of free black and brown children was three times that of the equivalent white group. In one parish, St. Thomas in the East, the number of free black and

TABLE 1. ESTIMATES OF THE POPULATION IN JAMAICA, 1768–1844

YEAR	WHITE	FREE COLORED		FREE BLACK	SLAVES	TOTAL
1768	17,000		3,700		167,000	187,700
1789	18,000		10,000		250,000	278,000
1807	30,000	—		—	300,000	—
1825	—	28,800		10,000	—	—
1834	16,600	31,000		11,000	310,000	368,600
Census	Whites	Colored		Black		Total
1844	15,776	68,529		293,128		377,433

SOURCES: John Stewart, *A View of the Past and Present State of the Island of Jamaica* (Edinburgh, 1823), p. 23; Edward Long, *The History of Jamaica*, 3 vols. (London, 1774), 2: 337; CO 318/76, Campbell to Hill, December 1825, Schedule B; CO 137/175, Lushington to Courtenay, September 17, 1826; Douglas Hall, "Jamaica," in David W. Cohen and Jack P. Greene (eds.), *Neither Slave Nor Free* (Baltimore, 1972), p. 194; Edward Brathwaite, *The Development of Creole Society in Jamaica, 1770–1820* (Oxford, 1971), p. 152; B. W. Higman, *Slave Population and Economy in Jamaica, 1807–1834* (Cambridge, 1976), pp. 142, 144; G. W. Roberts, *The Population of Jamaica* (Cambridge, 1957), p. 39; Sheila Duncker, "The Free Coloured and Their Fight for Civil Rights in Jamaica, 1800–1830" (unpublished M.A. thesis, University of London, 1960), p. 10.

The eighteenth- and early nineteenth-century figures are based on contemporary accounts of the period, and the 1825 figures for free colored and free black on John Campbell's "Memorandum" of that year. The 1834 figure for whites is based on B. W. Higman's calculation for 1832; the figures for free colored and free black in 1834 tally roughly with the census of 1844, assuming, as Higman does, that 10 percent of the slaves were colored in 1834 and adopting G. W. Roberts' calculation of a 1 percent per annum growth rate for coloreds between 1834 and 1844 (although Roberts' figure was worked out for a slightly later period). The figures for free colored and free black in 1834 are higher than Hall's total of 35,000 freedmen and closer to Duncker's calculation of 44,435 freedmen in that year.

TABLE 2. THE FREE POPULATION IN FOUR JAMAICAN PARISHES, 1812

PARISH	NUMBER			PERCENTAGE OF FREE POPULATION		
	WHITE	FREE COLORED*	FREE BLACK	WHITE	FREE COLORED	FREE BLACK
St. George	379	343	32	50.3	45.5	4.2
Westmoreland	688	790	119	43.1	49.5	7.4
Portland	415	180		70.0	30.0	
St. Thomas in the East	434	463		48.4	51.6	

*The figures for free colored for Portland and St. Thomas in the East include free black as well.
SOURCE: CO 137/136, Morrison to Bathurst, January 28, 1813, no. 21, enclosures in CO 137/137.

colored children was more than seven times that of white children. Since most of these children were free browns, the statistics must have caused concern among the whites about the future size of the free colored population.

The available figures are also suggestive about the sexual composition of the free brown population. According to John Campbell, a prominent free man of color from St. James, there were twice as many adult females as males among the free coloreds in 1825. Out of a total of 28,800 free people of color, Campbell estimated that there were 4,800 adult males and 9,600 adult females. G. W. Roberts has made use of more reliable statistics on the number and sex of slave manumissions to make a similar point. Lumping together free browns and blacks, Roberts found that 2,566 females were manumitted between 1817 and 1829 compared with 1,445 males during the same period. These statistics provide further evidence of the sexual imbalance in the freedmen population.[22]

The nature of the legislation against the freedmen as well as the statistics on

TABLE 3. FREE CHILDREN IN FOUR JAMAICAN PARISHES, 1812

PARISH	NUMBER		PERCENTAGE OF FREE POPULATION	
	WHITE	FREE COLORED AND FREE BLACK	WHITE	FREE COLORED AND FREE BLACK
St. George	67	183	8.9	24.3
Westmoreland	127	373	8.0	23.4
Portland	102	49	17.1	8.2
St. Thomas in the East	16	114	1.8	12.7

SOURCE: CO 137/136, Morrison to Bathurst, January 28, 1813, no. 21, enclosures in CO 137/137.

their distribution make it clear that free blacks and people of color lived primarily in towns. The deficiency legislation meant that it was difficult for them to become landowners, and the law of 1761 limited this possibility even further. Moreover, the towns offered them the best chance of employment. Kingston had the largest number of free coloreds and blacks; an estimate in 1788 put their numbers at 3,280, or 12 percent of the city's population. Since more than 2,700 of the freedmen were brown, there was a high proportion of free coloreds among the urban freedmen.[23] St. Catherine also had a significant freedmen population. In 1796, there were 1,902 free coloreds and blacks in the parish, most of them from Spanish Town.[24] Thus, nearly half of Jamaica's freedmen lived in Spanish Town or Kingston at the end of the eighteenth century. Freedmen also made their homes in the other towns around the island and constituted an important segment of the population in the parish of St. Elizabeth.[25] The early nineteenth century witnessed their continued expansion in the urban areas of Jamaica. In Kingston, for example, the free blacks and coloreds were the fastest growing part of the city's population during this period, with one report suggesting a total of nearly 10,000 freedmen in 1825.[26]

In the towns, many of the freedmen performed the same work as slaves. They found jobs in shops, they acted as servants and porters, and they were employed as boatmen and sailors. As elsewhere in the British Caribbean, the more fortunate freedmen occupied a middle ground between the upper ranks of the slaves and the poorer whites.[27] Women in this category became shopkeepers and sold provisions, millinery, confectionery, and preserves. They usually had two or three slaves who traveled into the interior of the island to sell commodities on the estates. In addition, freedwomen owned and managed lodging houses throughout the island.[28]

Many free colored and black men also had a small number of slaves working for them; these freedmen were often mechanics, artisans, or tradesmen. Sheila Duncker has reported on the predominance of tradesmen among this group. In the St. Catherine Register of Free Persons, she found a list of freedmen and their occupations, which included "two taylors, three masons, a farrier, two planters, four carpenters, a wheelwright, a tavern keeper and a 'Butcher near the Race Course.' "[29] Other free coloreds were finding different kinds of work. During the first few decades of the nineteenth century, more free browns were becoming clerks and there was an increasing number of brown schoolmasters. A significant proportion of the local merchants involved in the American-West Indian trade were colored. Several became creditors of the estate owners and then planters themselves when difficult economic conditions after the Napoleonic Wars forced many plantations into near bankruptcy. Free coloreds and blacks also were acquiring property in towns, some of which provided income in the form of rents.[30] Most of the freedmen who remained in the country, on the other hand, grew provisions for the weekday markets, although the wealthier free blacks and coloreds tended to cultivate pimento and ginger or raise cattle. Despite the bias against them, there were some brown overseers as well as a few colored estate owners who had inherited their properties before the limitation on legacies.[31]

The influx of free coloreds and blacks from St. Domingue at the end of the eighteenth century increased the range of occupations among the freedmen in Jamaica. Many of the refugees from the Haitian Revolution were skilled craftsmen; these included goldsmiths, cabinet makers, shoemakers, dyers, tanners, and bakers. While the women often kept shops that sold provisions and liquor, agriculturalists among the immigrant freedmen had a more lasting effect on Jamaican produce. They significantly improved techniques for growing coffee and for irrigating land.[32]

The free coloreds thus worked in a variety of occupations. As a group, they were better off economically than free blacks, but it is important to note that most of the free browns were at the lower end of the economic scale. One measure of this relative poverty was their contribution to the island treasury. The duke of Manchester (William Montagu), who was governor of Jamaica from 1808 to 1827, pointed out in 1823 that their share of the taxes was less than 3 percent of the total amount paid by whites.[33] John Campbell also provided evidence that the overwhelming majority of the people of color were in a difficult economic position. In 1825, he estimated that 22,900 free browns were "absolutely poor," while only 400 were "rich" and 5,500 in "fair circumstances."[34] Although there were clearcut economic differences among the coloreds, they shared a common goal. As Duncker has noted, "fundamental to all free colored was a desire to be measured by the same yardsticks as those used for people in similar positions who were white."[35] The nature of Jamaican slave society meant that it would be difficult to attain their goal.

But what was the position of the free coloreds in Jamaican slave society? While the evidence is slight on the "absolutely poor" people of color, more information is available on the rest of the free colored population. Relations between browns and whites are also better documented than those between browns and blacks. In general, the free people of color were excluded from the high society that existed on the island as well as from the society of the lower class whites. It would not have occurred to the governor's wife, Lady Nugent, in 1803 to invite coloreds to her parties and dinners in Spanish Town, but she would receive brown women privately when visiting estates in the country. Even this behavior was not typical of that of less transient whites. The European Club, which admitted colonists of at least twenty-five years' residence in the island, pointedly invited *Europeans only* to an anniversary meeting in 1794.[36] Attitudes had not changed much three decades later. A Jamaican planter noted in 1827 that whites not only disliked "the contact and strong smell of a negro" but also had "been used from infancy to keep mulatto men at a distance."[37] The planters generally refused to mix with even wealthy or well-educated people of color, although this rule was relaxed in the case of a few privileged people of color.

Whites seem to have regarded the coloreds with a mixture of superstition and contempt. They maintained, for example, that the people of color were incapable of producing children. Although an absentee owner found that this was not the case, he concluded after a visit to Jamaica that coloreds were weak and effeminate. Governor Manchester also had doubts about the qualities of the people of color despite his numerous brown children. When the Colonial Office asked him to recommend free coloreds for overseas service in Africa, Manchester commented on their timidity and lack of resolution.[38]

Despite their belief that the people of color were inferior, the whites were uncertain whether the coloreds would prove a threat to their continued supremacy or a potential support for it. A well-traveled stipendiary magistrate, R. R. Madden, noted that the whites distrusted brown men because they were potential rebels in disguise.[39] Planters feared that the Jamaican people of color might follow the example of the Haitian coloreds and help to destroy the system of slavery. Some whites, however, argued that coloreds could serve as a protection against the slaves. The most important contemporary historians of eighteenth-century Jamaica and the British Caribbean agreed that the brown slaves should be freed and apprenticed in a trade or business. This would create a group between the whites and the blacks who "would naturally attach themselves to the white race as the most honourable relations, and so become a barrier against the designs of the Blacks."[40]

In spite of such ideas, the free people of color had little access to white society. Some groups of free coloreds, such as those who were educated abroad, were particularly bitter about their situation. Often accepted as whites in Britain, these coloreds were dismayed by their reception in Jamaica when they returned home. One of the most articulate of them who had spent time in England, Richard Hill, noted that the educated coloreds regarded themselves in Jamaica as "blasted trees—'barkless, branchless, and blighted trunks upon a cursed root.' " The reaction of another man of color traveling home from Europe was less literary but nonetheless indicative of what was likely to happen. On landing in Barbados, he went ashore to a tavern with his fellow travelers, only to be singled out by the waiter who informed him that he could not sit down with gentlemen. Astonished, the colored man followed the waiter to another room and "burst into tears."[41]

Usually barred from the society of whites and often rejecting the company of blacks, the people of color staged their own entertainments. Like the whites, they organized balls and dinners that were as expensive and often more lively than those they could not attend. The planter and writer Monk Lewis described a ball that was limited to brown people; more often, colored women sponsored dances specifically for white men.[42] While these social events upset any generalizations about racial segregation, they did not alter the prevailing views about the inferiority of the people of color.

Free browns were constantly reminded of their lower status. Coloreds entered the theater by a different door than whites and sat apart from them; sometimes there were separate performances for whites and free coloreds. The people of color faced similar restrictions in the Anglican church. Although they worshipped together with whites, coloreds occupied special galleries or pews. This was a cause of much complaint not only because of the supposed brotherhood of all men but also because whites were often allotted more space than they could use. The separation of browns and whites continued after death. Each group had its own burial ground, and church bells rang longer for whites than for people of color.[43]

The Methodists proved to be more popular among the free coloreds, in part because of the Dissenters' lack of exclusiveness in seating arrangements and in the church hierarchy. In Kingston, free coloreds comprised half of the membership and two-thirds of the attendance at the Wesleyan missions. They often donated land for new chapels and subsidized the building of churches. Free people of color also held prominent positions as society officials, sometimes advising the missionaries and holding the societies together when illness or death among the missionaries interrupted their work. Yet, despite this help, the free browns were not treated as the social equals of the European missionaries. No missionary married a free colored woman, and the missionaries were accused in the 1830s of being prejudiced against the people of color.[44]

In contrast to this situation, the opportunities for the education of colored children seemed to provide a measure of equality between whites and people of color. Free coloreds were occasionally admitted to formerly white schools. In the case of Wolmer's Free School in Kingston, colored pupils formed the majority of the student body by 1822, only seven years after the first brown student was admitted. But Wolmer's was an exception, and even there white students seemed to leave in preference for segregated schools once the color bar had been breached. Elsewhere in the island, the educational facilities for the people of color were limited. A missionary noted that the means of education in the western district were inadequate even for white children "and still more for free browns, who could not mix with the others, and had long been treated as if they had no right to be free."[45] In St. James, the free coloreds sought to establish a school for poor colored students largely from their own funds but were unable to get any help from the parish vestry. The situation improved by the 1830s as more schools were open to brown children, especially in Kingston. Nonetheless, several years after emancipation there still remained a small handful of private schools that were limited to whites.[46]

Like the students at Wolmer's, the colored "housekeepers" also appeared to be on an equal footing with whites. This pattern of black or brown females cohabiting informally with white men was so widely accepted that one observer noted that it involved nine-tenths of the colored women on the island. The practice enabled some brown women to become economically secure. Monk Lewis described the colored landlady of an inn who was the mistress of an English merchant in Kingston and who owned a house of her own. Brown mistresses could have certain customary rights: whites would in some cases contract to pay large sums of money to them in case they married or left the island. Such economic rewards were greater than brown men could usually offer, and there was the prospect for colored women of children who were lighter in color. As in the contemporary Caribbean, these considerations were often more important than the question of legitimacy.[47]

Despite these advantages, the housekeeping system was not an equal partnership. On the contrary, it was a further example of the subordinate position of the free coloreds. Brown women were never accepted in white society. Apart from rare exceptions, they could not marry the men they lived with. In addition, the system served to debase men of color who were forced to cohabit with free blacks or slaves. As in the case of the Portuguese colonists in West Africa, the Jamaican planters' informal relations with colored women did not overturn the prevailing pattern of white superiority. Instead, the system of concubinage reflected the social inferiority of the people of color and their general exclusion from white society.[48]

Yet, there were free coloreds—like the privileged brown man James Swaby—who were not subject to these restrictions. Swaby was a rich planter who owned at least two estates and several hundred slaves; he was educated at Charterhouse and served in the British army. In supporting his application for special rights, the attorney general of Jamaica reported that Swaby "is highly esteemed by the different white inhabitants of Manchester and is admitted to their society and treated in every respect as a white person."[49] Thomas Drummond was in a similar positon. He was also a wealthy colored planter who had inherited a large estate and was the proprietor in 1823 of a 1,200-acre estate and 115 slaves. Since he had "acquired the respect of the Community in which he has resided," Drummond believed he was "entitled to greater privileges than the general class of people of free condition."[50]

These examples suggest that it was possible for a few privileged browns to gain entry into white society in spite of their color. Unlike the colonists in the United States, white Jamaicans had begun to take account of class as well as color considerations in determining status. But the acceptance of a small number of brown people into white society did not improve relations between whites and browns as a whole.[51] The experience of a young man of color, Martin Halhead, was evidence that problems between free coloreds and whites would continue as long as most brown people were denied their rights.

In late May 1813, the Kingston Common Council declared that certain parts of the Anglican church in Kingston would be set apart for whites. It is unclear whether this was a new ruling or an alteration of an existing arrangement. A few weeks later, Halhead refused to leave a pew reserved for whites during a regular Sunday service. When he was eventually taken out, he warned white officials that "your power is over or at an end; take care how you act." Once in court, Halhead insulted the magistrates and was placed under custody. Another person of color who was willing to serve as Halhead's bail was also arrested.[52]

Although Halhead was soon released, he continued to be a problem for the authorities. Two years later, he was in jail again, this time because of a riot in front of the Kingston Theater. A group of coloreds led by Halhead had picketed the theater and collected signatures from people of color against possible new color bar restrictions. The riot that accompanied the demonstration required the military to quell the disturbance, and only the governor's clemency saved Halhead and a fellow agitator from the pillory.[53] Yet, while Halhead's response to the segregation of the coloreds attracted considerable attention, his actions were not directed toward a fundamental reform of the society. He was not attempting to abolish slavery or even to ameliorate the condition of the slaves. Instead, Halhead joined the overwhelming majority of coloreds who accepted the divisions between slave and free and who wanted to have the same rights as whites.

Coloreds thus emphasized their affinity with the whites in a variety of ways. For example, they sought to imitate European fashions, often in an exaggerated form. Brown women frequently dressed in the latest and loudest English clothes to outdo their white competitors. In addition, the people of color formed the largest church-going group in Jamaica in proportion to their numbers and were more interested in European literary and cultural developments than were the white creoles. They established various educational societies, including the Society for the Diffusion of Useful Knowledge and the St. James Institute for Promoting General and Useful Knowledge.[54] Even though whites probably did not participate in these organizations, the societies were another way for brown men to differentiate themselves from blacks and to assimilate aspects of European civilization.

Free coloreds not only adopted white values but also tended to compensate for their lower status by abusing slaves. Many travelers reported that brown men were harsher masters than whites and were more likely to mistreat their slaves. A common Jamaican saying reflected the feeling that slaves preferred white owners: "If me for have massa or misses, give me Buckra one—no give me mulatto, dem no use neega well."[55] Even so, brown slaveowners were concerned about being identified with the slaves and refused to do any work on the estates that could link them with slavery. Free coloreds would not "cut cane, load carts, drive mules, carry trash" or perform any other tasks which in their mind belonged to slaves.[56] A white planter claimed that "they would rather starve than engage in agricultural labour—of course I mean manual labour."[57]

Coloreds also frequently sought to maintain the same distinctions toward slaves which characterized relations between browns and whites. Two abolitionists who visited Jamaica in the 1830s reported that free brown settlers in St. Elizabeth refused to send their children to a school where brown and black pupils were treated equally. Similarly, the Baptist missionary William Knibb encountered problems with free colored parents who were opposed to sending their children to schools that mixed freedmen with slaves.[58] There were exceptions. Recent evidence suggests that the free colored men in Kingston and Spanish Town often mated with black slaves. As there were more whites in the towns, the coloreds had difficulty competing with them for free colored women and turned to blacks.[59] But the racial attitudes of the coloreds who sought to keep black and brown students apart were probably more typical. This type of prejudice was not confined to browns and blacks. Since browns themselves differed in shade and in status, those who were most like the whites emphasized their distance from the rest of the free colored population.

Governor Manchester was aware of the tensions between the lighter and darker brown people. In a dispatch to the Colonial Office, he noted that the dark coloreds and blacks were "indignant at the superiority which those of fairer complexion claim over them."[60] More than a decade later, the lighter complexioned coloreds were still maintaining the same posture. A letter writer to *The Herald and Literary Journal* directed his anger at the offending browns: "You boast of personal attractions, but even after you have added to your loveliness by the application of patent washes for the improvement of your skins, I can discover nothing in you but your ignorance and conceit."[61] As in the case of brown attitudes toward blacks, light-colored freedmen assumed a superiority on the basis of their superficial closeness to whites.

Thus, considerations of color were crucial to the people of color. The light-complexioned browns, the free coloreds who abused their slaves, and the privileged people of color all sought to identify with the whites and generally to distance themselves from the blacks. The result was not a closer union of whites and browns, but rather the advancement of a small group of coloreds who were legally differentiated from the people of color as a whole. Although the whites allowed a tiny fraction of the people of color to enjoy a special status in Jamaica, this did not alter the plight of the overwhelming majority of coloreds. The petitions and campaigns of the free coloreds for an improvement in their legal condition highlighted this situation even further.

NOTES

1. John Stewart, *A View of the Past and Present State of the Island of Jamaica* (Edinburgh, 1823), p. 179.
2. Ibid.; W. J. Gardner, *A History of Jamaica* (London, 1873), p. 155.
3. Although there were separate groups of West Indian merchants and planters

who met on occasion during the eighteenth century, the West India Committee was first established in 1775. For more information on it, see Douglas Hall, *A Brief History of the West India Committee* (Barbados, 1971) and Lillian Penson, *The Colonial Agents of the British West Indies* (London, 1924), Chapter 10.

4. The House of Assembly was an all-white body elected on a £10 franchise. Each parish in Jamaica was allowed two representatives; exceptions were Kingston, Port Royal, and St. Catherine which had three.

5. Stewart, *A View of Jamaica*, Chapter 12; Gardner, *History*, p. 120.

6. Edward Brathwaite, *The Development of Creole Society in Jamaica, 1770–1820* (Oxford, 1971), Chapter 10; Lowell J. Ragatz, *The Fall of the Planter Class in the British Caribbean, 1763–1833* (New York, 1928), p. 9.

7. Lowell J. Ragatz, "Absentee Landlordism in the British Caribbean, 1750–1833," *Agricultural History* 5 (January 1931): 7–9. For a critique of Ragatz's view on the effects of absentee landlordism, see Douglas Hall, "Absentee-Proprietorship in the British West Indies," *Jamaican Historical Review* 4 (1964): 15–35.

8. For a discussion of the effects of absenteeism, see Orlando Patterson, *The Sociology of Slavery* (London, 1967), pp. 38–44. Edward Brathwaite has critically examined Patterson's work in "Jamaican Slave Society, A Review," *Race* 11 (1968): 331–42.

9. Winthrop D. Jordan, "American Chiaroscuro: The Status and Definition of Mulattoes in the British Colonies," *The William and Mary Quarterly* 19 (April 1962): 195–98.

10. Arnold A. Sio, "Race, Colour and Miscegenation: The Free Coloured of Jamaica and Barbados," *Caribbean Studies* 16 (April 1976): 7. For a discussion of brown slaves and their greater chance of becoming free in the Leeward Islands, see Elsa V. Goveia, *Slave Society in the British Leeward Islands at the End of the Eighteenth Century* (New Haven, Conn., 1965), pp. 231–32.

11. Douglas Hall, "Jamaica," in David W. Cohen and Jack P. Greene (eds.), *Neither Slave Nor Free* (Baltimore, 1972), p. 195; Gardner, *History*, p. 171.

12. A mulatto was the result of a union between black and white, sambo between mulatto and black, quadroon between mulatto and white, mustee between quadroon and white. The union of a mustee and a white produced a musteefino who was legally white and enjoyed full civil rights. Samboes, mulattoes, quadroons, and mustees were legally classified as mulattoes and were subject to the same disabilities.

13. CO 137/91, Williamson to Dundas, June 4, 1793, no. 10, secret, enclosure: Memorandum by Bryan Edwards, May 16, 1793.

14. 6 George II, c. 2 of 25 April 1733; 10 Anne, c. 4 of 19 May 1711; 11 Anne, c. 3 of 14 November 1712; [Richard Barrett], *A Reply to the Speech of Dr. Lushington* . . . (London, 1828), p. 36; Hall, "Jamaica," p. 202. I have adopted Barrett's date of 1715 for the deficiency legislation, although the act does not appear in the *Acts of the Assembly* for that year.

15. Edward Long, *The History of Jamaica*, 3 vols. (London, 1774), 2: 321. Bryan Edwards noted that by 1790 the law was no longer enforced. It was also questionable how rigorously it had been applied earlier. See Edwards' memorandum in CO 137/91, Williamson to Dundas, June 4, 1793, no. 10, secret, enclosure.

16. CO 137/91, Williamson to Dundas, June 4, 1793, no. 10, secret, enclosure: Memorandum by Bryan Edwards, May 16, 1793.

17. 21 George II, c. 7 of 13 August 1748; CO 318/76, Sympson to Hill, n.d. [1825], p. 7; [Barrett], *A Reply*, p. 22.

18. 2 George III, c. 8 of 19 December 1761; Gardner, *History*, p. 172.

19. CO 318/76, Sympson to Hill, n.d. [1825], Appendix: "A Table shewing the private privilege bills passed by the House of Assembly from time to time on the free blacks and coloured inhabitants of Jamaica"; *JAJ*, February 4 and 7, 1708, p. 438.

20. For a critical view of the privileged coloreds on this point, see the letter from a nineteenth-century brown man, Cato, in *The Watchman and Jamaica Free Press*, December 17, 1831.

21. Sheila Duncker, "The Free Coloured and Their Fight for Civil Rights in Jamaica, 1800–1830" (unpublished M.A. thesis, University of London, 1960), p. 37; CO 318/76, Sympson to Hill, n.d. [1825], Appendix.

22. CO 318/76, Campbell et al. to Hill, December 1825, Schedule D; G. W. Roberts, *The Population of Jamaica* (Cambridge, 1957), p. 71.

23. Wilma R. Bailey, "Power Relations in Pre-Emancipation Kingston," Paper presented to the Eighth Conference of Caribbean Historians (1976), p. 17.

24. Gerad Tikasingh, "A Method for Estimating the Free Coloured Population of Jamaica" (unpublished paper, University of the West Indies, Department of History [1968]), pp. 14, 16.

25. Brathwaite, *Creole Society*, p. 169.

26. Bailey, "Pre-Emancipation Kingston," p. 17; CO 318/76, Sympson to Hill, n.d. [1825], Appendix: Remark.

27. Goveia, *Slave Society*, p. 227. Goveia's discussion of the Leeward Islands parallels the situation of the freedmen in Jamaica on this point. See also the useful discussions in Jerome S. Handler, *The Unappropriated People* (Baltimore, 1974), Chapter 6 and Edward L. Cox, "The Shadow of Freedom: Freedmen in the Slave Societies of Grenada and St. Kitts, 1763–1833" (unpublished Ph.D. thesis, Johns Hopkins University, 1977), Chapter 4.

28. CO 318/76, Sympson to Hill, n.d. [1825], p. 12.

29. Duncker, "The Free Coloured," p. 79.

30. Ibid., p. 78; Hall, "Jamaica," pp. 202–203; Gardner, *History*, p. 371; CO 318/76, Sympson to Hill, n.d. [1825], pp. 12–13.

31. Brathwaite, *Creole Society*, p. 172; CO 318/76, Sympson to Hill, n.d. [1825], p. 12.

32. CO 318/76, Sympson to Hill, n.d. [1825], p. 13; Duncker, "The Free Coloured," pp. 85–86.

33. CO 137/154, Manchester to Bathurst, December 23, 1823, private.

34. CO 318/76, Campbell et al. to Hill, December 1825, Supplement to Schedule D. "Rich" meant those owning property worth more than £5,000, while those "in fair circumstances" had property valued between £1,000 and £2,500. Many of the "absolutely poor" free people of color possessed property worth £500.

35. Duncker, "The Free Coloured," p. 244.

36. Maria Nugent, *Lady Nugent's Journal*, edited by Philip Wright (Kingston, 1966), p. xxix; *Postscript to The Royal Gazette*, March 15, 1794.

37. [Barrett], *A Reply*, p. 48.

38. M. G. Lewis, *Journal of a West India Proprietor, 1815–17*, edited by Mona Wilson (London, 1929), pp. 94–95; CO 137/165, Manchester to Bathurst, April

1827, private; CO 137/163, Manchester to Bathurst, August 28, 1826.

39. R. R. Madden, *Twelve Months' Residence in the West Indies During the Transition from Slavery to Apprenticeship*, 2 vols. (London, 1835), 1: 113. Stipendiary magistrates were appointed to help adjudicate disputes between masters and their apprentices during the apprenticeship period which followed the abolition of slavery in 1834. Slaves were freed but served as apprentices to their former masters until 1838. For further background, see Chapter 8, pp. 97–98.

40. Bryan Edwards, *The History, Civil and Commercial, of the British Colonies in the West Indies*, 2 vols. (London, 1793), 2: 310; Long, *History*, 2: 333–35.

41. Richard Hill, *Lights and Shadows of Jamaica History* (Kingston, 1859), p. 104; Robert Renny, *An History of Jamaica* (London, 1807), p. 190n. Edward Long elaborated on the belief in England that colored schoolboys were really whites who had been tanned by the sun in *History*, 2: 274.

42. Lewis, *Journal*, p. 143; [J. Stewart], *An Account of Jamaica and Its Inhabitants* (London, 1808), pp. 302–303.

43. CO 137/175, Lushington to Courtenay, September 17, 1826; Brathwaite, *Creole Society*, p. 187; *The Watchman and Jamaica Free Press*, May 15, 1830; Duncker, "The Free Coloured," p. 119; David Lowenthal, *West Indian Societies* (New York, 1972), p. 49.

44. Mary Reckord, "Missions and Slavery, A Study of Protestant Missions in Jamaica, 1815–34" (unpublished manuscript), p. 38. Later controversies among the Methodists reinforced this view of the treatment of free coloreds. See, for example, the correspondence of the M.M.S., Edmondson to Beecham, July 20, 1837.

45. Reverend Hope Masterton Waddell, *Twenty-Nine Years in the West Indies and Central Africa* . . . (London, 1863), p. 34; *Appendix to the JAJ* (1841), p. 54; Brathwaite, *Creole Society*, pp. 173–74.

46. CO 318/76, Campbell, et al. to Hill, December 1825; James A. Thome and Horace J. Kimball, *Emancipation in the West Indies* (New York, 1838), p. 88.

47. Stewart, *A View of Jamaica*, pp. 326–27; Lewis, *Journal*, p. 142; Mavis Campbell, *The Dynamics of Change in a Slave Society* (Rutherford, N.J., 1976), p. 54. For the modern West Indies, see Edith Clarke, *My Mother Who Fathered Me: A Study of the Family in Three Selected Communities in Jamaica* (London, 1957), and Fernando Henriques, *Family and Colour in Jamaica* (London, 1953).

48. Duncker, "The Free Coloured," pp. 58–59; James Kelly, *Voyage to Jamaica and Seventeen Years' Residence in That Island* (Belfast, 1838), p. 31; C. R. Boxer, *Race Relations in the Portuguese Colonial Empire, 1415–1825* (Oxford, 1965), p. 40; Goveia, *Slave Society*, p. 217. In his study of *Creole Society*, pp. 188–89, Brathwaite documents some exceptions to the rule against mixed marriages. See also *VAJ*, November 12, 1796, p. 43, for an example of a petition by a colored man who was married to a white woman.

49. Duncker, "The Free Coloured," pp. 42–43. Duncker claims that Swaby was a sambo, but this was unlikely. See [Barrett], *A Reply*, pp. 8–9.

50. *Postscript to The Royal Gazette*, November 8–15, 1823, Debates: November 12, November 13.

51. Duncker, "The Free Coloured," pp. 245–46.

52. *Postscript to The Royal Gazette*: May 29–June 5, 1813; June 12–19, 1813; August 21–28, 1813.

53. Brathwaite, *Creole Society*, p. 196.

54. William Beckford, *A Descriptive Account of the Island of Jamaica*, 2 vols. (London, 1790), 1: 389; M. G. Smith, "Some Aspects of Social Structure in the British Caribbean About 1820," *Social and Economic Studies* 1 (August 1953): 63; *The Watchman*, February 12, 1834.

55. Stewart, *A View of Jamaica*, pp. 331–32; CO 137/112, Nugent to Cooke, August 30, 1804, private; Edwards, *History*, 2: 25; H. T. de la Beche, *Notes on the Present Condition of the Negroes in Jamaica* (London, 1825), pp. 34–35.

56. R. C. Dallas, *The History of the Maroons*, 2 vols. (London, 1803), 2: 402–403.

57. [Barrett], *A Reply*, p. 29.

58. Joseph Sturge and Thomas Harvey, *The West Indies in 1837* (London, 1838), p. 247; Reckord, "Missions and Slavery," p. 115.

59. B. W. Higman, *Slave Population and Economy in Jamaica, 1807–1834* (Cambridge, 1976), pp. 146–47.

60. CO 137/154, Manchester to Bathurst, December 23, 1823, private.

61. CO 137/225, *The Herald and Literary Journal*, May 9, 1836. ·

Part I: The Campaign for Civil Rights, 1792-1830

2

The Free Coloreds as Loyal Petitioners, 1792–1823

During most of the eighteenth century, the people of color were barely visible in Jamaican politics. When they appealed to the Assembly for an improvement in their rights, coloreds proceeded as individuals; they were not seeking changes in the general condition of the people of color. But the revolution in St. Domingue altered this situation. Although requests for special privileges continued, coloreds also organized petitions and campaigns to better the condition of their people as a whole.

Events in the 1790s thus had a profound impact on the free coloreds as well as on the rest of Jamaican society. The spread of the French Revolution to St. Domingue, the equality of the freedmen, and the abolition of slavery represented a complete reversal of the social order. The massacre and expulsion of the whites and the ruin of the wealthiest sugar colony in the New World were further results of a revolution that West Indian planters had long feared. For the Jamaican people of color, the experience in St. Domingue was both an example and a warning. It was evidence that other free coloreds were able to overcome similar legal limitations. It also demonstrated the danger of tampering with a social structure which at the very least guaranteed them the right to own slaves.[1]

While the Jamaican people of color wanted to preserve the slave system, a group of them also sought to gain many of the privileges that the freedmen in St. Domingue had acquired. They were led by a man named Dickson, a quadroon who had studied at the bar in England. Some time in 1792, Dickson drafted a petition on behalf of the coloreds, but he died before it could be presented to the House. The people of color who had been associated with him carried on the campaign by circulating the petition among the legislators.[2] In it, the free coloreds complained about the laws specifically directed against them. They felt particularly hampered by their inability to give evidence in court, by the different punishments accorded to whites and to browns for the same offenses, and by the limitation on inheritance. The people of color paid taxes, but they maintained that they were not obtaining the protection of British law. On the contrary, its partiality meant that they were "rendered the reproach and bye word of their native land for what they cannot amend."[3]

The petition worried the assemblymen who claimed that the appeal was "expressed in the language of fanaticism." The legislators were concerned about the power of the coloreds and about the danger they posed.

From what has happened at Hispaniola [St. Domingue], we have every reason to believe that these free people of colour have it in their power to lead our Slaves into rebellion by false representations. Their object would not be to make them free but to distress us and thereby oblige us to comply with their demand to be put upon an equal footing with the White Inhabitants.[4]

Others, such as Lieutenant-Governor Adam Williamson, were less afraid of the people of color. He argued that the free browns were dependable; they had family ties with the whites and would therefore come to the defense of the island or help to put down internal rebellion.[5] Many representatives shared this view. Nevertheless, the delegates concluded that the times were too dangerous to take any positive steps on behalf of the coloreds: "but such are our fears and apprehensions in consequence of the Spirit of Innovation which now prevails everywhere and is so distressing to the Government of every Country that we cannot attempt it at present."[6] The free people of color were thus cast in a strange light. Some planters clearly regarded the people of color as a potential threat; at the same time, the values and behavior of the free browns provided evidence of their allegiance to the whites. As the attitudes of the whites oscillated between these two views, the coloreds were never entirely free from suspicion.

Yet, the coloreds' role in helping to suppress the 1795 Maroon rebellion was further proof of their loyalty to the whites. The Maroons were descendants of the Spanish slaves who had escaped from their masters before the British army had invaded Jamaica. Since they had established communities in the mountains and attracted other runaways, they had proved to be a constant danger to a society based on slavery. The threat became especially grave when the Maroons organized an attack against the whites; the support of the colored as well as the black militia companies was at that point critical to the colony's continued stability. In the 1795 outbreak, brown militiamen were heavily involved in the fighting and were among the first groups to sustain any casualties.[7]

The whites therefore sought to reward the freedmen for their help in suppressing the rebellion. Soon after the Maroons had surrendered, the Assembly enacted a measure proclaiming that free coloreds and free blacks "should be protected by law against all violences that may be committed against them."[8] Passed in 1796, the bill allowed freedmen to give evidence before the courts in all cases of assault against them. This was an important concession; all the same, it was less than the coloreds had sought and was surrounded by procedures they found humiliating.[9] While freedmen could now appear in court against whites, they could do so only in certain cases. Moreover, free blacks and coloreds could not testify unless they had been baptized in the Anglican church and were able to produce their certificates of freedom. The coloreds were opposed to these discriminatory procedures, and one brown politician later claimed that the provisions condemned the statute to be "null and void."[10] Nonetheless, the Assembly did not take any action to improve the situation. Despite the backing of the freedmen at a time of great danger, the planter class was afraid of any changes that might upset the established social hierarchies in the island.

The whites' refusal to create a black and colored regiment was further testimony of their fears about the situation. In 1797, the duke of Portland (William Henry Cavendish Bentinck) suggested that a force of freedmen be stationed in the island instead of the usual European troops. The plan had a number of advantages. Local soldiers would not suffer the appalling mortality rate of Europeans in Jamaica, and it would be possible to augment their numbers more easily in an emergency. In addition, Portland hoped that the Assembly would pay a considerable share of the costs for the troops.[11] But the Assembly turned down the request, partly on the grounds that a corps of freedmen would simply reduce the number of blacks and coloreds already in the militia. More significantly, the legislators claimed that armed free coloreds were dangerous: "People of colour with Arms in their hands are a more dangerous body than purchased Slaves. People of colour . . . look up to Rights and Privileges; a Negroe looks to indolence."[12] The Assembly therefore proposed a different scheme: it would pay the entire bill itself for 2,000 European troops. The delegates preferred to incur the extra costs rather than allow freedmen to replace whites as a major line of defense.[13]

At the end of the eighteenth century, then, it appeared that the free people of color had little hope of improving their situation. Despite their support of the whites in overcoming a dangerous internal rebellion, the coloreds found that their legal status had not altered significantly. Notwithstanding the ample evidence of the coloreds' loyalty and dependability, the white ruling class argued that the continued social and political debasement of this group was essential to the maintenance of the slave system.[14] The growing attacks on the institution of slavery as well as the increasing population of the coloreds gradually changed this attitude.

In 1787, British humanitarians established the Society for the Abolition of the Slave Trade. Their goal was limited. They were not seeking an end to slavery, but they believed that the destruction of the British slave trade would lead inevitably to the amelioration of slavery in the West Indies. According to this view, planters would find it in their own interest to improve the condition of the slaves when it was no longer possible to replenish the supply. As a result, slaves would be better housed, better fed, and encouraged to marry; morally and physically, their lives were bound to improve.[15]

The planters did not share this view and voiced their opposition to abolition in Parliament. With strong support in the Lords, the anti-abolitionists were able to delay passage of any legislation, even a compromise bill that passed the Commons in 1792 and was designed to end the traffic in slaves gradually. At that point, the French Revolution and the war with France put off serious consideration of the measure for a decade. In 1804, the abolitionists changed their tactics by appealing for a suspension of the trade on the strictly practical grounds of national interest rather than on humanitarian principles. For example, they argued in favor of partial measures such as blocking the supply of slaves to newly conquered territories since these colonies were likely to be surrendered when peace was restored. The strategy worked. When the Lords finally agreed with the Commons to abolish the slave trade in 1807, three-fourths of the traffic had already been brought to a halt.[16]

Although the humanitarians had won their campaign, they became concerned after 1807 about the possibility of slaves being imported into the West Indies illegally. If new slaves continued to arrive in the colonies, the planters would have little incentive to improve the condition of their existing work force. The humanitarians therefore pressured the government for a registry of slaves to make certain no slaves were being brought into the island secretly. An Order in Council in 1812 ensured that Trinidad would establish such a registry, and three years later, the Crown asked the Jamaican Assembly to pass similar legislation.[17] The request met with strenuous opposition from the members of the House, who not only denied that illegal importations were taking place but also claimed that the registry bill was an interference in their local affairs. More importantly, the legislators regarded the measure as a further step on the road to emancipation. Since the registers would indicate that the slave population was declining, whites were afraid of further attacks once the statistics became known. Humanitarians could then argue that the planters were unable to look after the slaves and that more parliamentary legislation on their behalf was necessary.[18]

Although the Assembly passed a registry bill in 1816, the plantocracy was on the defensive. It was not just the issue of imperial interference; it was also a question of the economic outlook. Contrary to the views of Williams and Ragatz, Seymour Drescher has demonstrated that the West Indian economies were not in a state of collapse in the late eighteenth and early nineteenth centuries. Drescher has shown that the abolitionists were attacking a system that was gaining in economic strength rather than faltering.[19] By the 1820s, however, there is evidence that the planters were in serious difficulties. Low-cost sugar producers were making inroads in traditional West Indian markets, and the Jamaican producers suffered when prices in 1822 fell drastically.[20] Although the supply of African slaves had ceased, the humanitarians were continuing to express concern about the condition of the slaves. In this situation, the demands of the freedmen added further pressure on a society under increasing stress.

One of the problems for whites in the early nineteenth century was the rapid growth of the free colored population. In particular, some of the whites must have been alarmed by statistics published in 1813 on the island militia: these returns showed that 46 percent of the rank and file in the foot militia were free coloreds and blacks (Table 4). In the county of Middlesex, the figures may well have been more disturbing, as the nonwhite rank and file already exceeded their white counterparts by a slight margin. Whites still commanded the freedmen's regiments because of the rule that a brown or black man could not rise above the level of sergeant. With a growing free colored and black population, however, it was only a question of time before they would heavily outnumber the white militiamen. Members of the Assembly were concerned about this development and considered measures to counteract it, including a proposal to grant full rights to those closest in color to the whites, "the mestizoes." On learning of the proposed extension of privileges, the Colonial Office approved the plan.[21] But the measure never materialized, and in 1813 the House was instead faced with two petitions from the free people of color asking for an extension of their privileges.

There were a number of reasons why the free people of color chose to peti-

TABLE 4. FOOT MILITIA IN JAMAICA, 1813

COUNTY	COMMISSIONED & STAFF WHITE	SERGEANT		RANK & FILE		OTHER	TOTAL
		WHITE	FREE BLACK & COLORED	WHITE	FREE BLACK & COLORED		
Middlesex	217	60	57	792	862	45	2,033
Surrey	252	91	68	1,115	1,042	82	2,650
Cornwall	314	87	49	1,225	801	74	2,550
TOTAL	783	238	174	3,132	2,705	210	7,233

Middlesex parishes: Manchester, Clarendon, Vere, St. Dorothy, St. John, St. Catherine, St. Thomas in the Vale, St. Ann, St. Mary

Surrey parishes: Kingston, St. Andrew, Port Royal, St. David, St. Thomas in the East, Portland, St. George

Cornwall parishes: St. Elizabeth, Westmoreland, Hanover, St. James, Trelawny

SOURCE: *JAJ*, November 26, 1813, "General return of the militia in the island of Jamaica," p. 534.

tion the House at that time. First, they believed that Governor Manchester had presented their case to Colonial Office officials while on temporary leave in England.[22] Second, the scattered demographic statistics collected in 1812, which highlighted their rapid numerical growth and their increasing proportion of the free population, must have encouraged them to make the request. They also noted that several educated free browns had returned from Europe and "found it impossible to remain satisfied under the existing laws."[23]

Signed by more than 2,400 freedmen, the two petitions were directed at specific grievances: the coloreds asked for an end to the limit on inheritance and to their continued exclusion from giving testimony in court.[24] Although the members of the Assembly were sympathetic to these requests, the whites made it clear that they were opposed to any alteration in the political rights of the freedmen. The House resolved "that the free people of colour in this island have no right or claim whatever to political power, or to interfere in the administration of the Government, as by law established in the Governor, Council, and Assembly."[25] But the Assembly conceded the major points the coloreds had sought in their petitions. It passed legislation allowing freedmen to give evidence in all cases and against whites as well as removing the restrictions on the amount of property and wealth that free blacks and browns could inherit. The delegates also made it possible for freedmen to "save deficiency" on estates owned by other free blacks and coloreds.[26]

Governor Manchester was pleased about the new legislation. He regarded the reforms as an example of the legislature's generosity and believed that the laws would make the freedmen even more loyal: "it will produce in the minds of the coloured population a proper sense of gratitude for the considerate attention with which their claims have been admitted, and attach them more strongly to His Majesty's Government, and a Country in which they now possess an increased interest."[27] These measures were therefore designed to allow the free blacks and browns more economic and legal latitude, and to ensure the continued loyalty of a growing class of people.

After 1813, the free coloreds found that there were fewer limits to their economic advance. Because of the new legislation, they had a much wider choice of occupations. For example, coloreds were no longer barred from captaining sea-going vessels and quickly became involved in the island's coastal trade. Within three years, they had almost entirely dominated it.[28] This was also true for brown clerks. They had worked in merchants' counting houses and in solicitors' offices before 1813, but their functions had been limited because they could not give evidence in court. When the new statutes came into force, the colored clerks were able to take on larger responsibilities.[29]

These changes worried the island's representatives because of the effect on white employment. Since more positions were open to the freedmen after 1813, the legislators sought to safeguard the jobs of whites. They passed a bill to establish a quota system for clerks which required employers to keep half of their office staff white. But the duration of the law was only a year, and the Assembly chose not to renew the measure. It may have been this decision which encouraged a group of coloreds to petition the House in 1816 for a further extension of their rights.[30]

Unlike the two previous free colored petitions, this one did not appeal for partial improvements in the legal condition of brown people. Instead, it sought all the privileges which whites enjoyed: ". . . your Petitioners with the deepest sorrow have to state, that they are in great degradation and contempt, and are still excluded from the just rights and privileges of white subjects, to which your petitioners must ever consider themselves as a free people entitled." The people of color complained that the legislation in 1813 had not materially changed their situation and that they remained subject to a "humiliating system of exclusion and reproach." Accordingly, the coloreds appealed for their political rights, for an end to all deficiency restrictions, and for access to courts without having to produce expensive baptism and privilege papers.[31]

Both the timing and the tone of the petition were surprising. In 1816, the Assembly was facing the attacks of British reformers over the registry bill and was unlikely to be receptive to an appeal from the people of color. Moreover, the petition's claim for full rights and its criticism of the 1813 legislation were not well calculated to produce positive results. As expected, the report of the committee charged with examining the document dismissed it, noting that the Assembly had expected the people of color to be satisfied with the measures enacted in 1813. The representatives, while disapproving of those who had taken part in the petition, did not censure the majority of the free colored population. The report instead exempted "the very large proportion of the free people who have refused to concur in it [the petition] and who have thus shewn themselves, by a very meritorious example of correct and decorous demeanour, deserving of those privileges which they enjoy."[32]

The committee's report exposed a split among the free people of color. Later in the session, a group of free coloreds presented a counter-petition which expressed gratitude for the concessions of 1813 and concern about the possible effects of the 1816 petition. Since the counter-petitioners feared that their relationship with the whites might be harmed and that the whites' good opinion of them might be altered, they hoped that the Assembly would regard the petition seeking full rights as an example of human error rather than as an expression of "any latent desire of disturbing the peace and good order of society."[33] The two groups of coloreds thus disagreed over tactics.[34] The more conservative people of color were willing to accept their position in society rather than create the possibility of bad feelings with the whites. Those who had first petitioned the Assembly in 1816, however, were determined to be treated as the equals of the whites. Yet, even they sought to appear moderate and respectable.

John Campbell expressed the views of this group in a memorandum he forwarded to Earl Bathurst, the colonial secretary. Campbell was careful to emphasize the coloreds' loyalty to the Crown and to discount the Assembly's portrayal of them as seeking "to create anarchy and confusion." He also pointed out that the people of color wanted to maintain good relations with the whites. For Campbell, the coloreds'

attachment to His Majesty's Government, as it has ever remained unshaken, will ever remain fixed and unalterable: they wish that the degradation under which they labour may be removed as far as possible; but they wish it to be done in that way that will afford satisfaction equally to the White population as to themselves.[35]

Campbell highlighted the grievances of the people of color and stressed their powerlessness at law as well as their exclusion from the island's schools. His frustration at the plight of the coloreds is evident throughout the memorandum, particularly in his description of the relationship between whites and browns. Campbell found that "from some unaccountable fatality, from some undefinable reason and although they have sprung from the Whites, are they exposed to every indignity, to every illiberality; so much so, that the White Parents in public, will scarce notice his coloured Son or Daughter, which, in private are perhaps his only care and companion."[36] In the light of these disabilities, Campbell asked whether it was really possible for the counter-petition to express the attitude of the people of color in general. He noted that there were only seventy-one signatures to it, although the appeal for full rights was signed by 2,700 colored men, some of whom owned a considerable amount of property.

Despite the obvious differences between these two petitions submitted in 1816, there was a common theme running through both of them. Each provided evidence of the coloreds' desire to maintain the harmony that existed between whites and browns, and each voiced the coloreds' strong attachment to the Crown as well as to their "native country."[37] Even those who sought full equality with the whites were proceeding by petition. They accepted the slave system and were seeking simply to improve their own position in it. But the assemblymen did not regard the coloreds' action in this light. The history of white-colored relations, the ambiguous attitude of the whites toward the people of color, and the increasing economic pressures on the white ruling class made it difficult for them to view the situation calmly.

By the beginning of the 1820s, the whites found themselves in a precarious position. It was no longer possible to disguise the crisis facing the plantations; at the same time, the planters' way of life was threatened by the continuing attacks on the slave system. The humanitarians had not yet begun their campaign to abolish slavery, but it was by now only a question of time. Within the island, the expansion of the freedmen population added further problems. In particular, the increasing wealth and numbers of the coloreds as well as their importance in the militia made it more difficult for the Assembly to deny them their rights. And yet, the representatives in the House regarded any attempt to alter the coloreds' position in society as a threat to the structure of the whole society. Since the whites sought to preserve the institution of slavery above all else, they were likely to act irrationally in the face of all the attacks against them. As the humanitarians were too far away, the free people of color were likely to take the brunt of white reaction.

NOTES

1. For a discussion of the revolution in St. Domingue, see James G. Leyburn, *The Haitian People*, rev. ed. (New Haven, Conn., 1966), Chapter 2 and C.L.R. James, *The Black Jacobins*, 2d ed. (New York, 1963).

2. CO 137/91, Williamson to Dundas, March 9, 1793, no. 1. Williamson was less than clear about these developments. He discounted the petition as the work of one man, Dickson; yet, other coloreds were clearly involved in the project.

3. CO 137/91, Williamson to Dundas, December 2, 1792, no. 1, enclosure: "The Humble Address and Petition of the Free People of Colour to the Honourable the Assembly of Jamaica."

4. Ibid., enclosure: Letter to Stephen Fuller from members of the House of Assembly, December 5, 1792, secret and confidential. Fuller was the island's agent in England.

5. CO 137/91, Williamson to Dundas, March 9, 1793, no. 1.

6. CO 137/91, Williamson to Dundas, December 2, 1792, no. 1, enclosure: Letter to Stephen Fuller from members of the House of Assembly, December 5, 1792, secret and confidential.

7. Bryan Edwards, *The Proceedings of the Governor and Assembly of Jamaica in Regard to the Maroon Negroes* (London, 1796), p. 56. For further background on the Maroons, see Barbara K. Kopytoff, "The Maroons of Jamaica: An Ethnohistorical Study of Incomplete Polities" (unpublished Ph.D. thesis, University of Pennsylvania, 1973); R. C. Dallas, *The History of the Maroons*, 2 vols. (London 1803); Carey Robinson, *The Fighting Maroons of Jamaica* ([London], 1969); A. E. Furness, "The Maroon War of 1795," *Jamaican Historical Review* 5 (1965): 30–49; and Robin W. Winks, *The Blacks in Canada, A History* (New Haven, Conn., 1971), pp. 79–95.

8. *The Royal Gazette*, April 30-May 7, 1796.

9. 36 George III, c. 23 of 25 March 1796; Sheila Duncker, "The Free Coloured and Their Fight for Civil Rights in Jamaica, 1800–1830" (unpublished M.A. thesis, University of London, 1960), pp. 22–23.

10. CO 318/76, Sympson to Hill, n.d. [1825], p. 15.

11. CO 138/42, Portland to Balcarres, January 10, 1797.

12. CO 137/98, Balcarres to Portland, May 23, 1797.

13. CO 138/42, Portland to Balcarres, September 12, 1797. For more background on this episode, see Roger Norman Buckley, *Slaves in Red Coats* (New Haven, Conn., 1979), pp. 43–52.

14. Elsa Goveia, *Slave Society in the British Leeward Islands at the End of the Eighteenth Century* (New Haven, Conn., 1965), p. 222. Some observers were prepared to make further concessions to the people of color. See, for example, Dallas, *The Maroons*, 2: 466.

15. Frank J. Klingberg, *The Anti-Slavery Movement in England* (New Haven,

Conn., 1926), p. 95; W. L. Mathieson, "The Emancipation of the Slaves, 1807–1838," in J. Holland Rose et al. (ed.), *The Cambridge History of the British Empire*, 8 vols. (Cambridge, 1940), 2, *The Growth of the New Empire, 1783–1870*, p. 308.

16. Roger Anstey, *The Atlantic Slave Trade and British Abolition, 1760–1810* (London, 1975), Chapters 12, 14, 15.

17. Mathieson, "Emancipation of the Slaves," p. 310.

18. John Stewart, *A View of the Past and Present State of the Island of Jamaica* (Edinburgh, 1823), pp. 236–37; Klingberg, *The Anti-Slavery Movement*, p. 175. Thomas Clarkson later admitted that there had not been any illicit imports (Mathieson, "Emancipation of the Slaves," p. 311).

19. Seymour Drescher, *Econocide* (Pittsburgh, 1977), passim, but especially Chapter 2. For the debate, see Eric Williams, *Capitalism and Slavery*, rev. ed. (London, 1964) and Lowell J. Ragatz, *The Fall of the Planter Class in the British Caribbean, 1763–1833* (New York, 1928).

20. Ragatz, *The Fall of the Planter Class*, pp. 337–38.

21. CO 137/136, Morrison to Bathurst, February 20, 1813, secret; CO 138/44, Bathurst to Morrison, May 10, 1813, secret.

22. CO 318/76, Sympson to Hill, n.d. [1825], p. 19.

23. CO 318/76, Campbell to Hill, December 1825, Schedule D.

24. *Postscript to The Royal Gazette*, October 30-November 6, 1813, Debates: November 5.

25. Ibid., November 13-November 20, 1813, Debates: November 12.

26. 54 George III, c. 19 and c. 20 of 4 December 1813; CO 137/136, Manchester to Bathurst, December 10, 1813, no. 17. "Saving deficiency" in this case meant that free blacks and coloreds could work on the estates owned by freedmen without forcing the planter to pay a deficiency tax for not hiring enough whites. Freedmen could still not work on white-owned estates without the payment of the deficiency tax.

27. CO 137/136, Manchester to Bathurst, December 10, 1813, no. 17.

28. Duncker, "The Free Coloured," p. 31; Charles H. Wesley, "The Emancipation of the Free Colored Population in the British Empire," *The Journal of Negro History* 19 (April 1934): 143. Wesley incorrectly claimed that the Assembly passed legislation in 1813 allowing coloreds to become pilots; this did not occur until 1816. See CO 318/76, Sympson to Hill, n.d. [1825], p. 21.

29. CO 318/76, Sympson to Hill, n.d. [1825], p. 19; Wesley, "Free Colored Population," p. 144.

30. *Postscript to The Royal Gazette*, November 27-December 4, 1813; CO 318/76, Sympson to Hill, n.d. [1825], p. 20.

31. CO 137/148, Hibbert to Bathurst, March 3, 1819, enclosure: Extract of the Report of the House, December 20, 1816.

32. Ibid.

33. Ibid.

34. Duncker, "The Free Coloured," p. 161.

35. CO 137/145, Campbell to Bathurst, n.d. [April, 1817].

36. Ibid.

37. Ibid.; CO 137/148, Hibbert to Bathurst, March 3, 1819, enclosure: Extract of the Report of the House, December 20, 1816.

3

The Response of the Whites: The Case of Lecesne and Escoffery

At the beginning of 1823, the free people of color in Jamaica organized a new campaign for their rights. For the first time, they resolved to draw up a petition that represented the sentiments of coloreds from the whole island. In addition, they corresponded with humanitarians in England and sought to gain the support of the British Government. The timing of their appeal and the coloreds' connections with some of the antislavery leaders suggest that they hoped their activities would coincide with the agitation in England. In England, the humanitarians also established a new organization in 1823, the Anti-Slavery Society, to press for the eventual abolition of slavery. Later that year, the society enjoyed its first success, as the Government promised to take decisive steps to ameliorate the condition of the slaves and to prepare them for their civil rights.[1]

In Jamaica, the people of color had more limited aims. A group of them met in January 1823 to consider "the best means of ascertaining the sentiments of the Island at large, on urging the claims of the People of Colour upon the Legislature of Jamaica."[2] The coloreds established a committee of correspondence which sent a circular around the island requesting the views of the people of color on a forthcoming petition. As a result, public gatherings were held in several parishes to discuss the circular, and a draft petition was prepared. In it, the coloreds repeated many of the requests they had made in earlier petitions: they appealed for their political rights, for the privilege of sitting on juries, for the repeal of the deficiency law, and for the right to work in the colony's public offices. The coloreds presented a more sophisticated justification for their petition than they had previously, claiming that the opportunity for employment in the public offices would act as an incentive for the people of color in general.[3] Similarly, the right to sit on a jury was a privilege that could "only be delegated to those of settled habits, and of fixed residence and interest in the soil." Since education and sound character were necessary qualifications for any juryman, the coloreds' right to occupy such a position "must greatly increase the morality of a people."[4]

At a meeting in May, the coloreds adopted the resolutions and appointed a twenty-one member organizing committee to circulate a final draft to the people of color for their approval. By August, coloreds from all over Jamaica had agreed to the wording of the appeal, and the committee was ready to submit it to the House. In order to gain as many votes in the Assembly as possible, the committee asked its correspondents in various parts of the island to present a copy of the petition to their own representatives in the House.[5] The brown leaders had thus publicly and methodically canvassed the people of color in Jamaica. They had also advertised meetings in the press and publicized details of the petition. Members of the Assembly were informed about these activities and were themselves lobbied for support.

The coloreds did not restrict their appeal to the House of Assembly. Aware of the strong prejudice against them in Jamaica, they sought the backing of the Crown in hopes that it would act directly or perhaps bring pressure on the Assembly to improve their condition. The people of color therefore appointed an Englishman, Michael Hanly, to serve as their agent.[6] Hanly corresponded with the Colonial Office and made repeated attempts to influence the Government on behalf of the people of color. In forwarding their resolutions of May 1823 to the colonial secretary, for example, he claimed that there was "no physical or moral cause, why the fourth in descent from a free man should alone be admitted to those rights which the whole should be partakers of."[7] Hanly also maintained that it was in the interests of the whites to grant the coloreds their rights. The browns would then have more reason to support the slave system and to defend it in case of a rebellion. But officials at the Colonial Office do not appear to have been convinced by Hanly's reasoning, and the initial harmony between Hanly and the people of color soon ended. By 1827, he was involved in a legal wrangle "of a pecuniary nature" with them.[8] Yet, it was still significant that the coloreds had hired Hanly at all. The Jamaican people of color were clearly directing their appeal to England as well as to Jamaica.

The coloreds did not rely solely on Hanly's efforts to sway Government policy in Britain; they also attempted to make use of their connections in the antislavery movement. In July 1823, Richard Hill[9] wrote to a leading English philanthropist, William Allen, to enlist his aid. Hill was disappointed that the humanitarians had not included the people of color in their campaign to ameliorate slavery in the West Indies, and he maintained that improving the condition of the free coloreds was "the first step towards any effectual remedy for the

evils incidental to a system of slavery." For Hill, there was little likelihood that
the whites would willingly alter a system that preserved their superiority.

The complexional misanthropes—the minions of the world's interest who are sent out
here to sap the vitals of the Country raised into a sort of Complexional aristocracy, have
too many incitements not strenuously to endeavour to perpetuate our misery and degradation by joining the cry for the perpetuity of that policy, which having excluded the
people from all political importance, makes themselves rich and powerful, and keeps us
poor and wretched.[10]

Since the House of Assembly was unlikely to be receptive to the petition of the
people of color, Hill asked Allen to bring their case before Parliament. If Hanly
was unsuccessful at the Colonial Office, the humanitarians could at least raise
the issue in Parliament.

In addition to Hanly and the humanitarians, the coloreds sought the aid of a
brown lawyer, Richard Wilson, who lived in England. Wilson had practiced
law in one of the Leeward Islands but had been forced to abandon his career
there because of his color. Since Wilson had successfully appealed for redress
in England and also acted as agent for the freedmen of Dominica, the Jamaican
free coloreds hoped he might use his influence on their behalf.[11] In a letter to
him, the coloreds enclosed a copy of their proceedings to help Wilson dispel
the Government's ignorance about the brown population of Jamaica. They
also hinted at their power to overthrow the system that kept the people of color
in a "disgraceful State of demi-Slavery."

Our long endurance of such grievous oppression while evincing our unwillingness to
adopt coercive Measures proves also our Loyalty and Devotion to the British Crown
and Government; for what else could induce submission to a System so tyrannical as
that we labour under. And which possessing as we do a great Physical Superiority, we
might by one energetic effort overthrow and destroy.[12]

These attempts by the coloreds to gain support in England involved them in
a number of contradictions. On the one hand, they were constitutionally appealing to the authorities in Jamaica for improvements in their legal status.
Brown men therefore presented themselves as loyal, subservient, and peaceful
members of society. On the other hand, they were seeking help from groups in
England that were dedicated to the eventual abolition of the slave system.
Even more at odds with the coloreds' stance in Jamaica was their claim that
they could topple the whites, now that they outnumbered them. This was a
dangerous argument to employ, particularly when the plantocracy was already
feeling threatened by the abolitionists.

Extremist white opinion was alarmed by the meetings and by the petition of
the coloreds. One of the spokesmen for this group was Reverend George

Bridges, an Anglican minister who served in Jamaica for many years and who strongly defended the local plantocracy. Bridges claimed that the people of color were not ready for their rights "while the blood of pagan Africa still flowed thick and darkly in their veins."[13] The whites' fears were compounded by the news of the initial success of the antislavery campaign in England. Since the Government had adopted a policy of amelioration and eventual emancipation of the slaves, the whites held meetings denouncing the colonial secretary and calling on the king to dismiss him.[14] Speakers denied that the slaves were oppressed, claiming that they were "more contented with their lot than the peasantry of Europe," and noting that the Assembly was prepared to improve the condition of the slaves as soon as their habits warranted it. Concern in white Jamaica mounted as rumors about the new policy spread. Many whites became terrified at the possible consequences of the proposals for amelioration, and some of them envisioned a rebellion of slaves and freedmen.[15] According to one observer, "the island was become the scene of conspiracy and rebellion; every class was reasonably looked upon with suspicion and mistrust."[16]

It was in this setting that a local magistrate, Hector Mitchel, reported that two of the free people of color involved in the preparation of the petition to the House were aliens and "persons of dangerous character to the peace and tranquility of the island."[17] Mitchel—a Kingston merchant as well as one of the city's representatives in the Assembly—identified the conspirators as Louis Lecesne and Edward Escoffery. Mitchel was aware that they shared a common background: each had a white father who had lived in St. Domingue and fled to Jamaica at the time of the revolution. Lecesne had a black mother while Escoffery's was sambo. Both carried on trade in Kingston, were sergeants in the militia, and were related, Lecesne having married Escoffery's sister. Lecesne was about twenty-five years old, and Escoffery roughly twenty-eight.[18]

Scenting a conspiracy, Mitchel succeeded in convincing Governor Manchester to arrest Lecesne and Escoffery and to deport them as aliens. In jail, however, the two men of color applied for a writ of habeas corpus and were released when their case was discharged by the chief justice. This did not stop Mitchel, who established a secret committee of the House to look into treasonable practices in the island and especially the activities of Lecesne and Escoffery.[19] Mitchel served as chairman of the committee and was the most important witness before the commissioners of legal inquiry who also investigated the matter. According to Mitchel, Lecesne and Escoffery were the principal leaders of a lodge of freemasons known as the Bienfaisance Society. Under the guise of meeting to collect contributions to bury foreign indigent people of color, "these bastard masons, as they are termed, meet in a political character and as masons, and hatch all matters concerning their objects of future purpose in obtaining privileges, etc. and in respect to foreign connections."[20]

In his testimony before the committee of the House, Mitchel described the activities of the organization. He noted that its meetings had been held at Lecesne's home until he had begun to investigate it. At that point, the group's proceedings were moved to the house of Alexander Sympson, who headed the general committee of coloreds. Mitchel maintained that there were other reasons to suspect the Bienfaisance Society: thus, its members always gathered behind locked doors and usually dressed in black. Although Lecesne was officially the society's secretary, Mitchel claimed that he was in fact its president and general orator. Mitchel was also convinced that Lecesne corresponded with people in Haiti and that whenever Lecesne received letters or emissaries from Haiti, he communicated the information to the society and to the members of the coloreds' committee. For Mitchel, this was proof that Lecesne was conferring with "accredited agents of the Government [of Haiti]."[21]

Apart from Lecesne and Escoffery and the leading colored politicians, the freedmen in general were implicated in the alleged conspiracy. Even though Mitchel believed that the majority of free coloreds and blacks were loyal, he claimed that they would join the revolution once it began.[22] He also testified that the free people of color had planned not to turn out for militia duty at Christmas. The agent of the island, George Hibbert, was more precise about their intentions: he maintained that Lecesne and Escoffery had supplied slaves with arms, had organized their drilling, and had set December 19 as the date for the general insurrection. According to Hibbert, Lecesne and Escoffery were "designated for preeminent stations in the new order of things they were to establish."[23]

The report of the secret committee embodied these views and was further proof for Governor Manchester that Lecesne and Escoffery were aliens and were dangerous to the peace of the island. In fact, it was not difficult to persuade Manchester that Lecesne and Escoffery should be ordered off the island. He regarded them as persons of little consequence who, like many others without capital, carried on a trade in Kingston.[24] While Manchester believed that respectable coloreds did not support the two men or the petition of the people of color,[25] he thought it necessary to take action.

The feverish state of anxiety in which the Public Mind had been held on account of the effect which the discussions in England had produced on the Slave Population. The audacious letters of the Committee (as they chose to style themselves) of the free Population—The concert they had endeavoured to establish throughout the Island amongst all belonging to their own Class: The admission into their Body and making common cause with those who were notoriously Aliens . . . all concur in proving that the Alarm, felt here, was not imaginary.[26]

For many whites in Jamaica, the threat posed by the people of color was clearly not imaginary. The demands of the browns challenged their superiority and endangered the racial hierarchy of the society. Since the whites feared that Jamaica might become another Haiti, many of them found it impossible to accept the coloreds' petition for what it was. A conspiracy then became the only plausible explanation for the activities of the people of color.

The reality of the situation was much different. Instead of concealing their motives, the meetings of the coloreds were open and well publicized. The coloreds were not planning to murder the whites but were appealing to them in the House of Assembly for their civil rights. There was also little likelihood of their uniting with the slaves in a plot against the whites, as the people of color had long emphasized their superiority over the slaves and in return were generally disliked by the slave population. The whites nonetheless overestimated the danger posed by the people of color and chose to direct their anger at Lecesne and Escoffery. Although the two coloreds maintained that they were born in Jamaica and could not be deported without a trial, they were rearrested on November 28, 1823, and sent to Haiti the next day. Their expulsion became something of a *cause célèbre*, which dramatized not only the position of the free coloreds but also the paranoia of the whites.

When Lecesne and Escoffery landed in Haiti, they immediately sent a petition to Manchester asking him to reconsider their case. This request proved unsuccessful, and since the men had arrived in Haiti with little money and few clothes, they were fortunate in securing the aid of several British merchants resident in Port-au-Prince. The two coloreds were therefore able to depart for England where they hoped their appeal would be more successful.

Lecesne and Escoffery arrived in London at an opportune moment, at least from the humanitarians' point of view. By the spring of 1824, the fortunes of the Anti-Slavery Society had declined dramatically after its initial success in convincing the Government to ameliorate the condition of the slaves. Whereas the planters had correctly predicted that there would be slave revolts as a result of this policy, the antislavery forces were unsure how to proceed without further inflaming the situation. The expulsion of Lecesne and Escoffery provided them with an example of the injustice inherent in a slave society without the risk of inciting further outbreaks in the West Indies.[27]

Stephen Lushington,[28] a leader of the antislavery movement, took charge of the case. He moved for the papers on the deportation to be printed for Parliament and submitted a petition from Lecesne and Escoffery to the Commons. When the papers were assembled a year later, Lushington called for a parliamentary committee of inquiry. Since commissioners investigating the state of criminal justice were already in the West Indies, Lushington agreed that they should first examine the case.[29] It was apparent from the outset, however, that Lushington and the humanitarians were convinced that the two brown men were innocent.

The Colonial Office was more skeptical about Lecesne and Escoffery. The under-secretary, Wilmot Horton, believed that both of them were aliens, and James Stephen, the legal counsel, noted that there was "abundant cause to justify great suspicion of their conduct and intentions."[30] Yet, Stephen regarded the deportation of the coloreds as unjust. Since Lecesne and Escoffery had been living in Jamaica for twenty-five years, expulsion meant ruin for both of them. There was no proof of their alleged involvement in a conspiracy and no evidence in writing against them. As a result, Stephen concluded that Lecesne and Escoffery would have been acquitted of seditious practices had they been tried in court.[31] Thus, officials in the Colonial Office sought to take a balanced view of the case, but the humanitarians adopted a very different approach to it.

They not only believed that Lecesne and Escoffery had been illegally deported; they also made use of the affair to argue for more imperial control of the slave society. In a parliamentary debate in 1825, William Wilberforce, still a leading figure in the Anti-Slavery Society, cited the case as "proof of the growing hostility entertained in the West Indies towards the African Race" and concluded that it was "in vain to hope that the colonial legislatures will be gradually led to imitate the reformation [in the laws governing slavery] to be exhibited in the island of Trinidad."[32] Lushington also regarded the deportation of Lecesne and Escoffery as a weapon in the antislavery drive and was willing initially to subordinate the real interests of the two coloreds to the needs of the antislavery cause. But while gathering evidence on the case, Lushington began to consider it less as a part of the antislavery campaign and more as an issue on its own.[33] He became concerned about the fate of Lecesne and Escoffery as well as about the general problem of the freedmen. As he noted in a letter to Bathurst, the action against the two men "involved questions of much greater importance than the fate of the individuals deported; that Mr. Mitchel had imputed treasonable designs to very many individuals, indeed I may say to the whole coloured class. . . ."[34]

Lushington's task was made more difficult when the report of the commission of legal inquiry supported the coloreds' deportation. This setback only served to reinforce Lushington's commitment to Lecesne and Escoffery, as he was determined to prove their innocence and by implication that of the free coloreds involved in the campaign for full civil rights. Since the issue was no longer an integral part of the antislavery drive and was not likely to interest public opinion, Lushington decided that an appeal to Parliament was of little use.[35] Instead he began collecting further evidence in an attempt to convince the Colonial Office of the mistake that had been made. He therefore invited several of the participants in the affair to England and examined them in the presence of a referee from the Colonial Office, William Courtenay.[36] From the interviews and from the papers at his command, Lushington compiled a lengthy and detailed report that condemned the Jamaican authorities and the commissioners of legal inquiry.

In reviewing the events in 1823 that had led up to the deportations, Lushington noted that neither Lecesne nor Escoffery had been original members of the coloreds' organizing committee of twenty-one and that no meetings had ever been held at Lecesne's home. Nor had any of the local officials regarded the activities of the coloreds in the first half of 1823 as disloyal or dangerous. According to Lushington, the sudden shift in the attitudes toward the people of color occurred as soon as news of the amelioration policy reached Jamaica. The whites immediately lashed out at the activities of the coloreds and particularly at the Bienfaisance Society. But Lushington pointed out that the organization was established to relieve the poor people of color and that there was nothing to suggest it was the basis of a conspiracy. He also demolished Mitchel's later claim that Lecesne was commander-in-chief of the society by showing that Lecesne's use of the initials C.C. simply signified his position on its collecting committee.

Lushington demonstrated that much of the evidence was similarly distorted. Thus, Lecesne and Escoffery were not men without capital but prosperous shopkeepers; Lecesne, for example, was worth £4,832, considerably more than the few hundred pounds which Manchester had estimated. In addition, the two coloreds did not have any correspondence with the agents of the Haitian Government and were not welcomed by the Haitians when they arrived at Port-au-Prince. Not only was one of the leading witnesses against Lecesne and Escoffery personally interested in their deportation, but also Mitchel had concocted some of the evidence after the events and had accepted evidence from perjured witnesses, including his own mistress.[37]

Lushington contended that the commissioners of legal inquiry were also guilty of serious errors. Wilmot Horton agreed. He questioned one of the commissioners, Mr. Henry, about his report because he wondered why the witnesses for Lecesne and Escoffery were so rigidly cross-examined while those in support of the deportation had escaped such close scrutiny. According to Henry, that arose "from the Aliens and their friends being all a set of infamous rascals from one end to the other."[38] It would appear that the commissioners had made up their minds before hearing the evidence, were openly partial, and drew erroneous conclusions from the testimony.[39] Lushington himself was not free from some of the same faults. Wilmot Horton maintained that Lushington's innuendos "must be received with great distrust, not from any suspicion of his bad faith of which I have *none*, but of his possibly exaggerated views and more probably exaggerated information which he may have received."[40] Officials at the Colonial Office believed that Lushington had overstated the case, but their referee, William Courtenay, agreed with Lushington's report.[41]

Faced with the contradictory conclusions of the commission of legal inquiry and of Lushington and Courtenay, the Colonial Office referred the issue to an arbiter. Their eventual choice, Mr. Sergeant Bosanquet,[42] disposed of the question by suggesting that Lecesne and Escoffery's place of birth was not the most important point to be considered. Since their dates of birth coincided with the British occupation of Haiti, Bosanquet concluded that the two coloreds were life-long subjects of the Crown, whether they were born in Haiti or in Jamaica. Either way, the men were not liable to the Jamaican Alien Law. Although the attorney-general for Jamaica, William Burge, appealed the decision, Bosanquet and the law officers adhered to their opinions.[43] As a result, Lecesne and Escoffery were compensated for their losses, Lecesne ultimately receiving £11,622 2s. 3d. and Escoffery £4,654 17s. 2d. Not surprisingly, the Jamaican people of color regarded the two men as heroes when they returned to the island in 1830.[44]

The case of Lecesne and Escoffery proved to be an important development for the coloreds. First, it won the support of the humanitarians and dramatized the problems of the free browns. Second, the publicity which the events generated and the efforts of men like Lushington may well have had an effect on British policy toward the freedmen in general. On January 15, 1829, the Government issued an order declaring them the legal equals of whites in the Crown Colony of St. Lucia. Two months later, a similar decree was put into effect in Trinidad.[45] Although Jamaica was unlikely to face imperial intervention on this issue, attitudes toward the people of color there had changed since the meetings of the committee of twenty-one and the expulsion of Lecesne and Escoffery. In view of the continuing campaign of the abolitionists, many whites had begun to believe that the coloreds could be useful allies in the struggle to protect the slave system. Even in 1823, there were planters who were prepared to grant several demands in the petition of the people of color. Lecesne and Escoffery therefore represented only part of a more complicated picture.

NOTES

1. Howard Temperley, *British Antislavery, 1833–1870* (London, 1972), pp. 9–10; D. J. Murray, *The West Indies and the Development of Colonial Government, 1801–1834* (Oxford, 1965), pp. 128–29; *Hansard*, New Series 9 (May 16, 1823): 360.

2. CO 137/175, Lushington to Courtenay, September 17, 1826, enclosure: Minutes of the proceedings of the Kingston Committee of the People of Colour, January 23, 1823.

3. Ibid., enclosure: *Statement of the Proceedings of the People of Colour of Jamaica in an Intended Appeal to the House of Assembly of 1823, for the Removal of Their Political Disabilities* (1823), pp. 5–8.

4. Ibid., p. 9.

5. CO 137/175, Lushington to Courtenay, September 17, 1826, enclosure: Circular no. 8, Kingston Committee of Color, August 26, 1823.

6. Sheila Duncker, "The Free Coloured and Their Fight for Civil Rights in Jamaica, 1800–1830" (unpublished M.A. thesis, University of London, 1960), p. 163. Apart from Hanly's involvement with the coloreds and his later difficulties with them, there is no further biographical evidence about him or any suggestion about why the people of color chose him as one of their spokesmen in England.

7. CO 137/155, Hanly to Bathurst, September 23, 1823, private.

8. CO 137/161, Hanly to Huskisson, March 23, 1825; CO 137/176, Hanly to Manchester, June 30, 1827.

9. For more information on this prominent man of color, see Chapter 5, pp. 59–60 and Chapter 8, p. 99.

10. CO 137/175, Lushington to Courtenay, September 17, 1826, enclosure: Hill to Allen, July 18, 1823.

11. For more information on Wilson, see CO 137/175, Lushington to Courtenay, September 17, 1826; and Charles H. Wesley, "The Emancipation of the Free Colored Population in the British Empire," *The Journal of Negro History* 19 (April 1934): 137–70.

12. CO 137/174, Sympson and Scholar to Wilson, July 14, 1823.

13. Reverend George W. Bridges, *The Annals of Jamaica*, 2 vols. (London, 1828), 2:371.

14. W. L. Mathieson, "The Emancipation of the Slaves, 1807–1838," in J. Holland Rose et al. (ed.), *The Cambridge History of the British Empire*, 8 vols. (Cambridge, 1940), 2, *The Growth of the New Empire, 1783–1870*, p. 318.

15. See Reverend R. Bickell, *The West Indies as They Are* (London, 1825), pp. 122–23, for a description of the reception in Jamaica of Bathurst's instructions.

16. Bridges, *Annals*, 2: 371.

17. CO 318/66, The Report of the Commissioners of Legal Enquiry, First issue, February 28, 1826.

18. CO 137/175, Lushington to Courtenay, September 17, 1826.

19. Ibid.; Mavis Campbell, *The Dynamics of Change in a Slave Society* (Rutherford, N.J., 1976), p. 96.

20. *PP*, 1825, 25 (74): 137.

21. CO 137/174, Manchester to Horton, December 27, 1824, enclosure: Mitchel's testimony before the secret committee of the House of Assembly, November 18, 1824.

22. Ibid. Mitchel believed that all the foreign blacks and people of color were implicated. He also claimed that the usual toast at meetings of the free blacks was "Destruction to the Whites and success to the Blacks and Mulattoes."

23. Ibid.; CO 137/176, Hibbert to Horton, June 7, 1824.

24. CO 137/157, Manchester to Horton, September 13, 1824, private.

25. CO 137/154, Manchester to Bathurst, December 23, 1823, private.

26. CO 137/174, Manchester to Bathurst, February 20, 1826, private.

27. David Eltis, "Dr. Stephen Lushington: Liberal Reformer and Radical Advocate of Negro Rights" (unpublished M.A. thesis, University of Alberta, 1969), pp. 82–83. In October 1823, there was a slave insurrection in Demerara; see Murray, *The West Indies*, pp. 130–31.

28. Lushington was one of the original vice-presidents of the Anti-Slavery Society. An MP, he also served as a judge in the London Consistory Court, the Admiralty Court, the Court of Delegates, and as a member of the Judicial Committee of the Privy Council. Lushington was particularly close to Thomas Fowell Buxton, the leader of the antislavery campaign. For more background on Lushington, see Eltis, "Lushington," especially Chapter 1.

29. CO 137/176, William Burge, *A Letter to the Right Honorable Sir George Murray, G.C.B., His Majesty's Principal Secretary of State for the Colonies, Relative to the Deportation of Lecesne and Escoffery from Jamaica* (London, 1829), pp. 7–9.

30. CO 137/174, Bathurst to Manchester, June 18, 1825, private and confidential; CO 137/176, Stephen to Horton, January 22, 1825.

31. CO 137/176, Stephen to Horton, January 22, 1825.

32. *Hansard*, New Series, 11 (June 15, 1824): 1411, 1414.

33. Eltis, "Lushington," p. 90. Eltis is correct in pointing out that the case was no longer significant in the antislavery campaign, but he underestimates the affair's importance in the struggle of the free coloreds to gain their rights.

34. CO 320/4, Lushington to Bathurst, October 24, 1826.

35. Eltis, "Lushington," p. 90.

36. CO 137/174, Lushington to Horton, August 16, 1826. Among those who came to England to testify before Lushington was A. D. Sympson, the chairman of the people of color in 1823. Richard Hill also made the trip as did a white youth who had lived in Lecesne's house and one of Lecesne's slaves who had been maltreated by Mitchel.

37. CO 137/175, Lushington to Courtenay, September 17, 1826.

38. CO 320/4, Horton to Bathurst, October 7, 1826.

39. Eltis, "Lushington," p. 93; *PP*, 1830–1831, 6 (280): 343.

40. CO 320/4, Horton to Bathurst, September 13, 1826.

41. CO 137/175, Courtenay to Bathurst, December 6, 1826.

42. Although Sir John Richardson, a former judge of the Common Pleas, had agreed to take on the case, he was forced to give it up because of ill-health and nominated Bosanquet in his place. See *PP*, 1830–1831, 6 (280), Estimates, etc. . . . , 343.

43. CO 137/176: Letter of S. B. Bosanquet, November 5, 1827; Scarlett and Tindal to Huskisson, January 24, 1824; *PP*, 1830–1831, 6 (280): 344–45.

44. See CO 137/172, Keane to Hay, December 26, 1830, enclosure: *The Watchman and Jamaica Free Press*, December 4, 1830. This issue contained the details of the public dinner held for Lecesne and Escoffery on their return to the island.

45. Wesley, "Free Colored Population," p. 159.

4

The Response of the Whites: Too Little, Too Late, 1823–1830

Richard Barrett was one of the Jamaican whites who in 1823 believed that the people of color should no longer be denied their civil liberties. Since Barrett was an important figure in planter society and a prominent member of the Assembly, the committee of color asked him to submit their petition to the House. Barrett agreed, but warned the coloreds that they could not expect the Assembly to grant many of their requests. He reminded them that "there were strong prejudices in the minds of many of the whites against the people of Colour and that if they got a little now the door would be open for future application."[1]

Barrett adopted the same theme when he presented the coloreds' petition to the Assembly in November 1823. Since they were "originally . . . few and contemptible, a most degraded race, even more wretched than the slaves from whom they sprang," the House had passed legislation suited to their condition. Now that the coloreds were more numerous and respectable, Barrett believed that the Assembly should concede additional privileges to them.[2] He also argued that it was in the interests of the whites to advance the cause of the people of color, as they were potential allies in the defense of slavery.

. . . we were called on by the threatening dangers of our situation, and by the uncommon character which the plans of our enemies had assumed, to establish our security on a broader basis, if possible, than that on which it had hitherto rested. This was only to be done by union amongst ourselves; and this union was only to be obtained by removing all causes of dissatisfaction which might have the effect of separating the interests of one class of the community from the other.

But Barrett acknowledged that the coloreds were not yet ready for full equality with the whites. Furthermore, he maintained that the people of color were aware that all their demands could not be met and that "they would be grateful for any boon the House might please to grant."[3]

The petition encountered considerable opposition in the House. William Rennalls, the representative from St. Catherine, summarized the attitude of many assemblymen when he objected to the petition because it was similar in spirit to the one the House had rejected in 1816. Although the people of color in 1823 were not seeking all the rights they had demanded in 1816, Rennalls declared that any concessions would "make them more confident in demanding further privileges." Rennalls also believed that many of the browns' claims were based on principles that threatened the peace and order of the society. The coloreds' argument that their inherent rights had been violated was a dangerous concept in a society that denied the liberty of the vast majority of the population. Rennalls saw their appeal for the franchise as "nothing short of universal suffrage!" and concluded that "every Member must, upon a first inspection of that petition, admit that, were the principles of the petition sanctioned, they would tend to the direct subversion of the established Constitution of the island."[4]

Although Rennalls was unwilling to consider any requests that might threaten the superiority of the whites, he was in favor of taking some legislative action on behalf of the coloreds. In their appeal, the people of color objected to the necessity of producing certificates of baptism and freedom before giving testimony in court cases involving whites. Since the requirement could be abolished without any danger, Rennalls introduced a resolution dispensing with it.[5] Like many other members of the Assembly, he was also prepared to entertain private privilege bills. These acts had virtually ceased in 1802;[6] however, delegates were now in favor of reviving private bills. One representative summed up the views of his colleagues when he warned that since "propositions were about to be made, tending to overthrow the established order of things in this island, it would be wise perhaps to return to the former practice of the House."[7] The Colonial Office echoed these sentiments. Bathurst regretted that private acts had been discontinued and noted that they "certainly tended to keep the coloured people quiet by letting them see that the door was open to those who by industry and good conduct were deserving of encouragement."[8]

When the Assembly formally agreed to receive private petitions, many coloreds applied for privileges. Between 1823 and 1830, there were 123 petitions to the House seeking rights for 200 people.[9] Most of the resulting acts did not allow the favored coloreds to sit in the Assembly or the Council, and the people of color who appeared before the commissioners of legal inquiry complained that "prejudice or the influence of public opinion cannot be obliterated by private bills."[10] Men of color were nonetheless clearly eager to obtain further rights.

The privilege bills were also a useful device for the legislators, since they made it possible for the whites to appear generous without forcing them to make concessions to the freedmen as a whole. Furthermore, the acts served to lessen discontent among the more educated and wealthier coloreds and to retard the political union of the people of color. Because of their favored position, the privileged browns were unlikely to participate in any campaign to remove the disabilities of the freedmen. On the contrary, many of them opposed the petitions of the free blacks and browns for further rights.[11] In a society based on legal inequality, the privileged coloreds sought to preserve their superiority as long as possible.

For much the same reason, the coloreds also had an uneasy relationship with the free blacks. As a result, the people of color did not include the blacks in their 1823 campaign. The coloreds instead maintained that they were petitioning for their own rights and that it was a matter for the Assembly to decide whether to extend any concessions to the free blacks. A meeting of the St. Elizabeth people of color expressed this point of view in a public notice:

Resolved, That in submitting an appeal to the Hon. House of Assembly, People of Color have done no more than stating their own grievances, leaving to the wisdom of the Legislature to extend to the Free Black Population, or not, as it may deem proper, the Privileges prayed for by the People of Colour.[12]

The free blacks resented this attitude and resolved to submit their own petition to the House. A group of them met in August 1823 and drafted the document as well as a letter to Hector Mitchel seeking his support.[13] In the letter, the blacks attacked the committee of color for its "avowed intention . . . to attempt the attainment of Rank and privileges. We know of no right to claim a preference pertaining to one freed man above the other—therefore we take the liberty of soliciting your support to the Petition of Free Condition so far especially as shall protect them from any foreign Infringement or attempt at preference."[14] Since the blacks' appeal was similar to that of the coloreds, the legislators considered the two documents together, thereby ignoring the differences of color among the petitioners. But in the 1820s, the free browns were unable to disregard the issue of color and to unite politically with the free blacks. As in the case of the privileged coloreds, any mark of superiority was regarded as important among people whose object was to be as much like the whites as possible.[15]

The petitions of the free blacks and the free coloreds and the campaign of the committee of color had thus achieved very little. Freedmen could now submit individual appeals to the House and were no longer required to produce certificates of freedom in court; however, they were still unable to participate in the political life of the colony. Furthermore, free blacks and browns continued to suffer from the effects of social and economic disabilities. A few whites were prepared to argue their case, but the overwhelming majority of assemblymen remained unwilling to make any significant changes in the status of the freedmen.

The House adopted a similar stance toward Government attempts to improve the condition of the slaves. Although the West India Committee supported the Crown's amelioration policy, the Assembly protested against it and refused to enact any meaningful legislation on behalf of the slaves. In 1824, the delegates threw out a bill that would have admitted slave evidence in court and that formed part of an Order in Council for the Crown Colonies. The Order in Council established new regulations concerning the treatment of slaves: it included provisions to appoint an official protector of slaves, to prohibit the use of the whip, and to prevent the enforced breakup of families by sale. When the governor submitted these measures to the Assembly in 1826, the representatives emphatically rejected them. Instead they devised their own codes which did little to protect the slave and proved unacceptable to the Government.[16]

Still, the continued attacks against slavery worried the whites and ultimately forced them to reconsider their tactics. As a result, more of them began to accept Richard Barrett's argument that the coloreds could be allies against the abolitionists. In 1826, a group of whites from St. James organized a meeting and resolved to petition the House in favor of removing the disabilities of the freedmen.[17] This attitude was also reflected in the report of a House committee which concluded that freedmen should be given the franchise under certain restrictions.[18] The committee made two other important suggestions: it recommended that free blacks and coloreds should have the right to work in any public office and that those who served in the militia should be permitted to "save deficiency."[19]

Although the suggested reforms were strictly limited, the committee's report met with considerable opposition in the House. Delegates continued to resist any improvements for the freedmen as a whole and sought to maintain the system of individual privilege bills. The representatives were no less eager to allow freedmen to "save deficiency." Hector Mitchel noted that the number of whites was already declining and that such a measure could only hasten the process. According to Mitchel, "the object of the Deficiency Bill would be entirely lost sight of if free persons were qualified to fill the places of whites upon properties. The axe would be laid to the root of the tree, and the constitution of the island, as by law established, would be overturned."[20] While most assemblymen agreed with Mitchel, the legislators were prepared to consider minor grievances. They therefore abolished the heavy fees on private privilege bills—which cost about £100 to get through the Assembly—because of the freedmen's reluctance to buy "the immunities they naturally considered their good conduct entitled them to."[21] The favorable report of the committee which had examined the situation suggested that several representatives wanted to better the condition of the free blacks and coloreds. As the pressure of the abolitionists mounted, members were becoming aware of their need for allies in the defense of slavery.[22]

The planters had to contend not only with the attacks against slavery but also with the support of the humanitarians for the freedmen. Lushington had already discussed their plight during a parliamentary debate in 1825.[23] In 1827, he presented a petition to Parliament from the free coloreds in Jamaica and was supported by a deputation of brown men led by Richard Hill, who appeared at the bar of the Commons and made a favorable impression on the House. Since Lushington believed that undue pressure from England at that point would have been counterproductive, he did not press the Government for any immediate measure on the freedmen, but he promised to raise the issue again if no action were taken on their behalf.[24]

The authorities in Jamaica were nonetheless slow to make any improvements in the condition of the free blacks and coloreds. In 1827, the Assembly rejected Barrett's bill to extend the privileges of the freedmen by a margin of more than thirty votes. While the vote was less one-sided a year later (twenty-six to fourteen), the Assembly remained opposed to legislation relieving the freedmen as a whole.[25] Lieutenant-Governor Sir John Keane was disappointed that the measure had not passed the House, especially since the colonial secretary, Sir George Murray, had issued a circular asking the governors of the legislative colonies to support the claims of the freedmen.[26] By 1829, the need for a bill to better the position of the free blacks and coloreds was becoming more evident. In the early part of the year, the Colonial Office conferred legal equality on all members of the free community in the Crown Colonies. A few months later, many whites in Jamaica were organizing petitions and were lobbying their delegates to remove the freedmen's disabilities. Wealthy planters reiterated the need for unity among the free population and called on the House to rectify the situation.[27]

Most assemblymen now favored legislation of this kind, but there still remained some resistance to any change in the freedmen's status. For example, the representative from Manchester, Curtis Berry, was afraid that Barrett's general privilege bill would allow unfit blacks and coloreds to control elections.

If the Bill now before the House should pass, at contested elections the People of Colour should so far outnumber the Whites, as to send to the House none but those who would favour their democratical views, and thus would they quickly fill all places of emolument and power.[28]

Augustin Beaumont, the member from Westmoreland, refuted Berry's claims. He pointed out that the proposed legislation would impose a high property qualification for the new voters and make it impossible for them to dominate the hustings. According to Beaumont, only seven freedmen would be permitted to vote in Spanish Town under the measure, which would hardly allow them to overwhelm the white electorate.[29]

The general privilege bill that eventually passed the House in February 1830 included a restrictive franchise for the free blacks and coloreds as well as other clauses intended to limit their political influence. Under its provisions, freedmen were not eligible to sit in the Assembly or the Council and could not fill any public offices unless they were qualified to vote.[30] During the session, the House also enacted a new election bill. Though ostensibly designed to equalize the franchise, the act retained the £10 franchise for whites until the next generation and protected the white majority at the polls.[31] The legislators were thus attempting to appease the aspirations of the freedmen, while introducing safeguards that would preserve the whites' continued supremacy. Since the governor, the second earl of Belmore (Somerset Lowry Corry), approved the bills, the Assembly did not expect the Crown to veto them. But when James Stephen reviewed the statutes a year later, he recommended that both the privilege and the election acts be disallowed.[32] As the privilege bill had already been superseded, Stephen focused his attack on the election law.

Stephen believed that the property qualifications for the franchise were too high and that only a small number of wealthy individuals would be able to vote. It was clear to Stephen that "the law was expressly intended to exclude from the Elective Franchise all that mass of Coloured Proprietors who would otherwise have participated in it." This was opposed to Government policy.

I humbly conceive that this Act is at variance with those principles respecting the equal rights of His Majesty's free Subjects of all Classes which have not merely been maintained in theory, but enforced in practice in those Colonies over which the legislative power of the King in Council extend.[33]

Stephen was not alone in denouncing the measure; the brown people in Jamaica were also disappointed by it. Since many of the coloreds regarded the laws as an insult, they resolved to carry on their struggle for full civil rights.[34] Instead of being pacified, the people of color were prepared for further agitation.

The coloreds' activities in February 1830 recalled their earlier campaign of 1823. A group of them met in Kingston and appointed four men to correspond with the people of color all over the island on "the expediency of petitioning the King in Council to withhold the Royal Assent from the 'Brown Privilege Bill.' "[35] In addition, they asked their supporters in England to publicize the true nature of the legislation. Since the browns believed that the statutes were intended "to throw dust into the eyes of the inhabitants of the mother country by a shew of liberality which really bestow very trifling and very restricted immunities,"[36] they were worried that the Crown would approve the new laws.

The people of color also claimed that the Assembly had passed the legislation "to divide the more wealthy Mulattoes from their brethren, in order to diminish the strength and influence of the body."[37] According to the colored press, the legislators had hoped that the acts would allow them to maintain "their political superiority, as well as their monopoly of every office of trust, honor, or emolument."[38] Henry Taylor, the senior clerk in the West India section of the Colonial Office, agreed that, while the law appeared to be an improvement for the browns, it would in practice separate the wealthy coloreds from the rest of the people of color.[39]

The delegates in the House were surprised by the opposition to a bill which they had regarded as a concession to the free blacks and browns. In addition, they were worried by the election in 1830 of a Whig administration that was more likely to intervene on behalf of the free coloreds. Since the whites also wanted to ensure the unity of the free community in the face of a more determined campaign by the abolitionists, the plantocracy resolved to take action.[40] In November 1830, William Grignon submitted a bill that granted freedmen all the rights whites enjoyed. He believed that the measure would remove the coloreds' grievances and unify the free population, "but should . . . the bill pass of one accord, granting them every privilege that we ourselves possess and show that we are their friends, the House would then draw the whole population together." Although there was still some fear of the possible consequences of the bill, it passed the House in December. The Assembly also approved an act that allowed free blacks and coloreds to "save deficiency" on the same basis as whites.[41]

By enacting this legislation, the whites hoped that the freedmen generally and the coloreds in particular would join them in the fight against abolition. But the legislators had acted too slowly to unite the browns with the whites. Instead of creating a sense of solidarity between the two groups, the Assembly's delay in removing the coloreds' disabilities had alienated the people of color. The deportation of Lecesne and Escoffery, the belief of many whites in a colored conspiracy, and the restrictions in the first general privilege bill had made any union of whites and coloreds that much more difficult. Since the people of color had found help in England, they were more likely to support British policy and to oppose the whites when they came into conflict with the Crown. The reluctance of the white ruling class to take positive steps on behalf of the people of color had thus rebounded against them.

The Assembly's resistance to the colored demands had led to other consequences: namely, it had forced the people of color to campaign for their rights and to develop organizational abilities that would be useful after 1830. As a result, the coloreds were more unified than they had been a decade earlier, although the privileged browns remained aloof from the activities of the people of color. In addition, the relationship between the free blacks and the free coloreds had also improved. *The Watchman* claimed that "the policy of the whites has occasioned an union between the blacks and browns which never before existed; and there is now so good an understanding between them as nothing will ever dissolve or injure." Events in the 1830s would impair this relationship, but for the moment, the long inaction of the whites had brought blacks and browns closer together.

By 1830, then, the people of color were a potentially significant political force. They were more numerous than the whites and could influence local elections as a result of the low property franchise. The coloreds therefore warned the whites to share the power they now held before it was too late.

If they lose their ascendency, it will be because they have clung to it with too great pertinacity, and viewed the coloured inhabitants with too great a degree of prejudice. Let them, for expediency sake, be liberal, and they may ensure, at any rate, a share of power. Let them give up a part of their long-enjoyed monopoly in order to secure the remainder.[42]

NOTES

1. CO 137/175, Lushington to Courtenay, September 17, 1826, enclosure: Minutes of the proceedings of the Kingston Committee of the People of Color, November 4, 1823.

2. *Postscript to The Royal Gazette*, November 15–22, 1823, Debates: November 13.

3. *The Jamaica Journal*, November 22, 1823.

4. *Postscript to The Royal Gazette*, November 29-December 6, 1823, Debates: November 27.

5. Ibid.

6. CO 318/76, Sympson to Hill, n.d. [1825], Appendix.

7. *Postscript to The Royal Gazette*, November 8–15, 1823, Debates: November 12.

8. Bathurst to Manchester, October 3, 1823, quoted in Sheila Duncker, "The Free Coloured and Their Fight for Civil Rights in Jamaica, 1800–1830" (unpublished M.A. thesis, University of London, 1960), p. 38.

9. Ibid., p. 47.

10. CO 318/76, Sympson to Hill, n.d. [1825], Appendix.

11. Duncker, "The Free Coloured," p. 231.

12. *Postscript to The Royal Gazette*, November 15–22, 1823.

13. CO 137/175, Lushington to Courtenay, September 17, 1826, enclosure: Circular no. 8, Kingston Committee of Color, August 26, 1823.

14. CO 318/66, The Report of the Commissioners of Legal Enquiry, First issue, February 28, 1826. Mitchel used this as evidence against the people of color, claiming that it referred to foreigners among the coloreds who were involved in the 1823 conspiracy. It is more likely that the free blacks were referring to foreigners who were hired because of the deficiency law. In their petition to the Assembly, the blacks noted that they were debarred "the use of their acquirements in mechanics, agricultural pursuits, as Overseers, Bookkeepers, etc., by the operation of the said Law, which to contem-

plate, evidently procures and grants a preference, even to Strangers, Foreigners, or Aliens." For their petition, see *The Jamaica Journal*, November 22, 1823, Debates: November 18.

15. Duncker, "The Free Coloured," pp. 198–99. In 1827, free blacks again petitioned the Assembly separately from the people of color.

16. *Proceedings of the Honourable House of Assembly of Jamaica, in Relation to Those Which Took Place in the British House of Commons, on the 15th of May last* ... (Jamaica, 1823), quoted in Lowell J. Ragatz, *The Fall of the Planter Class in the British Caribbean, 1763–1833* (New York, 1928), p. 417; Sir Reginald Coupland, *The British Anti-Slavery Movement*, reprinted (London, 1964), pp. 129–32.

17. For their petition, see *JAJ*, October 13, 1826, pp. 601–602.

18. The qualification for a free black or colored voter would have been a freehold worth £100 in a town or one valued at £50 in the country. See *The Royal Gazette*, November 18–25, 1826, Debates on the Claims of the People of Color.

19. This proposed amendment in the deficiency legislation would have extended the right of freedmen in the militia to "save deficiency" on white-owned plantations. See Chapter 2, note 26, p. 32.

20. *The Royal Gazette*, November 18–25, 1826, Debates on the Claims of the People of Color.

21. *Postscript to The Royal Gazette*, October 14–21, 1826, Debates: October 18.

22. In its search for support, the Assembly turned not only to the privileged coloreds but also to the Jews. In 1826, the House passed legislation making the Jews the legal equals of the whites. Since the Colonial Office was unwilling to strengthen the power of the whites, it refused to sanction this legislation until the Assembly had removed the disabilities of the free coloreds. For more details on the Jews, see Samuel J. and Edith Hurwitz, "The New World Sets an Example for the Old: The Jews of Jamaica and Political Rights, 1661–1831," *American Jewish Historical Quarterly* 55 (September 1965): 37–56.

23. *Hansard*, New Series, 13 (June 15, 1825): 1173–1205.

24. David Eltis, "Dr. Stephen Lushington: Liberal Reformer and Radical Advocate of Negro Rights" (unpublished M.A. thesis, University of Alberta, 1969), p. 102; Mavis Campbell, *The Dynamics of Change in a Slave Society* (Rutherford, N.J., 1976), p. 118; *Hansard*, New Series, 17 (June 12, 1827): 1242–49.

25. CO 137/165, Keane to Horton, December 24, 1827, private; CO 137/167, Keane to Murray, December 13, 1828, no. 31.

26. CO 138/51, Murray to Belmore, February 16, 1829, no. 3.

27. See, for example, the report of the meeting held at Montego Bay in *The Royal Gazette*, November 21–28, 1829.

28. Ibid., November 28–December 5, 1829, Debates: November 26.

29. Ibid.

30. *Postscript to The Royal Gazette*, February 6–13, 1830, Debates: February 10; CO 139/68, Jamaica Acts, 1830, Act no. 2055, "An act to remove certain disabilities of persons of free condition." Another bill, Act no. 2053, allowed coloreds who could qualify for the vote to "save deficiency."

31. CO 139/68, Jamaica Acts, 1830, Act no. 2048, "An act to regulate the elections in this island."

32. CO 323/48, Stephen to Goderich, June 6, 1831.
33. Ibid.
34. *The Watchman and Jamaica Free Press*, February 17, 1830.
35. Ibid., May 8, 1830.
36. Henry Duncan, *Presbyter's Letters on the West India Question* (London, 1830), p. 90.
37. Ibid.
38. *The Watchman and Jamaica Free Press*, August 7, 1830.
39. CO 137/180, Memo by Taylor on a letter by Mr. Gibbs, n.d.
40. Campbell, *Dynamics of Change*, p. 139. In 1830, the Anti-Slavery Society voted to press for immediate emancipation, though they had previously sought only gradual emancipation. See Frank J. Klingberg, *The Anti-Slavery Movement in England* (New Haven, Conn., 1926), p. 252; Coupland, *The British Anti-Slavery Movement*, pp. 134–35; and for a more recent assessment of the change in policy, see David B. Davis, "James Cropper and the British Anti-Slavery Movement, 1823–1833," *The Journal of Negro History* 46 (July 1961): 164.
41. *Postscript to The Royal Gazette*, November 13–20, 1830, Debates: November 17; CO 139/69, Jamaica Acts, 1830, Act no. 2092.
42. *The Watchman and Jamaica Free Press*, May 22, 1830.

Part II: Brown Men in the Assembly and in Society, 1830-1865

5

Coloreds and Blacks in the Assembly: A Biographical and Ideological Profile

By passing the final privilege act on behalf of the freedmen in December 1830, the white legislators ensured that it would be some time before many coloreds could win places in the House of Assembly. Since a general election had just been held in the island that fall, the opportunity for brown politicians to contest a large number of seats in the House was likely to be a few years away. The people of color had other political problems as well. For example, they were a significant element in several urban constituencies, but the towns on the island returned only a small fraction of the total number of assemblymen. Furthermore, the coloreds were new to elective politics. Although they had successfully organized a campaign for their rights, they did not have experience in getting out the vote or setting up a slate of candidates.

In spite of these obstacles, two brown men, Price Watkis (1831–1836)[1] and John Manderson (1831–1836, 1838–1841), were elected to the Assembly less than a year after the civil rights legislation had been passed. Both were returned as a result of by-elections held in October 1831, Watkis for Kingston and Manderson for St. James. Even voting together, they could hardly accomplish much in a House that consisted of forty-five members.[2] Since the two of them disagreed on some important issues, the impact they might have had was further diminished. Men of color were nonetheless present in the Assembly and expressed views there which were often very different from those of the white representatives.

Watkis was the more outspoken of the two colored delegates. The first brown barrister on the island, he had a large practice and successfully defended Edward Jordon during his trial for treason in 1832.[3] Moreover, Watkis generally sympathized with the editorial stance of *The Watchman*. Watkis was proud of his color and of his link with the people of Jamaica: "he *boasted* of being a coloured man,"[4] and during a debate in the House he noted: "I am one of the people. I am attached to the people by birth and every other sympathy."[5] Unlike the white legislators, he regarded himself "as the representative of the slave (a murmur from Mr. Brown, the Member for St. Ann's), yes, he repeated, as the representative of the slave, for such he considered himself as much as of the freeman...."[6] Watkis was also vocal about his support for the slaves outside the House. Soon after the slave rebellion of 1831–1832,[7] he was reported to have berated another brown man for not being concerned about the slaves. According to a witness, Watkis maintained that the people of color should "have entertained some sympathy for their origin, and that for his own part, he should labour by every means in his power in their [slaves] behalf." While Watkis corrected that statement by noting that he would use "every legal means" to free the slaves, the distinction was lost on those seeking to uphold the system.[8]

The other colored representative in the Assembly, John Manderson, did not agree with Watkis' views on emancipation. A comfortable merchant from Montego Bay, Manderson was to become the first brown custos on the island. In that capacity, he chaired meetings of the parish vestry and was effectively head of the parish. As a future custos and as one of the representatives from a sugar district, Manderson supported the whites in their resistance to abolition. *The Watchman* therefore identified him with the planter class. But the editors of the paper were apparently unaware of Manderson's financial support of *The Struggler*, the free colored newspaper for Montego Bay. Manderson was also prepared to take steps that could alienate him from the whites. After the 1831–1832 rebellion, he stood bail for the Baptist missionaries who were imprisoned in Montego Bay. Since his defense of the missionaries exposed him to the anger of the local white community, Manderson proved that he was more than a brown man striving simply to be white.[9]

Apart from Manderson, the other colored delegates returned in the 1830s tended to vote as a bloc and in opposition to the whites. However, only five more men of color were elected to the House between 1833 and 1837: John Campbell (1833–1834), Edward Jordon (1834–1852, 1854–1864), Robert Osborn (1835–1866), Aaron Deleon (1835–1837), and James Taylor (1835–1861). John Campbell was a retailer from Montego Bay who had been "extremely well educated in England," according to Lord Sligo (Peter Howe Browne), governor of Jamaica from 1834 to 1836. Campbell was involved in the early petitions of the free coloreds for their civil rights, but he had to resign his seat in the Assembly because of ill-health.[10]

Edward Jordon was elected to fill out Campbell's term and sat in the House with a short break for the next thirty years. Born in 1800, he was probably the offspring of a free black mother and a free colored father. Like many coloreds,

Jordon worked as a clerk to a Kingston merchant, but he lost the job because of his involvement in the coloreds' campaign for civil rights in the 1820s. Jordon later opened a bookshop in Kingston with Robert Osborn; its success enabled them to launch *The Watchman* in 1829. Although the newspaper campaigned successfully for the coloreds' civil rights, its anti-planter stance hardly made Jordon a popular figure among the white population. Yet, by 1834, he had already served as a Kingston alderman and was beginning a long career in Jamaican politics. Several later governors shared Sligo's view that Jordon's "character, and station as the head of the Coloured Inhabitants of this Island, entitles his opinion to the highest respect."[11]

Jordon's associate, Robert Osborn, was also born in 1800. His father was a wealthy Scottish planter who became speaker of the House. Osborn may have been born a slave, but because of his father's wealth he probably would not have remained one for long.[12] Trained as a printer, Osborn was later responsible for the printing of *The Watchman*; he also worked with Jordon on the paper's editorial content and on its successor, *The Morning Journal*. Osborn became involved in parish politics soon after the coloreds had gained the vote, and he was elected to posts in Kingston and St. Andrew. In 1835, he won a seat in the House which he held continuously until 1866. As a politician, Osborn was a passionate and outspoken partisan of the people of color. For example, in a speech after he had been returned to the Assembly for the first time, he "complimented the colored constituency on the independent manner in which they had come forward and asserted their rights. On taking his seat in the House of Assembly, he would endeavour to advance their interest in every possible way."[13] Such views did not endear him to the whites in the Assembly, but Osborn outlasted most of them and became one of the House's most important members.

The two other men of color elected to the House in 1835, Aaron Deleon and James Taylor, were both strong opponents of slavery. Sligo described Deleon as a man "formerly known as a decided radical . . . [who] will be a decided friend of the Government."[14] Taylor was an equally loyal supporter of the Government and remained in the Assembly for over a quarter of a century until his death in 1861. A Kingston merchant and clerk of the Kingston vestry, Taylor contributed heavily to the antislavery cause and freed the forty slaves he received as a legacy. He was also a very popular figure in the island.[15]

The number of coloreds in the House increased significantly as a result of the general election held in 1837. Osborn, Jordon, and Taylor were reelected and were joined by five new brown delegates, the most prominent of whom was Richard Hill (1837–1838). Hill was educated in England, had close connections with the Anti-Slavery Society, and visited Haiti on behalf of the society. The first colored stipendiary magistrate on the island, Hill eventually became secretary of the Department of Stipendiary Magistrates—a post that made him one of the more influential members of the administration. Although Hill was reviled by the planter press in the 1830s, a leading figure on the island more than half a century later described him as "one of Jamaica's most worthy and remarkable sons—philanthropist, politician, magistrate, author, poet, naturalist, draughtsman, and indefatigable worker, and a man of wide sympathies."[16]

Hill served in the House for only one brief term, but two other men of color who worked for the Government, Robert Russell (1837–1838, 1841–1847, 1850–1854, 1855–1860) and William Thomas March (1837–1863), remained in the Assembly until the 1860s. Russell was a barrister who was employed in the governor's office from 1832 to 1836 during the administrations of Mulgrave and Sligo and later became registrar in chancery. He corresponded with members of the Anti-Slavery Society and was regarded as an articulate spokesman of the people of color.[17] William Thomas March, also an attorney, served in the 1830s as a defender of slaves and later as clerk of the Supreme Court. Sligo described March as "a man of excellent character, a great enemy to oppression, and always a decided advocate for the Slave."[18] March ended his career as island secretary.

The occupations of the other new colored representatives, Charles Lake (1837–1850) and J. S. Brown (1837–1838, 1844–1851), are less clear. Both may have been Kingston merchants, although they were involved in other activities as well. Lake was elected to offices in Kingston and was later appointed stipendiary magistrate for Portland. Brown was the secretary of the Jamaica Mutual Life Assurance Company and a director of the Planters' Bank and the Water Company.[19]

The coloreds in the Assembly during the 1830s, then, were men of some standing. Two were editors, two were attorneys who worked for the Government, one was an important Government official, one was a barrister, and several were apparently merchants. Russell, Jordon, Osborn, and Hill corresponded with British abolitionists and were visited in Jamaica by representatives of the antislavery societies who came to examine the workings of apprenticeship. The coloreds' connections in England as well as their more urban and often professional occupations in Jamaica reflected a very different orientation from the majority of the whites. This pattern continued after the ending of the apprenticeship system and into the post-emancipation period.

Several men of color who were returned in the 1840s enjoyed lengthy terms in the House. Among this group, Charles Jackson (1845–1866) served the longest; he remained a delegate until the Assembly was abolished. Jackson came from a prominent local family—both his father and grandfather had been chief justices of the island. Born in 1817, the younger Jackson was articled to solicitors in Kingston and Spanish Town and later became clerk of the peace for the parish of Manchester. He was known for his independence in the House as well as for his knowledge of its rules. Jackson's pivotal position during the 1860s and his skill in the House led to his appointment as speaker in 1864.[20]

Jackson was not the only colored attorney-at-law to become an assembly-man for the first time in the 1840s. Both Peter Moncrieffe (1842–1849) and Alexander Heslop (1849–1860) were barristers who had been educated abroad and had distinguished professional careers in the island.[21] Henry Franklin (1844–1857) was a wealthy solicitor for a firm of mortgagees as well as a director of the Planters' Bank. At his death, Franklin left nearly £14,000 in personal property apart from his freehold estates and lands. Another lawyer, Foster March (1851–1860, 1861–1862), served as an alderman and a common councillor in Kingston; like Franklin, he died while still a delegate to the Assembly.[22]

The brown attorneys in the House augmented an already sizable group of barristers and solicitors. Fourteen lawyers were returned to the two Assemblies which lasted from 1838 to 1849, though not all of them practiced law. During this period, the number of brown attorneys rose from two to six. The high proportion of lawyers was not that surprising. Their work was often centered around the capital, and their skills were important in ensuring the smooth flow of legislation.[23] The presence of so many attorneys in the Assembly nonetheless became an issue on the hustings. A successful candidate for a by-election claimed that he was prompted to run because a lawyer was seeking the seat and there were already too many of them in the House.[24]

Apart from the brown lawyers, two colored merchants who had extensive landholdings also became delegates to the House in the 1840s. Alexander Forbes (1844–1845) was the founder of a Kingston firm and owned property principally in St. Andrew. After serving on the Kingston Common Council for many years, he died only a year after he was returned to the House.[25] George William Gordon (1844–1849, 1863–1865) had a longer and more documented career. Born a slave, he was freed by his father who was a wealthy planting attorney and proprietor. The younger Gordon eventually opened a produce store in Kingston which proved successful and enabled him to purchase large plots of land all over the island. The land was apparently intended to provide small holdings for the peasantry, and Gordon's will made it clear that some of his remaining estates were to be sold in lots to the laborers who worked the land. Yet, when he was elected to the Assembly in 1844, there was little evidence of Gordon's later development as a radical politician or his concern for the peasantry. In the election, he defeated a rival who was supported by a radical Baptist missionary. Moreover, he generally voted in the 1840s with the planters on immigration and on retrenchment, although he joined the colored party in its opposition to the plantocracy in 1848.[26]

While nearly all of the colored assemblymen were characterized by their wealth or education, one candidate returned in 1842 represented a departure from this tradition. Hugh Henry (1842–1843) was a small provision shopkeeper who defeated a well-known planter in a by-election for Hanover.[27] Henry's appeal was to the recently enfranchised voters. His advertisements were directed to the "Independent Electors," and his spokesman at the hustings described the parish as a "rotten borough."[28] When Henry lost the election, a planter paper concluded that "radicalism has thus been signally defeated; and it is hoped for ever silenced." However, irregularities during the election voided the result and forced a second poll which Henry won.[29] Henry proved to be an inactive delegate and resigned after only one term in office. But his election was significant, as he was the first brown man who emerged from the class of shopkeepers and artisans to be returned to the Assembly. By the end of the decade, there were other representatives who shared his background.

The new type of assemblyman elected primarily in the late 1840s and early 1850s included brown tradesmen and shopkeepers as well as blacks. Edward Vickars (1847–1860), a Kingston alderman and magistrate, was the first black man who sat in the House.[30] Although his occupation is not clear, Vickars owned slaves in 1834 and held office during the 1850s as a commissioner of the Ferry Toll Road. At his death, he had several houses in Kingston and land in the city and in St. Andrew.[31] Another black member of the House, Charles Price (1849–1863), was a master carpenter and builder who served on the Kingston Common Council and as a justice of the peace.[32] Price characterized himself as a tradesman and a member of the laboring class, but he also noted that his family had been "free from slavery and born in legitimacy" for five generations.[33] A prominent Jamaican doctor, Lewis Bowerbank, described Price as "perhaps in intelligence the first of his class in Jamaica."[34] Yet, in spite of his color, Price was killed by rioters at Morant Bay in 1865. The other representative who may have been black, Christopher Walters (1851–1865), was a cobbler from Port Antonio. A trustee of the Titchfield School and a churchwarden of his parish, he had amassed enough capital by 1860 to become the proprietor of a sugar estate.[35]

Several brown members of the Assembly who were elected around 1850 also worked with their hands or owned small businesses. Samuel Q. Bell (1849–1853) was a carpenter, John Nunes (1852–1866) owned a livery stable in Kingston, and Robert L. Constantine (1854–1859) was the proprietor of a store in Trelawny.[36] All three men served as vestrymen in various parishes, and Constantine was a collecting constable in Trelawny. Like the black men in the House, Bell, Nunes, and Constantine represented a different class of assemblyman than had formerly sat in Spanish Town. At the same time, colored professionals and officials continued to be elected to the House.

A few of the wealthier men of color who were first returned to the Assembly in the 1850s often voted with the planters. Wellesley Bourke (1851–1866), a solicitor and clerk of the peace, was one of them. A vestryman for St. James, Bourke owned some land and buildings in Spanish Town.[37] The editor of *The Falmouth Post*, John Castello (1853–1860), was also a member of the Country party, the faction associated with the plantocracy. An early ally of the

Baptist missionaries, his relations with them deteriorated sharply after the end of apprenticeship. Moreover, he generally opposed the politics of Jordon and Osborn.[38] Another colored representative, Stephen Weise Mais (1851–1866), held office as master·in chancery and as road commissioner. The son of a planter and member of the Assembly before abolition, Mais became custos of Port Royal and served in a variety of other parish posts.[39]

The number of brown assemblymen declined during the late 1850s and 1860s; however, three new colored members who practiced law or owned land managed to win seats to the House. The most prominent was Samuel Constantine Burke (1863–1866). A lawyer, Burke was educated at Harrow and Cambridge and became an important figure in island politics. Although he opposed the abolition of the House in 1865, Burke served on the Legislative Council which replaced it and became the leader of the unofficial members on the new legislative body.[40] D. P. Nathan (1863–1866) was also a lawyer who practiced in Kingston; he held the usual parish offices and rose to become mayor of the city.[41] Unlike Nathan and Burke, John Pillon (1860–1863) was a minor official, serving as an inspector of weights and measures and clerk of the market in Port Antonio. Pillon nonetheless owned a considerable amount of property and established a scholarship fund for the sons of army officers from his father's former regiment.[42] The last brown man elected to the Assembly, James Mitchell Gibb (1865–1866), was a planter as well as a harbormaster and collecting constable. He later became a banker and served as the custos of Clarendon; in addition, he joined Burke as an unofficial member of the Legislative Council.[43]

Although nearly all the brown men in the House were considered respectable members of society, two of them—at various times in their careers—had been accused of misappropriating funds. Foster Davis (1849–1852, 1855–1860, 1862–1863) was a lawyer and held office as master extraordinary of the chancery. In 1852, he was expelled from the House for refusing to refund money that had been allocated for improving the parish roads. His expulsion did not prevent him from running again for a different constituency and sitting in several other sessions.[44] Robert A. Johnson (1861–1866) was involved in a similar case: he had been forced to resign as a Wesleyan minister for mishandling church funds. He later became a schoolmaster and was a newspaper editor during his years in the House.[45]

The black and brown men in the House of Assembly during the period from 1831 to 1866 were clearly a diversified group: more than a third of them were lawyers, and several were merchants, editors, and officials. The blacks and nonprofessional brown men elected around 1850 represented a departure from their predecessors, who were generally more educated and wealthier men of color. Nevertheless, nearly all the coloreds shared an urban orientation; not one of them was solely a planter, and only a few had any significant connection with the land.

The increasing number of brown representatives in the Assembly represented a dramatic shift in the composition of the House. While there were only seven colored assemblymen in 1841, fourteen browns and three blacks occupied places in the House ten years later. The number of Jews also rose dramatically during this period: four sat in the House which lasted from 1838 to 1844, but sixteen won seats in the shorter term from 1860 to 1863 (Figure 2). The result was a membership that was less directly attached to the land and more distinctly creole. In addition, it meant the expression of an alternative set of political ideas in the House.

The brown politicians were creoles above everything else. They were committed to the country in which they had been born, and they were dedicated to its future. For the coloreds, this loyalty to Jamaica was in marked contrast to the attitudes of the planter class. This theme surfaced repeatedly in the Assembly. For example, during one of the recurring political crises in the postemancipation period, Robert Osborn argued for the need to maintain government, particularly in the face of a proposed legislative strike. Osborn noted that other delegates might be able to board ships and travel elsewhere if the situation on the island became too dangerous, but he and his creole friends had nowhere else to go. Since Jamaica was their home, they did not wish to see it ruined.[46]

The coloreds in the House also complained that the white delegates were prepared to damage the financial well-being of the colony in order to influence the British Government. While the browns were concerned about the threat to Jamaica's solvency, they claimed that the planter representatives were continuing to rely on a Home Government whose colonial policy was no longer in their favor. According to the colored newspaper, *The Morning Journal*, the white assemblymen would follow the same line "until the popular voice shall be more distinctly heard within our Legislative hall." Such delegates would protect local institutions from abuse and attempt to solve the problems in Jamaica without counterproductive attempts to sway Parliament.[47]

The brown politicians were thus linking themselves to the people. Robert Osborn often reminded audiences of his ties to the working class. At a meeting in 1851, he described his long-standing commitment to them. According to the *Daily Advertiser*, Osborn asserted that

he had been fighting for the people for the last twenty-five years; he lived among them and was taxed in the same manner as everybody else, and he hoped they would have confidence in him. . . . From the time that he hoisted his flag, he has always stuck to it, and never deserted it.[48]

Although much of this was political rhetoric, Osborn and his political allies shared the view that they alone would work in the best interests of the majority

Figure 2. COMPOSITION OF THE ASSEMBLY: BLACKS, COLOREDS, AND JEWS, 1838–1866

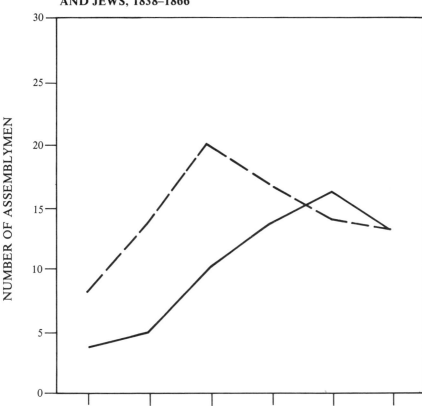

Coloreds and Blacks

Jews

The chart represents the number of coloreds, blacks, and Jews elected during the life of each assembly.

SOURCE: See Appendix B.

of the population. In part, this attitude reflected the coloreds' ideas about the future: they believed that blacks and browns would one day take over from the whites. Osborn was more precise about when the transfer of power would occur. He claimed in 1858 that "the Government of the country within twenty-five years will be left to brown and black men."[49] *The Morning Journal* also warned the whites that it was useless for them to worry about the rise of blacks and coloreds in island politics. After all, Bryan Edwards had long ago predicted that "the West Indies are destined to be governed by the children of its soil."[50] Charles Jackson agreed. During a debate in the House, he pointed out that

if we enquire into the facts which relate to the intermixture of Negroes and Europeans, it will be impossible to doubt the tendency of the so termed Mulattoes to increase. The men of colour, or the mixed race between the Creoles and the Negroes, are, in many of the West India islands, a rapidly increasing people, and it would be very probable that they will eventually become the permanent masters of the island, were it not for the great numerical superiority of the genuine negroes.[51]

In light of Jackson's prediction, the coloreds maintained that the best preparation for the future was to educate the people for it.

The brown delegates therefore appealed to the whites in the House to pass the appropriate measures. Charles Jackson was speaking particularly to the planter representatives when he exhorted them to take action:

Let them do the people, the great body of the people, whose rights they hypocritically pretend to regard, the justice that was due to them . . . educate them, moralize them, treat those who are advanced in the world well, and endeavour to infuse a spirit of emulation among them, and fit them morally to occupy positions to which in the nature of things, they must arrive.[52]

The Morning Journal argued along similar lines but was especially concerned about the education of the future voters. The newspaper noted that the 3,000 voters registered in 1853 were an insignificant number compared to those who would soon be qualified. Since the new electors would be primarily black and brown, the editors of the paper concluded that the only way of "providing for the well-being of our Constitution" was to educate and elevate the new constituencies.[53]

But the brown politicians wanted time to prepare for the future. They were in favor of gradual political change, although Osborn declared that the brown leaders had the option of speeding up the process. He suggested that they could have brought out all the half-acre landowners to vote in elections and swamped the Assembly with blacks. As conservatives, however, the colored representatives were opposed to this development: "If it were not because many of us are of conservative feelings, you would have this place long ago, deluged with negroes; but I don't think this desirable. If the thing must come, let it come naturally."[54] In the coloreds' view of the future, blacks and browns would dominate politics and society, but there was also a place for the whites. Brown delegates blamed the planter class for its dependence on England, for its failure to prepare the people to exercise power, and for its class legislation. Nonetheless, for the colored representatives, the plantocracy still represented European values. This meant that the planters should continue to have an important role in post-emancipation Jamaica.

On the one hand, then, the brown assemblymen continued to attack the planter representatives for their waste and extravagance. Osborn was among several coloreds who noted that the white ruling class was unwilling to make any lasting improvements in the colony:

The history of the country shows the indelible fact that it has been the system of the planters, for three-quarters of a century past to take everything away from the country and to return nothing to it, except what is necessary to keep up their estates. . . . What have they done for the country? Nothing.[55]

Such criticism was frequent. On the other hand, when the coloreds considered changes in the plantation system, they were more careful. Even for them, sugar was still king.

Like so many critics of the way sugar was grown in Jamaica, the brown delegates complained about the problem of absentee ownership. In their judgment, absenteeism deprived the island of its natural leaders and seemed highly uneconomic as well. Since sugar profits were spent elsewhere, Jamaica gained little from its most valuable resource. The alternative—a locally resident class of estate owners—would fill an important vacuum in the society while paying attention to the needs of the colony.[56] The coloreds were also worried about the consequences of Jamaica's heavy dependence on sugar. They argued that it made the economy overly vulnerable to fluctuations in the metropolitan market and led to the importation of large quantities of foodstuffs that could be raised locally. For these reasons, the colored leadership advocated a more diversified economy. Elaborating on this theme, *The Morning Journal* maintained that the production of ground provisions, cotton, corn, and honey could be undertaken by the temporarily unemployed or by those who did not work for the estates. These new sources of wealth would help to create a middle class tied to the land.[57]

The plantocracy was unhappy about these proposals. Sir Henry Barkly, governor of Jamaica from 1853 to 1856 and himself a sugar planter, was strongly opposed to any attempt to displace the sugar industry. For him, the departure of European capital, energy, and intelligence would mean the economic ruin of the island. Barkly supported plans for some diversification, but he argued that minor products could never take the place of sugar.[58] Like many planters, then, Barkly misunderstood the coloreds' proposals. The brown politicians were not in favor of dismantling the sugar estates; on the contrary, the coloreds believed that the plantations were still at the heart of the economy. In addition, the planters and the plantations were the bearers of European civilization. Without their influence, many colored delegates feared that the mass of the population would recede into barbarism.[59]

The coloreds thus sought to have a prosperous sugar industry as well as a diversified economy. Richard Hill was an exponent of this approach. He advocated a balance between the estates and the small farmers, although he recognized that this balance had been made more difficult by the planters' refusal to sell land on their estates to the ex-slaves after emancipation. In Hill's view, the peasants and small farmers should have worked part-time on the plantations, thereby helping to keep the estates going and also bringing the former slaves "into the mainstream of Jamaican life."[60]

On the question of the plantation system as well as on other general issues, the colored delegates often disagreed with the representatives of planters. This was hardly surprising, since the coloreds were not usually connected with the estates, and their electoral support tended to come from blacks and coloreds rather than from whites.[61] But although the brown representatives considered the needs of the ex-slaves, they were often unsuccessful in translating their ideas into legislation. In part, this was because they did not always agree among themselves on specific policies. More importantly, the coloreds had to confront a strongly entrenched plantocracy that sought to retain the political power and the social privileges it had acquired during slavery.

NOTES

1. The dates here and elsewhere in the text after the names of assemblymen refer to their respective terms in the House. See Glory Robertson (comp.), *Members of the Assembly of Jamaica* (mimeo, Institute of Jamaica, 1965), pp. 50–59.

2. In 1842, the number of assemblymen increased to forty-seven because of the creation of a new parish, Metcalfe.

3. Sligo Papers, MS 228, Public Letters, II, Sligo to Glenelg, August 11, 1835, no. 84, 117. For more details on the trial, see Chapter 7, p. 88.

4. *The Falmouth Post*, May 4, 1836, cited in Marlene Manderson-Jones, "Richard Hill of Jamaica, His Life and Times, 1795–1872" (unpublished Ph.D. thesis, University of the West Indies, 1973), p. 211n.

5. *The Watchman and Jamaica Free Press*, May 26, 1832, Debates: April 23.

6. *Supplement to The Royal Gazette*, October 5–12, 1823, Debates: October 3.

7. The rebellion is treated in greater detail in Chapter 7, pp. 85–86.

8. *Supplement to The Royal Gazette*, February 4–11, 1832.

9. *The Watchman and Jamaica Free Press*, July 9, 1831; Mary Reckord, "Missionary Activity in Jamaica Before Emancipation" (unpublished Ph.D. thesis, University of London, 1964), p. 289n.; Thomas F. Abbott, *Narrative of Certain Events Connected with the Late Disturbances in Jamaica* . . . (London, 1832), pp. 10–12; Philip Wright, *Knibb, 'the Notorious' Slaves' Missionary, 1803–1845* (London, 1973), pp. 98–99.

10. Sligo Papers, MS 228, Public Letters, I, Sligo to Stanley, June 13, 1834, no. 27, 21.

11. CO 137/209, Sligo to Glenelg, January 21, 1836, no. 286. For more background on Jordon, see Mavis Campbell, *The Dynamics of Change in a Slave Society*

(Rutherford, N.J., 1976), passim; W. Adolphe Roberts, *Six Great Jamaicans* (Kingston, 1952), pp. 4–24; W. A. Feurtado, "MS notes on official and other personages in Jamaica" (hereafter referred to as MS notes); James A. Thome and Horace J. Kimball, *Emancipation in the West Indies* (New York, 1838), p. 88.

12. CO 137/235, East to Glenelg, August 28, 1838, enclosure; John Bigelow, *Jamaica in 1850* (London, 1851), p. 35.

13. *Supplement to The Royal Gazette*, October 17–24, 1835; Feurtado, MS notes. For further background on Osborn, see Gad J. Heuman, "Robert Osborn: Brown Power Leader in Nineteenth Century Jamaica," *Jamaica Journal* 11 (August 1977): 76–81.

14. Sligo Papers, MS 281, Private Letter Book, Sligo to Glenelg, October 26, 1835.

15. Ibid.; H. P. Jacobs, *Sixty Years of Change, 1806–1866* (Kingston, 1973), p. 142; Feurtado, MS notes. Taylor's obituary is in *The Morning Journal*, September 30, 1861.

16. Frank Cundall, *Biographical Annals of Jamaica* (Kingston, 1904), p. 29; Manderson-Jones, "Richard Hill," passim.

17. Feurtado, MS notes. Russell's brief correspondence with L. A. Chamerovzow, the secretary of the British and Foreign Anti-Slavery Society, is in the Anti-Slavery Society Papers, Rhodes House, Oxford.

18. Sligo Papers, MS 228, Public Letters, II, Sligo to Glenelg, August 11, 1835, no. 84, 117–18; Feurtado, MS notes. March's birth certificate is available in the IRO, Registry, vol. 2, f. 141, and indicates that he was born a free mustee.

19. Feurtado, MS notes.

20. [Augustus C. Sinclair], *The Political Life of the Hon. Charles Hamilton Jackson* . . . (Kingston, n.d., circa 1878), pp. 1–24; Feurtado, MS notes; CO 137/351, Darling to Newcastle, November 24, 1860, confidential.

21. For Moncrieffe, see Feurtado, MS notes. For Heslop, see MSS, West India Reference Library, Institute of Jamaica: William Cowper, "A Catalogue of Men Born in the Island of Jamaica who matriculated at Oxford, 1689–1855 . . ." (n.d.); Feurtado, MS notes; CO 137/374, Eyre to Newcastle, September 29, 1863, confidential. Heslop is discussed in more detail in Chapter 6, p. 77.

22. For Henry Franklin, see Feurtado, MS notes; IRO: Will (entered November 14, 1857); Inventory 159–152. For Foster March, see Feurtado, MS notes; CO 137/351, Darling to Newcastle, November 24, 1860, confidential; *Daily Advertiser*, November 17, 1851.

23. In "Politics as a Vocation," Max Weber describes the importance of the lawyer in politics. See Max Weber, *From Max Weber*, edited by H. H. Gerth and C. Wright Mills (London, 1970), pp. 94–95.

24. *Postscript to the Cornwall Chronicle*, June 5, 1841.

25. Feurtado, MS notes; Slave Compensation Records; *Jamaica Almanac*, 1840, 1845; IRO, Will: 123–217.

26. Feurtado, MS notes; *Jamaica Almanac*, 1840, 1845; *The Baptist Herald*, September 24, 1844; IRO, Will: 131–180; Inventory: 161–210; Ansell Hart, *The Life of George William Gordon* (Kingston, 1972), passim; Roberts, *Six Great Jamaicans*, pp. 25–29. Roberts provides some useful background on Gordon, but he is apparently unaware of Gordon's early political career in the Assembly. For some of Gordon's early votes on immigration and retrenchment, see *VAJ*, December 5, 1844, p. 346,

December 20, 1844, pp. 457–58; and *The Falmouth Post*, October 26, 1847, Debates.

27. Feurtado, MS notes; *The Falmouth Post*, September 20, 1843. There is little conclusive evidence that Henry was a brown man. However, the attacks on him in the press and the comment that the Democrats won "by reviving the forgotten distinction of colour" suggest that he was. See the *Jamaica Standard and Royal Gazette*, January 15, 1843.

28. *The Cornwall Chronicle*, December 25, November 24, 1841.

29. *Jamaica Standard and Royal Gazette*, November 26, 1841. Henry's petition claiming that his supporters were illegally deprived of their votes appears in *VAJ*, November 26, 1841, pp. 208–209.

30. Robert Clemetson, harbormaster and collecting constable, was also black and was returned to the House in 1841 and again in 1844. The Assembly voided his election on each occasion. Vickars was described as a black man in his obituary: *The Morning Journal*, April 20, 1867.

31. Feurtado, MS notes; Slave Compensation Records; IRO, Will: 130–182; Inventory: 161–113.

32. Feurtado, MS notes; CO 137/351, Darling to Newcastle, November 24, 1860, confidential.

33. Abraham Judah and A. C. Sinclair (comps.), *Debates of the Honourable House of Assembly of Jamaica . . .*, 13 vols. (Kingston and Spanish Town, 1856–1866), February 22, 1861, p. 473.

34. CO 137/390, Eyre to Cardwell, April 19, 1865, no. 90, enclosures: Bowerbank to Austin, March 15, 1865.

35. Feurtado, MS notes; *VAJ*, 1844, Appendix, p. 219; CO 137/351, Darling to Newcastle, November 24, 1860, confidential. For the view that Walters was brown, see Newcastle Papers, NeC 9553, Barkly to Roberts, March 10, 1854.

36. For all three, see Feurtado, MS notes. Jury lists suggest that Bell was a carpenter, and CO 137/351, Darling to Newcastle, November 24, 1860, confidential, and CO 137/380, Eyre to Newcastle, March 9, 1864, confidential describe Nunes. Nunes' inventory is available: IRO, Inventory: 160–198.

37. Feurtado, MS notes; CO 137/351, Darling to Newcastle, November 24, 1860, confidential.

38. Feurtado, MS notes; Obituary in *The Daily Gleaner*, April 2, 1877.

39. Feurtado, MS notes; CO 137/351, Darling to Newcastle, November 24, 1860, confidential; Obituary in *The Daily Gleaner*, November 22, 1900.

40. Biographical notes: West India Reference Library.

41. Feurtado, MS notes; *VAJ*, 1861, Appendix, p. 165.

42. Feurtado, MS notes; CO 137/351, Darling to Newcastle, November 24, 1860, confidential; CO 137/357, Darling to Newcastle, October 22, 1861, no. 151.

43. Feurtado, MS notes; Biographical notes: West India Reference Library.

44. Feurtado, MS notes: CO 137/380, Eyre to Newcastle, March 9, 1864, confidential.

45. Feurtado, MS notes.

46. *Daily Advertiser*, May 21, 1853, Debates: May 18.

47. *The Morning Journal*, October 22, 1850.

48. *Daily Advertiser*, December 8, 1851.

49. Judah and Sinclair, *Debates*, December 31, 1858, p. 309.
50. *The Morning Journal*, August 25, 1848.
51. Ibid., February 21, 1849, Debates: February 14.
52. Ibid.
53. Ibid., October 3, 1853.
54. Judah and Sinclair, *Debates*, December 31, 1858, p. 309.
55. Ibid., January 4, 1859, p. 317.
56. *The Morning Journal*, October 9, 1851. This was an interesting attack on the absentees because it attempted to divide the resident proprietary from the absentees.
57. Ibid., February 25, 1850.
58. CO 137/323, Barkly to Newcastle, May 26, 1854, no. 73.
59. *The Falmouth Post*, March 16, 1855; *The Morning Journal*, January 1, 1848.
60. Manderson-Jones, "Richard Hill," pp. 490, 411.
61. This point is discussed in more detail in Chapter 9.

6

White Over Brown
Over Black: The
Coloreds in Post-
Emancipation Society

Although brown men and a few blacks won seats to the House of Assembly after 1830, the people of color continued to feel the effects of segregation and discrimination in post-emancipation Jamaica. The problem was not the privilege bill on behalf of the people of color but rather its lack of effectiveness in altering their place in society. Many of the coloreds were therefore angry about their situation. Like Martin Halhead in 1813, they had expected more than white society was prepared to concede.

Brown men often publicized their protests through the free colored press. For example, one letter writer to *The Watchman* reported on a court of inquiry which examined the charge that coloreds were not being selected as officers for the militia. William Griffiths, a brown member of the militia, had lodged the complaint and had argued that men of color were capable of becoming officers "and besides that, this is our native country—we have nowhere to go; and consider it a hardship to be superseded by foreigners who have been in the country for 10 or 12 months and who brought nothing with them." Griffiths' plea was limited to colored companies. Although the militia was still segregated, he was apparently prepared to accept free colored units as long as brown men could lead their own groups.[1]

The Watchman supported the view that coloreds were not being promoted in the militia. It had earlier reported the situation in St. Andrew where a colonel's fourteen-year-old nephew had received a commission as an ensign. This was not the only case of its kind; brown men were also overlooked in favor of a temporary white resident in the parish. Unhappy about these appointments, *The Watchman* argued that selections should be made from the ranks of the militia rather than from the ranks of the officers' relatives and friends. The paper was disappointed that the new status of the people of color had not resulted in any positive changes for them in the district.[2]

The coloreds also complained about the lack of brown men in government positions. Two years after the privilege bill had been passed, *The Watchman* noted that there was only one black councilman and one brown alderman in Kingston. Despite the efforts of the sympathetic governor, Lord Mulgrave (Henry Constantine Phipps), people of color were finding it difficult to get jobs in the island bureaucracy. The parish authorities were equally slow in making colored appointments. In St. Thomas in the East, the custos had yet to elevate a brown man to the magistracy six years after the people of color had gained their rights. Elsewhere, the situation was much the same.[3] This reluctance to appoint men of color to office undermined the solidarity between whites and browns which the privilege bill had been designed to achieve. It also helped to create at least temporary alliances between the people of color and other groups in Jamaica who were the objects of racial or religious prejudice.

The political pact between the Jews and the coloreds in the 1830s was an example of this type of coalition. It would not have been possible even a decade earlier because the wealth and color of the Jews had linked them to the planto-cracy rather than to the people of color. Although the Jews themselves had been denied full civil rights, they had strongly opposed any improvement in the condition of the coloreds. When a member of the Assembly raised the possi-bility in 1812 that brown men should be treated equally with the Jews, three of them entered the House and threatened the offending member.[4] Jews con-tinued to harass the people of color after both sides had gained their privileges in 1830. During an election in 1831, for example, *The Watchman* accused the Jews of trying to split the free blacks and free browns. Jews were also active in the Colonial Church Union (a militant organization formed in the early 1830s to resist the abolition of slavery) at least in part because they sought to empha-size their identity with the other whites in the island.[5]

Despite this history of hostility, the two groups grew closer in the 1830s, for now that both could vote, each side appealed to the other for support. "A Denizen" writing in *The Watchman* hoped that the "gentlemen of color" would plump for a Jewish candidate seeking a seat on the Kingston Corpora-tion. Similarly, a successful brown candidate for the Assembly was grateful to the Jews for their votes which may well have made the difference between vic-tory and defeat.[6] However, it was not electoral politics per se that brought the Jews and coloreds together but rather their mutual exclusion from white society. No Jew or person of color was invited to an important ball in 1834 or to a similar function two years later which Governor Sligo attended. In response to these snubs, the Jews and the people of color asked Sligo to a public dinner they planned to sponsor exclusively themselves. Sligo turned down the invitation, hoping thereby to avoid the revival of what he called "complexional and other distinctions." The governor also noted that the Jews and the coloreds had formed a political league designed to defeat the most illiberal whites at the next general election, but he rightly predicted that "it would not come to much in the end."[7]

This temporary alliance between the Jews and coloreds was partly the result of the pattern of race relations that emerged after 1830. In the case of the Jews, they were "tolerated" by white society before they gained their full civil rights in 1830. Thereafter, however, the situation changed; whites were no longer prepared to accept them in society. As a correspondent for *The Falmouth Post* noted in 1836, the Jews "will not be endured" now that they were legally on a par with the whites.[8] The abolition of legal restraints meant that other kinds of limitations had arisen to take their place. This was even more applicable to the people of color who had to face psychological and social barriers despite their new legal status.[9]

While the coloreds continued to experience discrimination, their prospects after 1830, and particularly after emancipation, improved considerably. Brown men not only entered politics but also moved into jobs that had formerly been limited almost entirely to whites. The abolition of the deficiency acts helped to make this possible. In addition, there were a great number of openings for the people of color because whites were attracted to more prosperous areas of the empire. As the labor supply from Europe dwindled, planters began to hire more men of color as bookkeepers, tradesmen, and overseers.[10] Coloreds were branching out into new areas as well, especially in business. Before the 1830s, people of color had enjoyed little prospect of rising above a clerkship in a white-owned company. Even when they had gained their privileges, coloreds were often prevented from transacting business on their own because they could not obtain credit. Since whites generally regarded any attempt at advancement "as a kind of insurrection," the possibilities of promotion were limited. After emancipation, the people of color became more independent of the whites. As different needs developed for a considerably larger and more diverse freed population, brown merchants were able to import goods directly for themselves rather than being dependent on traditional patterns of doing business.[11] The result was that many of them prospered and helped to form a mainly new middle class which Herman Merivale, a permanent under-secretary in the Colonial Office, described as one of the most positive consequences of emancipation. Even before the end of apprenticeship in 1838, it was not an exaggeration to suggest that the general trade of the island was passing into the hands of colored merchants.[12]

Observers noted that the people of color were also playing a prominent part in government service. Although they complained about the lack of government posts in the early 1830s, coloreds served in the stipendiary magistracy during the apprenticeship period and advanced to the highest levels of local government after 1838. In the 1860s, for example, the attorney-general, the speaker of the House, and the chairman of the Quarter Sessions were all men of color.[13] As a result of their increasing wealth and political importance, coloreds appeared to be more respectable. Informal unions between whites and browns continued but often became permanent; in one district, a visiting Quaker counted three planters who had married their colored mistresses in 1840. Men of color were also becoming planters and were buying up land that whites were forced to sell. Robert Osborn claimed that by 1864 coloreds were responsible for almost all the coffee produced on the island and were "at the heels of the large proprietors in the cultivation of canes, and competing with them in the manufacture of sugar."[14]

Not all the free coloreds were as successful as the merchants, lawyers, and planters who prospered after emancipation. The worst sufferers seem to have been the brown women who had lived with whites and who had often received a little property and some slaves to support them. After abolition, these women had a difficult time: their properties depreciated, the compensation money for their slaves dried up, and many of them turned to needlework for a livelihood. By the 1860s, they were often destitute and dependent on private or public charity.[15] Similarly, the large majority of people of color who had been poor before 1830 did not necessarily fare that much better after their enfranchisement. Two American abolitionists noted that the urban coloreds continued to work as porters, servants, fruiterers, fishmongers, hucksters, and artisans.[16] Moreover, emancipation did not alter the attitude of many whites toward the people of color; as during slavery, Europeans continued to scorn the company of brown men. Coloreds could aspire to the most important positions in the island, but they were not usually admitted to white society. Whites continued to draw the line almost exclusively on the basis of color.

During the early 1830s, for a short time it appeared that the social isolation of the coloreds was slowly breaking down. Governor Mulgrave and his wife helped to establish a new precedent by inviting people of color to dinners and other events at King's House, the governor's residence. A perceptive Englishman observed that the coloreds' presence in King's House "had the effect of familiarizing the exclusives with the persons of the excluded, against whom in a short time, they were likely to jostle in every public situation."[17] Mulgrave's successor, Lord Sligo, not only continued this practice but also maintained that color prejudice was disappearing. Sligo wrote home rather optimistically that "on *the part of the Whites* all feelings of complexional distinctions had been done away [with] and except in two instances, the Browns seemed disposed to accede, and meet them half way."[18] A visitor to Jamaica in 1835 who had not been on the island for seven years agreed with Sligo and was heartened by one improvement in particular. He noted that "the first pleasing change which attracted my attention was the breaking down of Caste—In the same Pew I have seen persons of every grade and at the same sacrament table persons of all Colours."[19] Segregation in public places was no longer the rule; elsewhere, social patterns had changed very little.

Privately, whites generally refused to have any contact with the people of color, a policy that some observers believed to be unwise. For instance, Henry Morson, a member of the West India Association, was concerned about the whites' lack of foresight in refusing to mix with the coloreds. Writing in 1841, Morson warned the planters to modify their views because brown men would inevitably become one of the most important groups in the island. But relations between whites and coloreds did not improve. Although brown people were present at nearly every public gathering, Anthony Trollope noted almost twenty years later that planters in Jamaica had a greater fear and dislike of the coloreds than whites in any other West Indian island he had visited. The brown privilege bill and emancipation seem to have done little to affect the attitudes established during slavery.[20]

One reason for the continued exclusion of the people of color was a change in white society. After 1838, more absentees were forced to live in Jamaica because of the economic threat which emancipation posed to their survival. The decrease in absenteeism meant an increase in the number of white women on the island. As in nineteenth-century India, European women tended to introduce minute distinctions that could be carried to great lengths. Trollope noted the rationale of white women who would not entertain colored ladies: the problem was not the coloreds' respectability but rather their questionable ancestors.[21] The patroness of a ball in the eastern Caribbean provided a further example of the type of differences white women often sought to maintain. She strongly criticized a British captain for having danced with a "costie," a term describing a person who was one-sixteenth colored. The woman sponsoring the event then provided the captain with a list of the various castes between mulattoes and "costies" and presumably the proper rules of behavior for an English officer.[22] Thus, the increased presence of European women worked against the acceptance of browns in white society.

Nor had the attitudes of white males changed in the aftermath of emancipation; planters and government officials also continued to regard the people of color as inferior. Sir Charles Edward Grey, the governor from 1846 to 1853, held views that were typical. He believed it would be "a fearful misfortune" if coloreds gained control of local politics. In his view, browns lacked "that common understanding which results from a long continuance of homogeneous renewals of a people: . . . they have no traditional sentiments unless it be a sense of *injury* and a feeling of *resentment*, more instinctive than malignant against white persons."[23] Planters expressed even stronger feelings about the people of color. One who had served on the executive committee, George Solomon, claimed that whites were not prejudiced against the people of color but found that "there are so very few of the mixed race who are not of a treacherous disposition that they are naturally mistrusted as a rule." In any case,

Solomon's reading of Darwin had convinced him that mulattoes would not be a problem because they tended to die out after the third generation.[24] Most whites were not as hopeful as Solomon about the future and feared that browns would eventually supplant whites in Jamaica.

Despite the attitudes of men like Solomon and Grey, a small number of coloreds were accepted in white society. Like the privileged free coloreds during slavery, they were not necessarily distinguished by color but rather by education, wealth, and identity with the whites. Alexander Heslop was probably one of them. Born in Jamaica, Heslop studied at Oxford and returned to practice law in the island. He became a leading barrister and subsequently an attorney-general; he also sat in the Assembly and on the Legislative Council. Governor Edward John Eyre regarded him as the only brown man he had met who "comes up to the standard of a gentleman by education, in manners and feelings." Not surprisingly, Heslop included himself as a member of the upper class. Although he admitted that racial prejudice existed among the uneducated classes and among women, he claimed that he had never felt it himself.[25] Other people of color who enjoyed Heslop's privileged status included the Moncrieffes, a family that had applied for special rights under slavery and had already been welcomed in white society before abolition. Benjamin Moncrieffe was so closely identified with the whites that he served as treasurer of the St. Ann's Colonial Church Union. Peter Moncrieffe, who was probably Benjamin's son, became a barrister and sat in the Assembly during the 1840s. He also served as a judge and as a member of the Legislative Council.[26]

Unlike Heslop and Moncrieffe, Edward Jordon was neither a planter nor a barrister and had not been educated in England. As the leader of the people of color, he would not have been regarded as proper company in white society before emancipation. Yet, Jordon enjoyed the confidence of successive governors and became an important member of the government in 1853. When Governor Charles Henry Darling recommended him for the Order of the Bath, he noted that Jordon's position in society was already secure as he took precedence over everyone except the bishop, the chief-justice, and Darling himself.[27] The social pattern established during slavery thus continued almost unchanged after emancipation. A few brown men enjoyed a privileged status, while most of the free coloreds remained excluded from white society. Black-brown relations suffered from a similar problem: neither the general privilege bill nor abolition could offset the long-standing distrust between the two groups. The hostility between browns and blacks probably grew after 1830 and was the source of continuing tension throughout the post-emancipation period.

Local politics was the source of some of this friction. Since blacks had helped coloreds win seats to the Assembly, they expected that the people of color would also back their candidates for local offices. This was not always the case. After the 1832 municipal elections in Kingston, a meeting of black freeholders denounced the coloreds for having failed to support a black politician. Although their candidate had the necessary training and respectability, the blacks concluded that "prejudice still operates against us on every occasion by men bound in honor to support us, who, on the contrary, have basely sacrificed our interest at the shrine of subserviency and intolerance." The free-holders therefore resolved to oppose all future nominations and recommendations of the coloreds.[28]

In a society that valued lightness of skin color, problems between blacks and browns were bound to occur. Whites complicated the difficulties. On the one hand, the whites' hostility to British policy and to the Nonconformist churches brought the freedmen together. A meeting in 1832 of black freeholders in Spanish Town provided evidence of this potential black-brown unity: the blacks condemned the Colonial Church Unions, expressed their support for the amelioration and ultimate emancipation of the slave population, and noted their willingness to cooperate with the free coloreds.[29] On the other hand, whites also sought to break up any potential coalition between blacks and browns, sometimes by threatening economic reprisals against the freedmen who refused to support them. In addition, whites were often the beneficiaries of any electoral conflict between blacks and coloreds. When whites were successful in dividing the votes of the freedmen, it was the coloreds who were caught between black and white.

In the post-emancipation period, many travelers noted the antipathy of browns toward blacks, but Trollope was aware that it worked both ways. He observed that coloreds were "imperious to the black men, and determined on that side to exhibit and use their superiority." Blacks therefore preferred to work for whites rather than for people of color. The blacks found that coloreds were "sly and cunning; that they cannot be trusted as masters; that they tyrannize, bully, and deceive; in short, that they have their own negro faults."[30] Trollope too easily accepted Carlyle's assumptions about West Indian blacks, and yet, other visitors confirmed Trollope's observations about the lack of inter-racial harmony. A minister from Glasgow, Reverend David King, maintained that the browns despised the blacks and would not work with them in the fields. This was particularly the case for coloreds who had been enslaved with blacks and who would "scarcely stoop to shake hands with the blacks, whom they regarded with disdain."[31] The browns who were closest in color or in status to the blacks had the greatest fear of being associated with "an inferior caste."[32]

Brown politicians also abused blacks who were seeking office. For example, Jordon and Osborn were accused of failing to support black candidates for places on the Kingston Corporation. In addition, *The Falmouth Post* claimed that the two colored leaders opposed a black man as a representative for Kingston to the House of Assembly. The bitterness was not limited to politics: Osborn was apparently guilty of insulting the wife of a black member of the House when she attended a party in 1849 given by Governor Grey.[33] Even at this level, black-brown relations were far from harmonious.

It would appear, then, that the enfranchisement of the people of color in 1830 and the abolition of slavery four years later did not fundamentally alter either the place of the browns in Jamaican society or the racial attitudes of the majority of the population. Coloreds found that they could not generally associate on an equal basis with whites and were often unwilling to do so with the blacks. While considerations of class enabled a small number of browns to become part of white society, color continued to restrict the social mobility of most people of mixed race. Despite the increasing importance of the people of color, whites continued to dominate the economy, politics, and society of the island. The strong position of the whites ensured that the structure of society established under slavery would remain very much the same in the post-emancipation period. Yet, race relations probably became more strained after abolition than during slavery. Since legal criteria no longer separated whites from the rest of society, color considerations may have grown in importance. One student of West Indian societies has therefore concluded that emancipation served to increase racial prejudice rather than diminish it.[34] As elsewhere in the Caribbean, the racism of white society continued to affect the attitudes of nonwhites.

NOTES

1. *The Jamaica Watchman*, March 16, 1833.
2. *The Watchman and Jamaica Free Press*, September 7, 1831.
3. Ibid., August 22, 1832, October 19, 1833, July 20, 1836, May 3, 1834. See also the November 13, 1833 paper for a discussion of the coloreds' lack of advancement in St. Mary and Hanover.
4. Sheila Duncker, "The Free Coloured and Their Fight for Civil Rights in Jamaica, 1800–1830" (unpublished M.A. thesis, University of London, 1960), pp. 227–28. Samuel and Edith Hurwitz argue that the Jews attacked the Assembly member in his home. See Samuel J. and Edith Hurwitz, "The New World Sets an Example for the Old: The Jews of Jamaica and Political Rights, 1661–1831," *American Jewish Historical Quarterly* 55 (September 1965): 37–56.
5. *The Watchman and Jamaica Free Press*, November 9, 1831, March 24, 1832; Mavis Campbell, *The Dynamics of Change in a Slave Society* (Rutherford, N.J., 1976), pp. 203, 219.
6. *The Jamaica Watchman*, December 12, 1832; *Postscript to The Royal Gazette*, October 24–31, 1835.
7. *The Watchman*, February 22, 1834; CO 137/209, Sligo to Glenelg, February 26, 1836, private.
8. *The Falmouth Post and Jamaica General Advertiser*, February 17, 1836.
9. Philip Mason, *Patterns of Dominance* (London, 1970), p. 281.
10. A. Caldecott, *The Church in the West Indies* (London, 1898), p. 108.
11. James A. Thome and Horace J. Kimball, *Emancipation in the West Indies* (New York, 1838), p. 90.

12. Ibid.; Herman Merivale, *Lectures on Colonization and Colonies* (London, 1861), p. 337.

13. George Price, *Jamaica and the Colonial Office* (London, 1866), p. 7n.; R. Montgomery Martin, *The British Colonies*, 4 vols. (London, 1854), 4: 96.

14. John Candler, *Extracts from the Journal of John Candler Whilst Travelling in Jamaica* (London, 1840), p. 23; Abraham Judah and A. C. Sinclair (comps.), *Debates of the Honourable House of Assembly of Jamaica. . .*, 13 vols. (Kingston and Spanish Town, 1856–1866), November 3, 1864, p. 48. The Baptist missionary James Phillippo also confirmed that marriages between whites and browns were becoming more common; see Phillippo, *Jamaica: Its Past and Present State* (London, 1843), p. 137.

15. Add. MSS 40,863, Ripon papers, Mulgrave to Goderich, March 2, 1833, private and confidential; CO 137/391, Eyre to Caldwell, May 6, 1865, no. 128.

16. Thome and Kimball, *Emancipation*, p. 89.

17. R. R. Madden, *Twelve Months' Residence in the West Indies During the Transition from Slavery to Apprenticeship*, 2 vols. (London, 1835), 1: 208.

18. CO 137/192, Sligo to Stanley, May 8, 1834, private, no. 4.

19. ASSP, British West Indies, Jamaica General S22 G61, Trew to Buxton, December 31, 1835.

20. Henry Morson, *The Present Condition of the British West Indies . . .* (London, 1841), pp. 11–12; Anthony Trollope, *The West Indies and the Spanish Main*, 2d ed. (London, 1860), p. 74. For attitudes in the eastern Caribbean by a brown missionary, see Reverend John Horsford, *A Voice from the West Indies* (London, 1856), p. 56.

21. Philip D. Curtin, *Two Jamaicas* (Cambridge, Mass., 1955), p. 175; Trollope, *The West Indies*, p. 86. E. M. Forster's *A Passage to India* (London, 1924) is useful for examining the views of Englishwomen in India during a later period.

22. Horsford, *A Voice*, p. 62.

23. CO 137/313, Grey to Pakington, June 26, 1852, no. 53.

24. CO 137/398, Solomon to Cardwell, November 21, 1865.

25. MSS, West India Reference Library, Institute of Jamaica: William Cowper, "A Catalogue of Men Born in the Island of Jamaica who matriculated at Oxford, 1689–1885 . . ." (n.d.); Feurtado, MS notes; CO 137/374, Eyre to Newcastle, September 29, 1863, confidential; Lord Olivier, *Jamaica the Blessed Island* (London, 1936), pp. 180–81.

26. CO 137/182, Cuthbert to Goderich, July 12, 1832, no. 11, enclosures; Feurtado, MS notes.

27. CO 137/344, Darling to Bulwer-Lytton, March 12, 1859, confidential.

28. *The Watchman and Jamaica Free Press*, January 28, 1832.

29. Ibid., May 16, 1832.

30. Trollope, *The West Indies*, pp. 81–82.

31. Reverend David King, *The State and Prospects of Jamaica* (London, 1850), pp. 59–60.

32. John Bigelow, *Jamaica in 1850* (New York, 1851), pp. 26–27.

33. *The Falmouth Post*, September 14, 1849.

34. David Lowenthal, *West Indian Societies* (New York, 1972), p. 67.

Part III: The Politics of Opposition, 1830-1865

7

The Coloreds as Loyal Englishmen, 1830–1834

The 1830s witnessed the most important legal change in Jamaican history: the emancipation of over 300,000 slaves. In view of the whites' financial as well as psychological investment in the institution of slavery, it was not surprising that many of them resisted abolition. Some of the coloreds also owned slaves, but the majority of browns supported British policy on behalf of the slaves. By opposing the worst excesses of the whites' campaign to maintain slavery, the browns proved their loyalty to Britain while at the same time emphasizing their political distance from the whites on the island.

In 1831, the British Government decided to press ahead on its policy of ameliorating the condition of the slaves. Under pressure from the Anti-Slavery Society, the new Whig administration chose to revise an earlier Order in Council that had never been sent out. Designed originally to ensure the recognition of slaves as legal witnesses, the order was strengthened and dispatched to the colonies. In the Crown Colonies, it became effective immediately; in the chartered colonies, it had to be ratified by local assemblies. To gain their approval, the Government promised a considerable reduction in sugar duties if the island legislatures would adopt the order "word for word." This concession would have provided a substantial amount of relief to ailing West Indian economies. It was also a form of blackmail that the Jamaican planters were unwilling to accept.[1]

When news of the renewed antislavery drive and the intentions of the Government reached Jamaica in the late spring and summer of 1831, the whites immediately organized a series of island-wide protest meetings. As was usual on such occasions, these proved to be a forum for denouncing the interference of the Home Government in the island's internal affairs. But the tone of the protests was different that summer. Henry Whiteley, a Methodist bookkeeper who arrived on the island in 1831, was disappointed about the language of the gentlemen planters, but he sensed the determination in their speeches. Whiteley was particularly surprised to hear a representative to the Assembly "swear by his Maker that that Order should never be adopted in Jamaica; nor would the planters of Jamaica, he said, permit the interference of the Home Government with their slaves in any shape."[2]

The speeches and resolutions did much more than object to the Order in Council. As a result of the activities of the abolitionists, whites feared the outbreak of a servile war "of too horrible a nature to contemplate." Planters also predicted that they would be ruined if deprived of their slaves, and they demanded full compensation for the losses they would suffer. Since the British Government seemed prepared to endanger their lives, the whites began to reconsider their allegiance to the Crown. At a meeting in Falmouth, for example, freeholders resolved:

That we cling with the most filial affections and veneration to our beloved Sovereign and Mother-Country, a separation from which, though apparently desired by the latter, must fill our bosoms with the sincerest regret; but . . . we have no alternative but to resolve that the Governor should convene the Assembly . . . to pray that if the Crown consider us unworthy of the protection of our just rights, equally with all his Majesty's subjects, we may be absolved from our allegiance, and allowed to seek that protection from another nation, which is so unjustly and cruelly withheld from us by our own.[3]

The whites were no longer complaining merely about the infringement of their rights; they were now using the language of political separatism. If Britain would not safeguard their property, then perhaps the United States could be persuaded to do so.

The problem with this idea was that very few whites were actually willing to carry it out. England was still home for most of them, and their ideal continued to be the life of an absentee in Bath. But Britain was also the source of their difficulties. The result was the development of what one historian has called "a false nationalism." It was not a love for Jamaica that inspired the whites to seek independence from England but rather fear that Britain, and ultimately Jamaica, would soon be under the control of the humanitarians.[4] The economic and political weakness of the planters and the contradictions in their attitudes meant that separatism never really had much chance of success. Still, the whites hoped that the free blacks and coloreds would join them in denouncing British policy. Since this group owned an estimated 70,000 slaves, the whites believed that the freedmen would also resist any changes in the status of their slaves.[5] But the planters were mistaken about the depth of support among the newly enfranchised classes: only a minority of them were willing to oppose the Order in Council and other ameliorative legislation.[6] The coloreds who joined the plantocracy held meetings throughout the island and published their resolutions in the local press. Unlike the whites, the browns were not responding directly to the Order in Council; they were angered by a statement made by Stephen Lushington in April 1831. Speaking in the House of Commons, Lushington had claimed that the freedmen would be willing to release their slaves without compensation and that they were violently opposed to the whites on the issue of slavery. The people of color who attended the meetings disagreed on both points. At a gathering in St. George, for example, they "disclaim[ed] against that part of the Honourable Member, Dr. Lushington's speech, wherein he says we detest the whites." Since the interests of the browns and the whites were "so united and interwoven," the coloreds in St. George resolved not to emancipate their slaves independently of the whites. Public meetings held in other parishes came to similar conclusions.[7] Whites probably encouraged the people of color to pass these resolutions; even so, it was clear that a significant number of coloreds were anti-abolition, anti-British, and pro-planter.

Despite the publicity which these meetings received, the resolutions did not represent the sentiments of the majority of coloreds. The natural coalition between white and brown slaveholders had been weakened by the Assembly's strong opposition to the coloreds' campaign for privileges in the 1820s. Since the Crown was responsible for their success in gaining full equality with the whites, the people of color were generally more grateful to the Government than to the legislators in Jamaica. The coloreds' membership in the Nonconformist churches also brought them into contact with the views of the British humanitarians and the values of the British religious revival. As a result, it was less likely that they would share the outlook of the local plantocracy. Although most brown slaveowners wanted to receive compensation for their slaves, they believed that resistance to the Government would harm their chances and that only a more conciliatory policy could be successful.[8] *The Jamaica Watchman* articulated these views and expressed its opposition both to the separatist movement and to the men of color who supported it. The paper regarded the resolutions of the pro-planter coloreds as "sycophantic" and characterized one of the wealthy people of color allied to the whites as "whitewashed" and "no longer a mulatto." For *The Watchman*, these brown men were not representative of the people of color: they had adopted the values of the planter class and had lost their identity in the process.[9]

The debate among the free coloreds and the protests of the plantocracy received wide circulation in the local press. The whites' resolutions were debated throughout the island and apparently with little concern about the possible effects on slaves. Slaves were therefore aware of the growing antislavery sentiment in England and of the determination of the whites to retain the slave system, even at the cost of severing ties with England. The continuing agitation in the summer and fall of 1831 and the tone of the public meetings convinced many slaves that the Crown had already freed them. Coinciding with a severe drought and a poor crop of ground provisions, the rumors of freedom sparked one of the most serious slave rebellions in Jamaican history.

According to the leader of the uprising, Samuel Sharpe, the rebellion was initially planned as a strike. After the Christmas holidays of 1831 and before the harvest season began, slaves would refuse to work unless masters acknowledged their freedom. Since military preparations were also underway, the outbreak of the rebellion two days after Christmas was evidence of the lack of coordination rather than of a well-defined plan of operation. The slaves were involved in some initial skirmishes against the militia which included some free colored units. But the regular troops had little opposition, and the armed rebellion was over by the first week in January. The uprising nonetheless caused a great deal of destruction: a parliamentary loan of £500,000 for the entire island was barely sufficient to cover the damage recorded in St. James alone. The loss of life among the slaves was even more serious. Despite a free pardon for all those who went back to work, military operations, court martials, and individual vendettas resulted in the death of more than 500 slaves.[10]

The rebellion and the manner in which it was suppressed did little to support the planters' claims that their slaves were happy and well treated. However, the plantocracy contended that the rebellion had been the work of the Nonconformist preachers. Whites blamed the Baptists in particular for misleading the slaves; in fact, the uprising came to be known as "The Baptist War." For the planter class, the problem was not so much the institution of slavery as the European missionary.

While the whites' portrayal of the contented slaves was clearly inaccurate, there was some truth to their allegations about the preachers. The missionaries had exhorted the slaves to obey their worldly masters, but the doctrine of equality implicit in Christianity had provided inspiration for the rebellion. The Baptist system of class leaders had also indirectly supplied an organization around which the uprising could be planned.[11] It later became clear that the missionaries were innocent of any complicity in the rebellion, but the whites had already organized a campaign against them that again demonstrated the divisions among the people of color.

Soon after the rebellion was over, the whites established the Colonial Church Union to carry out their plans. Ostensibly a society created to support the Church of England, the Union was in reality a planter organization. Since the whites believed that the missionaries had been the cause of the rebellion, the Union's first priority was to expel the offending preachers and to destroy their chapels. The planters also hoped to delay the date of emancipation. The first branch of the organization was formed in St. Ann's at the end of January 1832, and by the beginning of March, there were chapters in eleven other parishes. During these few months, the Union was active in persecuting missionaries and destroying their chapels. In February and March, members of the organization wrecked seventeen churches, thirteen belonging to the Baptists and four to the Wesleyans. The leading Baptist missionary on the island, William Knibb, was arrested and other preachers jailed as well, although only two were ever tried and both of these were acquitted.[12]

The mobs which destroyed the chapels represented a cross-section of the free community. Predominantly white, these groups were made up largely of ordinary militiamen but frequently included their officers and prominent magistrates as well. Freedmen were also involved in the destruction of the chapels. On a tour of the island, Governor Belmore learned that one Baptist chapel had been pulled down in less than two hours by a "crowd of people including Negroes free inhabitants of all Classes and some Sailors from the Shipping." Many of the brown people in the mobs had taken refuge in Montego Bay during the rebellion; others who were in the militia reported that the slaves had destroyed their homes and small settlements.[13] These coloreds seem to have participated in the activities of the Union as a result of their own personal losses.

There were other reasons for joining the Colonial Church Union. Members of the organization had threatened to withdraw trade from the people of color who supported the missions, and there was the possibility of being accepted as an equal in the society. Belmore's successor, the second earl of Mulgrave, noted that some of the most violent supporters of the Union were the "idlest and worst" among the coloreds who were "vain of the equality with the White Persons and Gentlemen, which the paternity of the Colonial Union gives them."[14] As in the case of the separatist movement, some free browns joined the whites in their defense of slavery. But as before, most of the coloreds resisted the whites even though the consequences could be serious.

Like the opposition to the separatists, the campaign against the Colonial Church Union was led primarily by the people of color. Since the coloreds were generally Nonconformists, they opposed the Union because of its attempts to restrict religious freedom.[15] The people of color were also angered by the destruction of their chapels and the expulsion of their missionaries. They therefore protested by holding rallies and publishing resolutions. At one meeting in Montego Bay, a group of coloreds agreed that the Union was "guilty of gross intolerance, and such intolerance becomes exceedingly tyrannical and oppressive when manifested by men holding his Majesty's Commissions, Civil and Military." The coloreds pledged themselves "individually and collectively" to resist any illegal attempts to deny them "those Civil and Religious liberties, secured to them by the British Constitution."[16]

Resolutions and protests were not enough to protect the dissenting missionaries and churches from the activities of the Union. As a result of the organization's threats, the coloreds in many parts of the island put their chapels and ministers under guard. In Kingston, people of color as well as blacks armed themselves and kept nightly watch over the Wesleyan chapels there. Brown men also defended ministers from bodily harm. For example, when a Baptist missionary, Thomas Burchell, was released from a Montego Bay jail, a crowd of whites was waiting to tar and feather him. People of color came to his rescue, and he was able to make a hasty departure from the island. This was not an isolated incident: coloreds sheltered missionaries in their homes, sought to protect churches and chapels, and worked to secure the release of ministers from jail.[17]

The hostility between the Colonial Union and the people of color significantly heightened racial tensions during the first part of 1832. This ill-will threatened to escalate into violence in April when the attorney-general ordered the arrest of Edward Jordon, the leader of the anti-Union movement, who was charged with having published an antislavery article in *The Watchman* which endangered the security of the island. Since this was a treasonable offense and punishable by death, armed coloreds were present in the courtroom to make sure the sentence was not carried out. Jordon's acquittal may therefore have prevented the outbreak of racial warfare. Jordon was sentenced to a fine and six months in prison on a lesser charge later in the year. By that time, however, racial animosities had already begun to subside.[18]

The arrival of a new governor in the summer of 1832 helped to reduce the tension between the browns and whites. Unlike his predecessor, Mulgrave sought to support the missionaries as well as the free coloreds. Educated at Harrow and Cambridge, he had become an MP in the advanced Whig interest at the age of twenty-two. Before his appointment eleven years later to the Government of Jamaica, Mulgrave had also lived in Italy for a few years and had written several novels and sketches. He later served in Melbourne's cabinet and as the marquis of Normanby was colonial secretary for six months in 1839.[19]

Soon after landing in Jamaica, Mulgrave demonstrated his opposition to the Colonial Church Union. He reacted quickly to a Unionist disturbance in Westmoreland by sending two of his senior aides to the parish. They ordered the release of a free colored family and a missionary from jail as well as the arrest of several men involved in the riots. Mulgrave himself later appeared before the largely Unionist militia and warned them that he was prepared to use the army to enforce discipline.[20] The governor was not alone in helping to discredit the Union: the excesses of the organization also rebounded against it. The image in England of persecuted missionaries and wrecked chapels was bad enough; the reports of missionary agents to Parliament that further delays in freeing the slaves might lead to other damaging uprisings were even more serious. Officials from the Colonial Office also feared that the coloreds might react violently to any more attacks on their ministers. To avoid further friction among the free classes, the Government declared the Colonial Church Union illegal less than a year after it had been established.[21]

By this time, it had become clear that the whites could not count on the support of the free coloreds. Although the brown people were not united, the majority rejected the proslavery and anti-British stance of the Jamaican plantocracy. They had demonstrated their allegiance to England and to their own religious faiths, and in the face of considerable pressure, some were even willing to emancipate their slaves without compensation.[22] It was not surprising, then, that the people of color pursued their own brand of politics in the House of Assembly as well as in the colored press.

One of the brown delegates in the House, Price Watkis, was a consistent supporter of Government measures to improve the condition of the slaves. Although he found only one other assemblyman who would vote with him, he persevered with his minuscule minority in advocating the adoption of the 1830 Order in Council and compulsory manumission.[23] While the other colored representative, John Manderson, did not back Watkis on these issues, their votes in the Assembly suggest that they disagreed more with the whites than with each other.

Both demonstrated a particular interest in the legal and social status of the people of color. In the spring session of 1832, Manderson presented a bill designed to amend the Militia Act as well as to abolish all distinctions of color under the old legislation. The Civil Rights Act of December 1830 made his amendment unnecessary but left additional problems unresolved. Many coloreds were illegitimate and consequently suffered a variety of legal disabilities. In an attempt to improve the situation, Manderson and Watkis backed a bill designed to "encourage marriage and award justice to illegitimate children." Most of the representatives chose to ignore the problem. On another occasion, the two brown legislators unsuccessfully opposed a change in the franchise which Watkis believed was intended to limit the numbers of freedmen who could vote. Both coloreds also favored receiving a petition from people of color whose homes had been destroyed by the Colonial Church Union.[24] As in the other cases, Watkis and Manderson were in the minority, but they presented views and voted in ways which demonstrated that Jamaica was not a wholly white society.

The Watchman also articulated many of the social and political grievances of the people of color; however, the paper focused its attention on advancing the coloreds in local politics. *The Watchman* therefore worked to increase the size of the colored electorate as well as the number of brown men in political life. Since it sought to offset the political dominance of the whites, the paper encouraged an electoral alliance between black and brown voters. Though not always successful, *The Watchman* provided evidence of the increasing political importance of brown Jamaicans.

The 1832 election was *The Watchman's* first opportunity to exercise its influence in a general election. There were definite limits to what the paper could accomplish: only a few colored candidates were running for the Assembly, and most of the old members were likely to be reelected.[25] *The Watchman* nonetheless encouraged the freedmen to support brown men seeking office. In an issue several weeks before the election, the paper ran the appeals of the aspiring brown politicians from Kingston and St. Andrew. These notices requested that the black and brown freeholders reserve their votes for colored candidates who would be nominated at the hustings. The plea from St. Andrew also observed "that the White Planters, if they are really the friends of the BLACKS and BROWNS, can have no reasonable objection to their being represented by ONE White and ONE Coloured Gentlemen."[26] As it was unlikely that the whites would respond favorably to this appeal, *The Watchman* suggested that the coloreds in each parish agitate and demand pledges from their future representatives. In the face of attacks by a "prejudiced" and "vulgar" press, the paper counseled respect for the law and "a determination to maintain their rights inviolable as their watchword."[27]

The Watchman was not alone in appealing for the freedmen's votes. A group of whites also published a statement designed to win the support of the black and brown electorate. The whites claimed that they had long wished to abolish color distinctions and blamed the freedmen for keeping up differences based on color. In addition, they stressed the need for equality and common purpose among all the free classes.[28] This plea for unity, based on the traditional leadership of the white ruling class, was likely to win support among some coloreds and blacks. *The Watchman* therefore repudiated it and called for a different kind of unity.

In its "Counter Appeal to the Coloured and Black Constituency," the newspaper lashed out at the "motly and insidious *16*" who had signed the statement. For *The Watchman*, the whites were representative of those who had resisted the advance of the coloreds and who now sought to divide the freedmen: "The sting of oppression yet rankles—the voice of denunciation and insult still reverberates—brief, very brief is the period which has elapsed—and those who lately oppressed, denounced, and derided you, are they who now endeavour to entrap you." The paper not only attacked the whites but also appealed to the common racial background of the freedmen. It described blacks and browns as brethren who shared a similar past and a mutual responsibility. As descendants of slaves, they were obligated to improve "the condition of the race from which [they had] sprung." Unlike the whites, blacks and coloreds would seek "the gradual, but speedy explosion of that system—the early liberation of our kindred."[29] In the process, *The Watchman* hoped they would vote for colored candidates.

The Watchman thus worked to develop an alternative to the politics of the plantocracy. It supported the election of colored candidates and sought to create a black and brown political alliance. In addition, the paper's opinions on the issues of the day probably reflected the general sentiments of the people of color. Like the votes of the colored politicians, the newspaper's views suggest that the people of color had a distinct outlook on the problems of their society. In the early 1830s, the extent of the franchise was one of the most important questions being debated on the island. For the first time, freedmen had the power to affect the representation in the House and in local politics. Legislators were also concerned about the prospect that many of the slaves might be able to vote after emancipation. When the whites were no longer able to restrict the franchise to wealthy freedmen, they attempted to control it by introducing a taxpaying qualification. Since taxpayers were often salaried employees or clerks who would vote in accordance with the wishes of their employers, white delegates hoped in this way to maintain a predominantly white Assembly.[30]

The Watchman expressed greater faith in the new electorate, contending that the "enlarged constituency" could return "liberal and enlightened" representatives to the House.[31] At the same time, the paper argued that there should be a property qualification for the vote. Its insistence on even a small freehold requirement had a twofold objective. First, it sought to differentiate those who regarded Jamaica as merely a temporary place of exile from those who were more concerned about the colony's future. For *The Watchman*, ownership of land implied a sense of permanence and a commitment to the country. Second and more importantly, the editors of the paper believed that the property qualification would encourage the poor to acquire land. In their view, the poor would want to own land in order to exercise the franchise.[32] The argument seems to have ignored the desire of most Jamaicans to own land for its own sake. It was indicative, however, of the paper's interest in encouraging the development of a small settler society. This was in marked contrast to the planters' vision of Jamaica's future.

The Watchman also expressed its differences from the views of the whites in other ways. During the legislative session in the fall of 1833, the paper opposed a bill that sought to place a higher duty on dry and pickled food. Since this was a tax on a necessity of life, it would have been felt more directly by those who could least afford it. As an alternative, *The Watchman* advocated higher taxes on linens, woolen goods, and fancy articles used by the middle and upper classes. The paper expressed its anger at a system that prevented the growing of food locally and then attempted to import foodstuffs beyond the buying power of a large proportion of the population.[33] During the same session, the paper vigorously opposed another measure favored by the whites: a vote of thanks to William Burge, the island agent. Since Burge had defended the deportation of Lecesne and Escoffery and had later resisted the coloreds' campaign for their rights, it was not surprising that Price Watkis shared *The Watchman*'s hostility to the legislation on behalf of the agent. According to the paper, the Kingston representative "felt as none but a coloured intimately acquainted with the circumstances to which we refer could feel. . . ."[34]

The Assembly's delay in recognizing the coloreds as equals and its hostility to the Crown meant that *The Watchman* had few kind words for it as well. For *The Watchman*, the Assembly was unrepresentative, tyrannical, and disloyal. The paper did work for the election of brown representatives to the House, but described the House as it was then constituted as a "curse to the constituency of the country." *The Watchman* was opposed to the Assembly's resistance to British policy and to its discussion of a possible transfer of sovereignty:

> In a word, the coloured class, although determinedly loyal and devotedly attached, to the Crown and Government of Great Britain owe no allegiance to their high mightinesses of the Assembly! Indeed they cannot acknowledge any; for loyalty to the King and to the Jamaica Assembly is perfectly incompatible; and to hold the former the latter must be renounced.[35]

It was clear that *The Watchman* was more interested in the humanitarian and reformist ideas of the British Government than in the predominantly pro-slavery arguments of the local plantocracy. For the British, this meant the possibility of political allies in a colony where the government had few friends; for the coloreds, loyalty to England was an important weapon with which to overcome the limitations of being brown.

Although the British Government was ultimately responsible for the political liberation of the people of color, it did not immediately recognize the coloreds as political allies. The passivity of Governor Belmore partly explains its failure to do so. A partisan of the planters, Belmore did little to advance the claims of the people of color. Instead, his administration witnessed the unchecked growth of the Colonial Church Union and increasing friction between coloreds and whites.

Belmore's successor, Lord Mulgrave, had a different set of priorities. On the one hand, he sought to encourage the political and social development of the coloreds, and he appears to have been genuinely concerned about the condition of the free coloreds. On the other hand, his overtures to them were partly motivated by political considerations. The governor was seeking support in an Assembly that was otherwise hostile to his Government. When Mulgrave dissolved the House in December 1832 and called for a general election, he was therefore hopeful that the coloreds would have some impact on it. This was particularly true in the towns where they could often influence the outcome of an election.[36] Although Lord Goderich (Frederick John Robinson), the colonial secretary, disapproved of the dissolution, his dispatch made it clear that the Colonial Office had also become aware of the potential political importance of the people of color. Since the coloreds were enjoying the franchise for the first time in a general election, Goderich thought that the new Assembly might be "distinguished from the Body which preceded it, by a greater desire to cooperate with His Majesty in his efforts for improving the condition, not merely of the Slaves, but of all classes of his subjects in Jamaica."[37] Like Mulgrave, the Colonial Office believed that the people of color were more sympathetic to its cause than the whites.

The results of the election were as one-sided as Mulgrave had feared. Although both sitting colored delegates were returned, only one additional brown representative was elected.[38] In speculating on the reasons for the poor showing, Mulgrave provided an interesting insight into the voting behavior of the colored electors. According to the governor, the brown voters had become disheartened when they had learned that the Colonial Office disapproved of Mulgrave's appeal to the enlarged constituency. Long dependent on the whites and easily discouraged, the coloreds had simply "deserted their promises" in at least three parishes.[39]

Mulgrave had been unsuccessful in creating a sizable colored faction in the House, but he had made some progress. By the end of 1832, there was a recognizable group both within and outside the Assembly. Mulgrave's reception in the spring of 1833 on a trip to Montego Bay provided evidence of the growth of pro-Government sentiment. On his arrival in the harbor, a *Watchman* correspondent observed that the "would-be Aristocrats" were not prepared to receive him "but 'the Radicals,' however, or 'the government party,' or whatever else you may choose to call them, so that it is understood I mean *our* party, assembled a goodly number to meet him as he landed from the ship's barge."[40] The governor encouraged this development by nominating men of color to positions in the government service. A week before traveling to Montego Bay, Mulgrave appointed T. R. Vermont as island secretary and notary public for the port of Falmouth. A strong supporter of the Government, Vermont was to become publisher of an important colored newspaper on the north coast, *The Falmouth Post*.[41] A year later, the governor named Richard Hill to his first post in the Government.

As a result of Mulgrave's efforts on their behalf and, more importantly, their own desire to take an active role in the politics of the island, brown men were soon jostling with whites on many public boards and vestries that had formerly excluded them. Not long after the civil rights legislation of 1830, people of color as well as blacks were sitting on the Kingston Common Council. Two years later, the Council included both editors of *The Watchman*. In 1833, freedmen were able to run almost full slates against white candidates for the Kingston municipal offices. While Kingston was highly politicized and a stronghold for the coloreds, the pattern was being repeated in other parts of the island as well. By 1834, there were five coloreds in the vestries of Hanover and Westmoreland, three in St. Ann and St. Andrew, and at least two in Spanish Town. One brown man was acting as churchwarden in Spanish Town, and people of color were beginning to sit on juries in significant numbers.[42] In addition to their representatives in the Assembly, then, the coloreds were occupying other important elective offices.

When Mulgrave was replaced by Lord Sligo as governor of Jamaica in April 1834, much had changed since 1830. Men of color who had been denied access to official positions of any kind occupied seats in the Assembly and in parish offices all over the island. Although there were less than a handful of brown legislators in the Assembly, colored politicians were able to voice sentiments that were often very different from those of the plantocracy. The local whites had exerted great pressure on the people of color to resist the Government, but the coloreds in general remained loyal to England and to British policy. In return, the Crown recognized them as potential political allies, and the local executive appointed brown men to government positions and treated them as the social equals of the whites. Yet, there was also a hint of future difficulties between the coloreds and the Crown. Colored politicians were not in favor of the apprenticeship period which was to follow the abolition of slavery. Moreover, their opposition to this interim period was only the beginning of more serious differences between brown men and the Government. But in 1834, these problems were not as apparent as they would be a few years later. Rather than prepare for the future, the people of color were pleased by how far they had come so quickly.

NOTES

1. D. J. Murray, *The West Indies and the Development of Colonial Government, 1801–1834* (Oxford, 1965), pp. 189–90; W. L. Mathieson, "The Emancipation of the Slaves, 1807–1838," in J. Holland Rose, et al. (ed.), *The Cambridge History of the British Empire*, 8 vols. (Cambridge, 1940), 2, *The Growth of the New Empire, 1783–1870*, 325–26.

2. Henry Whiteley, *Three Months in Jamaica in 1832* (London, 1833), p. 2. For more on the protest meetings, see Mary Reckord, "The Jamaica Slave Rebellion of 1831," *Past and Present* 40 (July 1968): 110 and Henry Bleby, *Scenes in the Caribbean Sea* (London, 1854), p. 15.

3. *Supplement to The Royal Gazette*, July 9–16, 1831.

4. Philip D. Curtin, *Two Jamaicas* (Cambridge, Mass., 1955), p. 78.

5. *The Watchman and Jamaica Free Press*, June 4, 1831. The paper changed its name to *The Jamaica Watchman* in the spring of 1832, probably as a result of legislation directed against it. While the figure of 70,000 was in all likelihood no more than a guess, it was accepted by the British abolitionists as well. See *Hansard*, 3d series, 3 (April 15, 1831): 1459.

6. Curtin, *Two Jamaicas*, p. 46.

7. CO 137/179, Belmore to Goderich, September 6, 1831, no. 88. This dispatch also contains the resolutions of several free coloreds from Clarendon. For a stronger statement of support for the whites from a group in St. Mary, see *The Watchman and Jamaica Free Press*, July 30, 1831. The island agent described the meetings in an interesting dispatch: CO 137/180, Burge to Goderich, September 5, 1831 (filed under Agents). Lushington's statement can be found in *Hansard*, 3d series, 3 (April 15, 1831): 1456.

8. Charles H. Wesley, "The Emancipation of the Free Colored Population in the British Empire," *The Journal of Negro History* 19 (April 1934): 162–63; Curtin, *Two Jamaicas*, p. 46; *The Watchman and Jamaica Free Press*, November 9, 1831.

9. *The Watchman and Jamaica Free Press*, July 9, June 18, June 22, 1831.

10. For a discussion of the rebellion, see Reckord, "The Jamaica Slave Rebellion," pp. 108–20 and Philip Wright, *Knibb 'the Notorious' Slaves' Missionary, 1803–1845* (London, 1973), Chapter 5. The role of the planters' protest meetings is discussed in Henry Bleby, *Death Struggles of Slavery* (London, 1853), p. 127 and Thomas F. Abbott, *Narrative of Certain Events Connected with the Late Disturbances in Jamaica* . . . (London, 1832), pp. 37–38.

11. Reckord, "The Jamaica Slave Rebellion," pp. 109–10; W. L. Burn, *Emancipation and Apprenticeship in the British West Indies* (London, 1937), pp. 92–94.

12. Curtin, *Two Jamaicas*, pp. 87–88; Burn, *Emancipation and Apprenticeship*, p. 95; Lord Olivier, *Jamaica the Blessed Island* (London, 1936), p. 92. For more background on Knibb, see Wright, *Knibb*, passim.

13. CO 137/181, Belmore to Goderich, February 10, 1832, no. 152. See also [William Knibb], *Facts and Documents Connected with the Late Insurrection in Jamaica* (London, 1832) for a list of the properties that the militia had destroyed and for a list of some of the prominent men who participated in the destruction of the chapels.

14. CO 137/183, Mulgrave to Goderich, October 7, 1832, no. 25; Mary Reckord, "Missionary Activity in Jamaica Before Emancipation" (unpublished Ph.D. dissertation, University of London, 1964), pp. 337, 356.

15. Reckord, "Missionary Activity in Jamaica Before Emancipation," p. 73.

16. *Supplement to The Royal Gazette*, August 25–September 1, 1832.

17. Bleby, *Death Struggles*, p. 156; Abbott, *Narrative*, p. 38. For an example of a person of color securing bail for missionaries, see Abbott, *Narrative*, p. 2 and for an instance of a colored family protecting a missionary in their home, see *Supplement to The Royal Gazette*, August 18–25, 1832.

18. Bleby, *Death Struggles*, pp. 274–75; Mavis Campbell, *The Dynamics of Change in a Slave Society* (Rutherford, N.J., 1976), pp. 163–67. Campbell incorrectly suggests that Jordon was sentenced for one year in his second trial. For information on this trial, see *Postscript to The Royal Gazette*, August 4–11, 1832. The fine was remitted and Jordon was released early; this is described in CO 137/188, Mulgrave to Goderich, January 3, 1833, no. 69. For more background on the first trial, see *Supplement to The Royal Gazette*, April 14–21, 1832.

19. Sir Leslie Stephen and Sir Sydney Lee (eds.), *The Dictionary of National Biography* (London, 1921–1922), 15, 1116–17 [hereafter cited as DNB].

20. Reckord, "Missionary Activity Before Emancipation," pp. 357–60.

21. Reckord, "The Jamaica Slave Rebellion," p. 124; Burn, *Emancipation and Apprenticeship*, pp. 96–97; CO 138/53, Goderich to Mulgrave, December 7, 1832, no. 47; Wilbur D. Jones, "Lord Mulgrave's Administration in Jamaica, 1832–33," *The Journal of Negro History* 48 (January 1963): 51.

22. *The Watchman and Jamaica Free Press*, June 4, 1831.

23. *VAJ*, November 15, 1831, p. 86; *Postscript to The Royal Gazette*, November 19–29, 1831, Debates: November 22.

24. *Postscript to The Royal Gazette*, March 24–31, 1832, Debates: March 28; ibid., March 31–April 7, 1832, Debates: April 5; *VAJ*, December 11, 1832, p. 182; *Postscript to The Royal Gazette*, October 27–November 3, 1832, Debates: November 1; *VAJ*, November 22, 1833, p. 182.

25. CO 137/183, Mulgrave to Goderich, December 16, 1832, no. 49.

26. *The Jamaica Watchman*, December 19, 1832.

27. Ibid., December 22, 1832.

28. Ibid., December 26, 1832.

29. Ibid.

30. For a legislator's attempt to include forty shilling taxpayers in the franchise, see ibid., November 23, 1833.

31. Ibid., April 20, 1833.

32. Ibid., November 23, 1833.

33. Ibid., October 19, 1833.

34. Ibid., October 12, 1833.

35. Ibid., December 11, 1833.

36. CO 137/183, Mulgrave to Goderich, December 16, 1832, no. 49.

37. CO 138/53, Goderich to Mulgrave, February 5, 1833, no. 59. For Mulgrave's correspondence with Goderich, see Jones, "Lord Mulgrave's Administration in Jamaica," pp. 44–56.

38. Even the additional colored representative, John Campbell, had sat briefly in the House. He had won a Kingston by-election held during the fall legislative session of 1832, but the House had declared his opponent "duly elected." See Glory Robertson (comp.), *Members of the Assembly of Jamaica* (mimeo, Institute of Jamaica, 1965), p. 28.

39. Add. MSS 40,863, Ripon Papers, vol. 2, 1833–1842, Mulgrave to Goderich, May 13, 1833, private.

40. *The Jamaica Watchman*, March 16, 1833.

41. CO 137/204, Sligo to Glenelg, November 22, 1835, no. 208, confidential; *The Jamaica Watchman*, March 13, 1833.

42. It is not always possible to be accurate on the number of coloreds in a vestry or any political body. In some cases, they are identified by color in the account describing their positions. Otherwise, the information comes from a variety of sources, including secondary works, newspapers, and Colonial Office records. For the information on local offices, see the following: for Kingston, *Postscript to The Royal Gazette*, January 5–12, 1833; for Hanover and Westmoreland, *The Jamaica Watchman*, January 11, January 18, 1834; for Spanish Town, ibid., January 8, 1834; and for early reports of some coloreds as jurors, ibid., September 26, 1832.

8

The Coloreds as Creoles, 1834–1838

In the period immediately after the emancipation of the slaves, the number of coloreds in the House of Assembly continued to increase. Although still in a small minority and outvoted by the planter delegates, the browns in the House generally shared the Government's concern about the condition of the ex-slave population. However, the colored representatives also opposed the Crown, particularly over the future of the Assembly. When the House went on strike in 1838, the Colonial Office resolved to suspend the Assembly and rule directly from England. Faced with this possibility, the colored leadership refused to support British policy. In Edward Brathwaite's terms, these coloreds were acting as "creoles": they were resisting an imposed solution from London and defending a local institution, the Assembly.[1] Since the House offered the coloreds their only chance to participate in island-wide politics, brown leaders were unwilling to see the Assembly abolished or its powers reduced.

The coloreds were also unhappy about the establishment of the apprenticeship system in 1834. During this interim period between slavery and freedom, slaves were to serve as apprentices to their former owners for a period of either four or six years, depending on the nature of their jobs.[2] Apprenticeship was designed to ensure a peaceful transition from slavery to freedom as well as to provide a guaranteed labor force for the estates. Officials also hoped that it would train the ex-slaves to work regularly for wages. Although the intent of the system was to create the conditions for a free plantation economy, the result was to exacerbate the relations between masters and laborers and between the local legislature and the Crown. Since the colored politicians had foreseen some of these problems, they strongly disagreed with the idea of slaves becoming apprentices.[3]

Brown politicians argued in the press and in the House of Assembly that free labor was more profitable than the work of slaves. They had therefore favored immediate emancipation, and some had even questioned the necessity of compensation for the owners of slaves. More importantly, coloreds pointed to many of the difficulties that later became associated with apprenticeship. For example, *The Watchman* noted that there would be an insufficient number of specially appointed stipendiary magistrates to adjudicate disputes between masters and their apprentices as well as a shortage of apprentice labor during crop time. The paper also predicted the problem of excessive litigation as a result of the new system and the general difficulty of forcing free men to work as apprentices. For *The Watchman* and for the Anti-Slavery Society, apprenticeship was not only too complicated, it was slavery in another form.[4] But the coloreds' opposition to the plan was quickly overshadowed by the arrival of the governor who did more for the people of color than any other executive who served in Jamaica.

The marquis of Sligo became governor at one of the most difficult times in Jamaica's history. Arriving in the colony at the beginning of April 1834, Sligo faced the task of supervising the transition from slavery to freedom and of getting along with an Assembly that was hostile to Crown policy. In some ways, the new governor was ideally suited for the job. He owned property in Jamaica, and he had been a member of the West India Committee. On the other hand, Sligo's support of the reform bill and his recent conversion to abolition would hardly have been welcomed by the Jamaican planters. Since Sligo was excessively concerned about maintaining the dignity of his office and also lacked the necessary degree of tact in dealing with members of the Assembly, he became the object of abuse both in the planter press and in the House.[5]

The governor's relations with the Assembly were complicated by a fundamental difference over the nature of apprenticeship. While Sligo was concerned most about the future of the ex-slave population, the Assembly was attempting to retain as much of the past as possible. Jamaica's Constitution did not provide a means to reconcile these divergent views, as the constitutional history of the island was largely a struggle between the legislature and the executive.[6] Since reform was a long way off for Jamaica, Sligo took the only step that was really open to him: he sought to create public opinion outside the House and a group within it that would support Government measures. Brown politicians were the obvious basis of any pro-Government grouping in the House because they had been the only consistent supporters of Crown policy in the period leading up to abolition. But there were limits to what Sligo could accomplish. He was restricted in making appointments by the small number of positions available in Jamaica and by the necessity of obtaining Colonial Office approval for nearly every position he sought to fill. In practice, there was nothing Sligo could do about the size of the official establishment, although he could influence the selection of officeholders. The case of Richard Hill illustrates the willingness of the Colonial Office to accept Sligo's recommendations as well as the governor's attempts to reward his supporters. Hill had resigned from the special magistracy over differences with Sligo about the administration of justice in Montego Bay. But Sligo sought to retain Hill in the Government because he regarded Hill as an able man who deserved a job and because of Hill's previous record of consistent support. Since James Stephen at the Colonial Office agreed with Sligo's assessment of the former special magistrate, he authorized Hill's appointment to a post in the Kingston customs department. Hill's age then became an issue: he had just turned forty and was over the permissible age for beginning work in customs. In a letter to Lord Glenelg (Charles Grant), the colonial secretary, Sligo discounted this problem and emphasized Hill's politics. Hill was a Liberal who had been "the rallying point for the friends of the Government on the Northside of the Island, and being a Colored Man is of a class fast rising into importance in this Colony."[7] A few months later, Sligo returned to the same theme. He noted that Hill's transfer from the northern part of the island had been "an injury to the Government as he was the head of that party in that District," and he hinted that Hill should be promoted to a position there. The issue was resolved when Sligo nominated Hill to be secretary of the stipendiary magistrates' department.[8]

Hill was the most important colored who was appointed, but he was far from the only one. The creation of a stipendiary magistracy and the death of many European magistrates in Jamaica encouraged Sligo to recommend several coloreds for appointment as specials. R. B. Facey, for example, was a brown man who, like several other colored magistrates, had been educated in England. He was popular, able, and, perhaps most importantly, a native. Unlike British magistrates, Facey was likely to survive in Jamaica; Sligo was quite serious when he observed that Facey's ability to bear the climate was "not to be overlooked in such appointments." The governor chose at least six other men of color as special magistrates, all of whom were approved by the Colonial Office.[9]

It was not only their ability to withstand the heat that prompted Sligo to elevate these men to Government posts. Since Sligo wanted to create a Government party, patronage even in so limited a sense was a useful tool to encourage and reward support. The governor also believed that the coloreds would soon dominate island politics. He asserted that they "are rapidly rising in power here" and that the "house will presently be formed all of Brown people."[10] As a result, it was necessary to create a strong bond between the Government and the coloreds. The governor's selection of John Manderson as the first brown custos of St. James was recognition of the coloreds' increasing importance and of Sligo's willingness to nominate men of color to positions formerly reserved for socially prominent planters.[11]

While he appointed many brown men to official positions, Sligo's early efforts to create pro-Government sentiment in the House are more difficult to discover. At the very least, he would have encouraged men of color to run for office, and toward the end of his term in the island, he more openly sought support for them. Yet, even without his direct intervention, the coloreds were able to return candidates in the parish elections as well as for seats in the Assembly. In 1835, the leading votegetters in the Westmoreland vestry were the free coloreds who three years previously had been attacked by mobs for protecting missionaries in their homes. Across the island in St. Thomas in the East, the three brown Liberal party candidates also gained places on the vestry. A pro-colored reporter on the scene was gratified by the support of several white freeholders and the success of the "enlarged" electorate.[12] The strong showing of the Liberals was rather short-lived. A conservative vestry dominated the parish after the end of apprenticeship and was one of the causes of the Morant Bay Rebellion. But the election of brown men and probably some blacks to local offices continued a process that was already underway during Mulgrave's administration. The Assembly election of 1835 confirmed this trend.

Sligo called the election rather hastily after concluding that he had been deliberately insulted by the Assembly and that he was the object of an organized attack led by the speaker of the House.[13] Although he predicted that the new House would not be very different from the old one, there were ten changes among the members, including the addition of three colored members, raising the total number of brown delegates to six. This increase may not seem significant, but the colored representatives could have been more influential than their numbers suggest. Since most of them lived in Spanish Town or Kingston, it was easier for them to attend the meetings of the House than the planters who sometimes had to return to their estates during the session. In a sparsely attended House, a block of six votes could affect important divisions. But the coloreds were not always united; Manderson, for example, often voted with the planters, especially on issues concerning immigration.[14] Their numbers were also reduced by deaths, resignations, and absences. Watkis died in 1836, Manderson resigned in the same year, and Deleon—who may have become ill—rarely attended the sessions.[15] As a result, the effective strength of the brown politicians was usually only three votes during the two years before the 1837 election.

The coloreds in the House were known as the King's House Men, the Liberals, and finally as the Town party. Despite these labels, brown politicians did not have the organization of a modern political party. Instead, they were part of a floating faction that generally supported the Government.[16] An examination of the coloreds' votes in the House is nonetheless suggestive about the politics of the brown delegates.

Brown men voiced their disapproval of much that went on in the Assembly. In October 1834, for example, Price Watkis and Edward Jordan failed to persuade other representatives to amend a statement that attacked the stipendiary magistrates. The two coloreds were also the only delegates to vote against imprisoning a Baptist missionary when he refused to be examined on oath before a special committee of the House.[17] As in the period before emancipation, brown politicians continued to resist the planters' vendetta against the missionaries. Furthermore, they were reluctant to support an immigration scheme that would benefit the planters at the expense of the rest of the community.

For the planters, European immigration was the panacea that would save the plantations after the end of apprenticeship. The plantocracy also believed that immigrants from Europe would offset the demographic decline in the white community and prove a more reliable labor force than the ex-slaves. The coloreds, however, argued that immigration was an extravagance that would ruin the economy. They asserted that the yearly costs of the scheme would be greater than the island's annual revenue, and they also claimed it would not work. The experience of a recent group of German immigrants who had joined the police force rather than remain on the plantations was evidence that whites would not perform the same labor formerly assigned to slaves.[18] Consequently, the coloreds in the House sought to reduce the flow of immigrants, although they could not stop it completely. They voted in the minority to cut a planned outlay from £100,000 to £50,000 and to have the cost of immigration paid by those who employed the immigrants. Brown delegates also questioned the importation of only Europeans. Osborn, for example, wondered why immigrants from Africa could not be encouraged as well as those from France and Germany. Despite their opposition, the coloreds were unable to limit the Assembly's plans for "pauper emigration."[19] In addition, they could do little to spare Governor Sligo from the verbal abuse of other members of the House.

The governor encountered serious political problems in February 1836 when the House considered one of his messages a breach of its privileges and refused to meet until he apologized. Sligo's offense was to interfere with the Act in Aid of Abolition while it was under review by the Council as well as the Assembly. Since the Assembly regarded itself as a miniature House of Commons, it maintained the parliamentary precedent denying the Crown the right to send messages on a bill that was before both the Commons and the Lords. The vote on the breach of privileges was more interesting than the constitutional issue: the coloreds all agreed with the majority that Sligo had violated the rights of the Assembly. As in the crisis of 1838 and similar issues in later years, brown politicians were eager to assert the privileges of the House, in part because they hoped one day to dominate it. But the coloreds did not agree with the House's refusal to carry on business with Sligo. After the House had been prorogued, four of them voted together in a minority of five to reconvene.[20] Although the colored delegates had been willing to uphold the Assembly's privileges, they did not wish to embarrass the governor any further. It also seems likely that the coloreds were instrumental in organizing the meeting of six or seven assemblymen in 1836 which resolved to form a Government party in the House. Sligo was pleased about this development and hoped to generate support for it on a forthcoming tour of the island.[21]

The coloreds did disagree with Sligo on some important matters of policy. For example, Edward Jordon appealed to the Colonial Office to disallow the 1834 franchise act Sligo had approved. Jordon argued that the bill would enable the planters to multiply their votes and would therefore serve to reduce the number of brown delegates in the House. Richard Hill also criticized the governor. Writing to friends in the antislavery campaign, Hill complained that Sligo had mishandled apprenticeship and that the governor was "nothing less than a curse to the country."[22] In general, however, the browns remained loyal to Sligo. Even Hill later changed his mind and accepted a job working closely with Sligo, and Jordon became a consistent supporter of the governor in the Assembly. When rumors persisted in April 1836 that Sligo had resigned, the people of color organized a meeting in Spanish Town that passed resolutions praising his administration.[23] They also submitted petitions from various parishes applauding Sligo's efforts on behalf of "the dark-hued sons of Africa and their descendants."[24] The planters were not sorry to see Sligo leave the island; the coloreds were aware of what they were losing.

The planters not only had opposed Sligo's apprenticeship policy but also had worried about his encouragement of the people of color. The whites, fearing that the coloreds might dominate the Assembly and perhaps even force them to leave Jamaica, attempted to pass legislation that would ensure their continued control of the island. Apart from the franchise bill of 1834, the white representatives sought to limit the number of brown men appointed to Government posts by levying a tax on all new commissions. But Sligo vetoed the measure, and brown politicians continued to win seats in the Assembly.[25]

As in the 1820s, the fears of the whites were misplaced. Coloreds wanted to participate in politics, but they had no intention of evicting the whites. Instead The Watchman expressed the same fears as the whites: the paper did not want the House of Assembly overrun by uneducated blacks or coloreds. For The Watchman, "no ignorant mulatto or black should be selected to divide the contempt which men of mind and education must feel for the illiterate and ignorant. . . . Intellect and education and not creed or color are the proper qualifications for such as may aspire to office."[26] However, the paper was overstating its case. The color of prospective assemblymen did matter, and The Watchman's work on behalf of brown candidates was evidence of its wish to advance the people of color. Since Jordon and the colored men around him were concerned about the background of future representatives, they opposed any suggestions that blacks and coloreds should be represented on all public bodies in some proportion to their numbers in the population.[27] The demand for educated delegates was suggestive about the values of the people of color and would have served to keep many blacks from entering the House. It would also have guaranteed the continued dominance of the coloreds and the whites.

Blacks were therefore wary about *The Watchman*'s politics. In 1832, they had maintained that coloreds were unwilling to vote for blacks, and four years later they complained about the same thing. The problem was Jordon's refusal to support black candidates for local offices. In addition, black leaders claimed that Jordon had used his influence to keep blacks out of the stipendiary magistracy and out of commissions in the militia. Despite Jordon's denials, they refused to support the coloreds' candidate, J. S. Brown, in a by-election for an Assembly seat in Kingston. Instead the blacks backed a Jew, Daniel Hart, who had been described earlier by a Jewish freeholder as unfit and likely to be ridiculed in England because of his lack of education and ability. The split between the blacks and the browns prompted the whites to switch their support to Hart in an attempt to create a white-black coalition. Hart won the election.[28]

Brown politicians were thus unable to retain the support of either the whites or blacks. Although the coloreds appealed for moderation and respectability, they were deserted by the whites who continued to fear that brown men would supplant them. Yet, blacks remained suspicious of the close ties between coloreds and whites and did not believe that *The Watchman* would be "happy" to support "[a] black man possessing the necessary qualifications even in a moderate degree."[29] For *The Watchman*, the situation was "a delicate one" because "the ultratories, and ultraradicals will both find fault with us. The first think we are running too fast, the other creeping too slowly."[30]

The split between the blacks and the coloreds was partially resolved later in 1836 when one of the blacks whom *The Watchman* had earlier refused to support, David Lee, was elected to the Kingston Common Council. The whites on the Council sought to have Lee removed from office, and one white member declared that he considered the man "unfit from birth, education, and means." Osborn, however, defended Lee. It seems clear that the coloreds had backed Lee's election because they hoped to rejuvenate the black-brown political alliance.[31] It was not that easy, as the blacks had established a franchise organization that "had declared open hostility to the browns." The members of that organization, the United Franchise Society, probably violated their promise not to vote for any colored candidates. Even so, brown men were at least temporarily isolated between blacks and whites.[32] If the middle ground remains the usual haven for politicians seeking office, this was not the case in Jamaica during the period immediately after abolition. When Sligo resigned in 1836, his successor, Lionel Smith, made the situation of the coloreds even more difficult than it already was.

Smith arrived on the island in August 1836. He had spent almost all of his life in the military, although he had most recently served as governor of Barbados. Unlike Sligo, Smith saw his role as a conciliator and believed he could simultaneously carry out the aims of the Colonial Office and maintain good relations with the Assembly.[33] Each of these goals was difficult by itself;

the two together proved more than he or perhaps anyone else could handle.

Smith maintained that Sligo had been largely responsible for the difficulties in Jamaica. The new governor regarded Sligo's appointment of brown men to the special magistracy and his attempt to create a party based on the people of color as particularly serious errors.[34] Smith also attacked Sligo for encouraging the coloreds to run for seats in the Assembly. The result had been exactly what Smith hoped to avoid: the development of two parties in the House, one consisting of planters and people of property and the other made up of lower classes who lacked property and education. Since this second group could easily form a majority at parish elections, black and colored freeholders had already begun to control several vestries. For Smith, it did not take much of an imagination to predict the future: "It requires no prophecy to shew Your Lordship, what a few Years more would have produced, under the old Laws— Every White Gentleman and White man of Property would have been turned out of the House."[35]

The governor therefore proposed a new franchise for Jamaica that had already been accepted in Barbados. The law increased the freehold requirement from £10 to £30 and substantially raised the qualifications for sitting in the Assembly. Smith argued that the change in the franchise would reduce the preponderance of blacks and coloreds in the electorate and guarantee the time necessary for the improvement of the lower classes. Most importantly, it would avoid the danger of Jamaica becoming another Haiti.

... the time has now come, when, if this Colony is to be carried through its difficulties from the composition of its licentious Population: and the Constitution of England is to be preserved from the danger of its future intercourse with a neighbouring Black Republic [Haiti], we should lay the foundation of a strong and vigorous Government, or it must fall into a Waste, under all the Evils of Anarchy, Confusion, and Bloodshed.[36]

The outcome of the general election a little over a year after Smith had taken office provided evidence for the governor that his warnings had been justified. Smith reported that eight coloreds had been elected to the House, an increase of five from the previous Assembly. But Smith's figures were not wholly accurate. Six brown men had been elected to the House in the 1835 general election; hence, the increase of colored legislators in 1837 was only two. The governor nonetheless concluded that it would take only two more general elections before every white representative lost his seat in the House. For Smith, the consequence would be "the rapid sale of property and abandonment of the Island, by the few influential white Gentlemen who now reside in it."[37]

Smith's gloomy picture of colored magistrates and black and brown representatives in the Assembly did not raise the same spectre in the Colonial Office as it obviously had done in King's House. British officials were upset by the governor's attacks on Sligo and by the evidence of Smith's prejudice against colored assemblymen and officeholders. In a private dispatch to Smith, Glenelg noted that Sligo's appointment of six coloreds as special magistrates had reflected the former governor's "just and enlightened view of the subject." Since men of color might soon dominate island politics, it was important to encourage their participation in Government rather than exclude them from office.[38]

James Stephen, now the permanent under-secretary in the Colonial Office, elaborated on this view when he recommended that the franchise legislation Smith had approved be disallowed immediately. Inasmuch as the bill discriminated against the people of color, Stephen argued that the governor should have vetoed it. For Stephen, the act would have established a dangerous precedent because it was designed to retain political power solely among the whites. This not only violated the Government's pledge to abolish political distinctions based on color, but it also could lead to violence between a minority seeking to hold onto control and a majority frustrated by its inability to participate in local politics. Stephen was afraid that the attempt to maintain white supremacy would lead to racial war.[39]

The Colonial Office was not alone in rejecting Smith's views on the people of color: the coloreds themselves were bound to be unhappy with the new governor. In a letter to the secretary of the Anti-Slavery Society, Jordon and Osborn made it clear that the Liberals in the House would have nothing to do with Smith. Apart from his attitude toward them, the colored delegates also found it impossible to support a governor who approved legislation in violation of the Crown's instructions. Their differences with Smith put the coloreds in an awkward position. They continued to support the aims of the Government but not its representative on the island. Jordon and Osborn hoped that Smith would be recalled and that their former patron, Lord Sligo, could return as governor.[40]

The coloreds nonetheless progressed without Lord Sligo's help. Known generally as the Liberals during this period, brown politicians formed a more cohesive group than they had earlier, largely because of their increased numbers and their continuing concern for the apprentices. Despite abstentions, absences, and splits, the Liberals were usually able to muster at least seven votes in a division, although one of these votes often came from a white member of the House. While men of color were still unable to alter the course of legislation, their presence was a reminder that there was an alternative to the planter view of the world.

The brown representatives in the House thus sought to protect the apprentice. Accordingly, they opposed a police bill that was designed in part to limit the role of the stipendiary magistrates in certain cases involving apprentices. Since the measure would have increased the powers of the ordinary justices of the peace, the coloreds voted in a minority of seven against it. Like the Government, they were concerned about the impartiality of the planters who served as ordinary justices and the problems arising from masters judging the cases of their former slaves. The Colonial Office had already disallowed the bill, but Smith reluctantly approved it. For Jordon and Osborn, this was further evidence of the governor's increasingly difficult situation: Smith had alienated the planters and the coloreds and was now defying his instructions from the Colonial Secretary.[41]

There were other issues of this kind. The coloreds opposed a bill to recover the possession of premises because it allowed an owner to eject a laborer at once from his tenancy rather than through the usual legal procedures. Even though the brown politicians sought to amend the act, the legislation passed in its original form, with five coloreds and two white assemblymen voting against it.[42] The colored delegates were also unable to make any changes in a franchise bill that was almost identical to the measure disallowed in the previous session. Jordon and Osborn hoped that the new law would be vetoed in England because it would otherwise "destroy the influence of the Liberal or Government party in this Island and restore the absolute rule of the Planters."[43]

Brown men were not only unhappy about the legislation that was directed against the apprentices, but they were also concerned about the failure of apprenticeship in general. Jordon therefore proposed to abolish apprenticeship in 1838, two years ahead of schedule. In the debate on his motion, Jordon argued that apprenticeship had not satisfied the planters or the apprentices. He was also worried about the deteriorating relationship between England and Jamaica. But neither Jordon's arguments nor the chance of compensation altered the outcome of the vote: his proposal was defeated, even though five whites joined the six coloreds in the division.[44] Jordon was less interested in the actual result of his motion than in persuading the House "to admit the necessity" of ending apprenticeship. The coloreds hoped that this admission "would be of some service to the cause in England." Since Jordon and Osborn also asked to be appointed to the special magistracy, they may have expected that their action in the House might benefit them personally.[45] Although neither was ever invited to join the specials, both were pleased by the success of the anti-apprenticeship campaign.

The man who was most responsible for the early abolition of apprenticeship was Joseph Sturge, a wealthy Quaker from Birmingham. Sturge became impatient with a parliamentary commission on apprenticeship and organized his own investigation of the system. Not surprisingly, he concluded after a visit to the West Indies in 1837 that "apprenticeship is not emancipation, but rather slavery in another view."[46] Since Sturge was determined to end apprenticeship, he helped found the Central Emancipation Committee to create popular feeling against it. The result was a flood of petitions and large meetings all over Britain, designed to pressure the Government to free the apprentices.[47]

The Government's response was to introduce further amendments to the

Abolition Act severely restricting the powers of the planters over the apprentices and expanding those of its officials in the West Indies. Although the Crown maintained its pledge to retain apprenticeship until 1840, this legislation made it likely that West Indian Assemblies would themselves abolish the system. Planters faced the problem of continued parliamentary intervention; in addition, they were worried about the effect of freeing only the nonagricultural apprentices. The Jamaican Assembly therefore joined the other island legislatures in abolishing apprenticeship on August 1, 1838.[48] But it accompanied the measure with an even stronger protest than usual and laws designed to maintain the planters' power over their former slaves.

The debates in the Assembly reflected the planters' concern for the future of their estates. There was considerable discussion, for example, on the vagrancy legislation. A planter representative claimed that a strong bill was necessary to keep the former slaves on the plantations. Without it, he contended, the ex-slaves would abandon the estates and wander about the island under the pretense of peddling. The coloreds disagreed. Osborn argued that the planters were willing to sacrifice the people's liberties in order to protect the cultivation of sugar and coffee. When the Liberals' attempt to amend the bill failed with the usual minority, Jordon summarized the views of the brown delegates on a different issue the next day. Unlike the majority of the assemblymen, Jordon had not come to Spanish Town to legislate for himself or even for those who had elected him but rather "for the benefit of the island at large—of all classes of the inhabitants. . . . The House must now learn to legislate for the many—for the mass of the people [;] they had done so long enough for the few—for the handful of proprietors."[49]

Despite Jordon's warning, the bill to end apprenticeship contained provisions that were bound to lead to the deterioration of relations between planters and their ex-slaves. In particular, the measures to eject tenants after three months' notice and on the judgment of local magistrates suggested that the planters were intent on creating a landless proletariat that would be dependent on the estates. Similarly, the Assembly's attempt to transfer authority away from the stipendiary magistrates would have increased the planters' control over the former apprentices.[50] It was the "Protest of the House," however, that set the stage for the constitutional crisis later in the year. As in the case of the vagrancy legislation, there was little the colored delegates could do apart from indicating that the Assembly's actions did not represent the sentiments of the entire House.

In its formal "Protest," the House complained that the act to amend the abolition of slavery was "illegal, unconstitutional, and an usurpation of our legislative rights." Although Parliament could regulate commerce within the empire, the House claimed that it did not have the authority to enact other laws for Jamaica. If Parliament insisted on legislating for the island, the Assembly would cease to exist.[51] The "Protest of the House" was thus a strong denunciation of imperial intervention as well as an argument for the legislative independence of the colony. The problem for the Crown was the implication of the Assembly's future autonomy. Since the Colonial Office sought to protect the mass of the population, it could not give way to the House.

The coloreds in the Assembly also opposed the "Protest." Richard Hill, for example, disagreed with the petition and noted that it was well known "that he and his friends with whom he usually voted, held sentiments and cherished feelings on colonial politics, differing from those of the majority of the Assembly." He regarded Parliament's amendment of the Abolition Act and the end of apprenticeship as positive steps in raising all men to their proper level of dignity.[52] Despite the opposition of the brown politicians, the Assembly's petition was an indication of the House's strong feelings about imperial legislation. The next time Parliament sought to intervene, members would do more than simply protest.

The issue that led to further difficulties between the Government and the Assembly was the control of the island's prisons. This question aroused concern as a result of allegations that apprentices had been tortured in Jamaican jails. During the winter of 1837–1838, the Colonial Office therefore dispatched Captain J. W. Pringle to report on the state of the West Indian prisons. Pringle ran into trouble in Jamaica when the Kingston mayor refused him access to the city's house of correction. Since places of confinement were not always under the governor's control, Lionel Smith could not overrule the mayor. James Stephen regarded the incident as proof that a parliamentary bill was needed to enable a Government official to investigate prison conditions. The end of apprenticeship made a bill even more urgent because parish vestries would regain jurisdiction over the jails after August 1.[53]

The legislation to remedy this problem was the immediate cause of the 1838–1839 constitutional crisis. When the Assembly met in the fall, it ruled that the prisons bill was a violation of its Constitution and would not become law in the island. The House refused to conduct any legislative business "until it is declared by the Government whether the rights of the Assembly are, or are not, to be respected."[54] Although the overwhelming majority of the House supported this action, the coloreds were divided. Jordon, Osborn, and two other brown members voted with the majority, while three coloreds joined the minority of five in support of the Government's legislation. As a result of the Assembly's refusal to carry out its legislative duties, Smith first prorogued the House and then dissolved it.[55]

The new Assembly was virtually unchanged. Richard Hill was defeated for reelection, but the return of the governor's secretary, Charles Henry Darling, kept the minority who opposed the Assembly's stance at five.[56] Since the dissolution of the House had proved ineffective, Smith urged Parliament to maintain its "paramount Authority." He feared that the planters might otherwise reimpose slavery if the Assembly were left to conduct its own affairs. This was the only explanation he could offer for the House's "late perverse conduct."[57]

Smith's impression of the Assembly's proceedings was not all that far-fetched. There were members who believed that a successful resistance to the Crown would mean a free hand with their former slaves. A relatively independent Assembly, then, was one possible outcome of the constitutional crisis. Another was the suspension, or possibly the abolition, of the House. Many assemblymen found this a desirable alternative because the rise of the coloreds and the eventual enfranchisement of the emancipated blacks clearly endangered the whites' supremacy in the House.[58] Since more direct Crown Colony rule was preferable to black and colored control of island politics, some members were willing to take an extreme position. Either the Assembly emerged with its legislative independence intact, or the Government took over the island. In either case, the future of the whites would be assured.

The coloreds split on this issue but their arguments differed from those held by most of the whites. Brown men who opposed the majority maintained that their loyalty to the Crown was more important than their commitment to the Assembly. James Taylor told his constituents that the Crown had "every right to legislate for every portion of her widely extended dominions." By returning him to the House, they had proven themselves "what all Englishmen ought to be, faithful to your country, to the laws, and to your Sovereign."[59] *The Falmouth Post* agreed. It argued that "all Legislation for the good of the Island, for the preservation of Justice, and the conservation of Peace, must take place in England."[60]

The coloreds who supported the planters did not accept the view that England should be responsible for Jamaican legislation. On the contrary, the leadership of the people of color had worked to create a party in the House because they sought to exercise more influence over island legislation. Although the colored representatives were only a relatively small faction in 1838, they could foresee the day when they might dominate the House. In the meantime, the brown politicians in the Assembly symbolized the considerable progress of the people of color since 1830. The men of color who voted with the majority were not afraid of blacks and coloreds in the House. What they feared was a weakened Assembly in which brown representatives had no more power than parish vestrymen.[61]

Jordon and Osborn articulated these views in the press and in the Assembly's debates. Jordon stated that he had been a Government man and would remain one, but he could not support the Crown's interference in the island's Constitution. Osborn was more concerned about the effect of the Government's action on the people of color. He believed that the rise of the coloreds from political insignificance would mean very little if the Crown could ignore the wishes of the local Assembly. For Osborn, the prisons bill was "calculated to infringe the liberties of the very people it professed to serve." The Government had freed the slaves, but now it was "about to deprive them of [their] privileges, by curtailing the power of the representative assembly of those very people."[62] The coloreds who opposed the Government saw themselves as defenders of the privileges of the House. Despite their loyalty to the Crown throughout the 1830s, they opposed the imperial legislation on prisons in favor of the Assembly's autonomy. As "creoles," in Brathwaite's terminology, brown men were not following the advice of London-based officials but rather were rallying behind the local legislature.[63] In contrast, many of the planter representatives were acting on orders from absentee owners in England.

The split among the coloreds over parliamentary intervention was the forerunner of later divisions. It also led to attacks against those men of color who supported the planters. As the head of the people of color, Edward Jordon received most of the abuse. The colored editor of *The Falmouth Post*, for example, claimed that Jordon had turned against the Government that had raised him to his present position. The planter press regarded him as a "traitor" to his class, and Governor Smith wrote home that Jordon and Osborn had joined the enemy out of financial considerations. Smith also maintained that the two coloreds had begun publishing a paper in the planters' interest.[64] But these claims were exaggerated, partly because of the heated political atmosphere of the time and partly out of personal animosity. Smith's allegation that Jordon had joined the mayor of Kingston's party was in all likelihood not true, especially since the mayor had originally led the fight against the coloreds' rights and also voted in the minority against Jordon on the prisons bill.[65] Jordon's new paper, *The Morning Journal*, was not a planter paper; it probably drew its support from urban coloreds, professionals, and local merchants. *The Morning Journal* was also a daily and was presumably more popular than its predecessor, *The Watchman*, which had appeared twice weekly. It would not seem that financial considerations forced Jordon to maintain a point of view against his better judgment. Jordon opposed the Government legislation because he believed it was better to fight for an Assembly that was open to coloreds than to have no Assembly at all.

The Assembly's position left the Colonial Office little option except to consider suspending the island's Constitution. Although the Government had been moving steadily in this direction during the 1830s, it had been able to accomplish its aims by disallowing legislation that clashed with Government policy and by occasionally appealing to Parliament for measures the local legislature was unwilling to enact. The reluctance of the Assembly to legislate first for the apprentice and then for free Jamaicans made it clear that these steps would not be enough. The House's refusal to conduct business in 1838 confirmed what officials in the Colonial Office and Governors Sligo and Smith had been saying for several years: that the House of Assembly was unable to deal with the important problems of a postslave society and should be suspended or abolished.[66]

Henry Taylor at the Colonial Office summarized this attitude in an important memorandum on the subject. Taylor attacked the Assembly for wasting the island's resources and for refusing to deal with the problems of an emancipated population. In his view, representative government in Jamaica meant a white oligarchy. He was convinced that the policy of working through the assemblies had failed to improve conditions in the West Indies. Thus, James Stephen could advise changes in the laws or make recommendations, but "was there one case in ten, in which an Assembly has been either conciliated or brought to reason by such a process?" Although the Government was committed to the welfare of the ex-slave population, the planters were opposed to any significant improvement in their condition. Under the circumstances, Taylor's suggestion was to establish "at once and conclusively, a power which shall overrule all opposition and set the question at rest." Parliament should enact the laws the Jamaican House resolutely refused to consider.[67] Taylor's memorandum clearly reflected the strength of humanitarian feeling in the Colonial Office; it was also well argued and amounted to a damning indictment of the Jamaican legislature. At the same time, Taylor's analysis of the situation erred in several places and placed too much faith on the virtue of direct rule from London.

Taylor significantly underestimated the number of coloreds in the population and, more importantly, their political bias. In the memorandum, he observed that they "have naturally shewn themselves disposed to make an alliance with the dominant and aristocratic class, and to join them in trampling upon the blacks to whom they feel it to be their shame and misfortune to be allied in blood."[68] Yet, earlier in the decade, Taylor had praised the people of color for defending the missionaries against the whites following the 1831 slave rebellion and for promoting emancipation. Similarly, Viscount Howick (Henry George Grey), who was parliamentary under-secretary from 1830 to 1833 and a future colonial secretary, had looked forward to the day when brown men would play an important part in the Assembly. At that point, he believed, the Assembly would pursue a more rational policy. Taylor therefore misjudged the politics of the coloreds and overlooked a potentially useful group in implementing Crown policy.[69] He also overestimated the advantages of Crown Colony government. If the apprenticeship system was any test for the Colonial Office, it was questionable whether Jamaica would have profited from direct rule. Although the Crown had sedulously upheld the legal rights of the ex-slaves, it had done no more than the Assembly in improving health, transport, and agricultural facilities. By 1865, Taylor himself was less optimistic about the efficacy of control from London.[70]

The Cabinet discussed Taylor's memorandum and eventually agreed on a modified version. The Government decided to suspend the Jamaican Assembly for five years instead of abolishing it entirely. The Government could have gone much further; even so, Melbourne's shaky Whig-Radical coalition collapsed over this issue. The planters had proved correct: Parliament was reluctant to suspend the House. Melbourne resigned, but the Queen was distraught about losing her "dearest kind" minister. By refusing to part with her

Whig Ladies of the Bedchamber, she made it impossible for the Conservative Sir Robert Peel to form a cabinet. Melbourne returned to power, but his parliamentary weakness required him to give up the idea of altering Jamaica's Constitution. Thus, the Assembly had successfully maintained its legislative autonomy. The new governor who arrived in 1839 carried instructions to concilitate the House rather than to subdue it. This was not an easy task with an Assembly "irritated by opposition, insolent from a victory over the Government, and emboldened by a belief that Parliament no longer cares, or no longer dares, to interfere."[71]

The Assembly's victory over the Government in 1839 ensured the continued survival of the planter class in local politics. Whites were now in a position to alter the franchise laws and generally to impede the political rise of the blacks and coloreds. The Colonial Office had disallowed earlier legislation of this kind, but after 1839 its priorities shifted. It was no longer as concerned about the problems of blacks and browns in the West Indies, in part because slavery and apprenticeship had been abolished. As a result, the progress of the coloreds was markedly slower in the period after the end of apprenticeship.

Still, the people of color were in a very different position than they had been ten years earlier. They had gained their civil rights only four years before abolition, yet eight brown representatives were sitting in the House by 1837. Brown men occupied places in parish vestries and had been appointed to important Government posts. Not only had British abolitionists corresponded with coloreds and visited them in Jamaica, but also a governor had predicted that the browns might well control island politics in the next decade.

This was not what the planters had foreseen when they granted civil liberties to the people of color. On the contrary, the whites had assumed that the coloreds would join them in resisting the Crown and in helping to preserve the remaining vestiges of slavery. But the people of color had different ideas about politics and society than the majority of the planter class. Thus, brown politicians did not regard the House as a legislative tool to preserve the plantations at the expense of the rest of the community. Since the brown delegates were also concerned about the welfare of the blacks, they voted against the restrictive legislation directed against the apprentices. Unlike the planters, then, brown men generally supported Crown policy and emerged as the basis for the pro-Government faction in the House. The problem came when the coloreds had to decide between their loyalty to the Government and the claims of the House of Assembly.

Preservation of the House seemed critically important to the colored politicians because of the strong likelihood that they would eventually outnumber the whites in it. Brown representatives therefore faced a serious dilemma when British policy was directed against the powers of the House. Since coloreds could not support both the privileges of the Assembly and the Crown at the same time, they split over this issue. The brown men who voted for the prisons bill believed that the imperial legislation was necessary to protect the ex-slaves. While the colored leadership had also held this view, their first priority was the survival of the House of Assembly.

The colored delegates had other political difficulties as well. For example, they were unable to create an alliance with the blacks or to gain the support of the whites. The coloreds' appeals for respectable and educated officeholders served to alienate the blacks and to worsen the already strained relationship between blacks and browns. Although brown politicians sought to appear as moderates, whites were still prepared to sacrifice the House of Assembly rather than allow the coloreds to take it over. The browns had made dramatic progress in the 1830s, but the coloreds' politics—and their appeal for support among the ex-slave population—would aggravate the political situation even further.

NOTES

1. Edward Brathwaite, *The Development of Creole Society in Jamaica, 1770–1820* (Oxford, 1971), p. 98.

2. Slaves involved in nonagricultural work were to be freed in 1838, two years ahead of field slaves or praedials who would remain apprentices until 1840. The dividing line between praedials and nonpraedials was obviously open to abuse. See William A. Green, *British Slave Emancipation* (Oxford, 1976), pp. 132–33.

3. For more background on the apprenticeship period, see ibid., Chapter 5; W. L. Burn, *Emancipation and Apprenticeship in the British West Indies* (London, 1937), passim; D. G. Hall, "The Apprenticeship Period in Jamaica, 1834–1838," *Caribbean Quarterly* 3 (December 1953): 142–66.

4. *The Jamaica Watchman*, March 6, September 4, September 21, 1833.

5. R. Montgomery Martin, *The British Colonies*, 4 vols. (London, 1854), 2: 56; Burn, *Emancipation and Apprenticeship*, pp. 148–50.

6. For a study of the eighteenth-century conflicts between governors and the House of Assembly, see George Metcalfe, *Royal Government and Political Conflict in Jamaica, 1729–1783* (London, 1965), passim.

7. CO 137/198, Sligo to Aberdeen, March 20, 1835, no. 55; CO 137/202, Sligo to Glenelg, September 26, 1835, no. 135.

8. CO 137/205, Sligo to Glenelg, December 31, 1835, private; CO 137/210, Sligo to Glenelg, April 9, 1836, private.

9. CO 137/203, Sligo to Glenelg, October 12, 1835, no. 155. For some of the other appointments, see CO 137/192, Sligo to Stanley, June 13, 1834, no. 27; CO 137/193, Sligo to Stanley, September 14, 1834, no. 28; CO 137/202, Sligo to Glenelg, September 5, 1835, no. 102; CO 137/209, Sligo to Glenelg, January 21, 1836, no. 286; Sligo Papers, MS 281, Private Letter Book, October 26, 1835.

10. CO 137/193, Sligo to Stanley, September 14, 1834, no. 28; CO 137/209, Sligo to Glenelg, February 8, 1836, private.

11. CO 137/193, Sligo to Spring Rice, October 24, 1834, no. 49.

12. *The Watchman*, January 14, January 17, 1835. For Sligo's attempt to create a pro-Government party, see CO 137/211, Sligo to Glenelg, June 11, 1836, private.

13. CO 137/201, Sligo to Glenelg, August 12, 1835, no. 85; Burn, *Emancipation and Apprenticeship*, pp. 296–97.

14. See, for example, *VAJ*, December 14, 1835, p. 176. For Manderson's support of the planters on other issues, see ibid., October 23, 1834, pp. 53–54.

15. Glory Robertson (comp.), *Members of the Assembly of Jamaica* (mimeo, Institute of Jamaica, 1965), pp. 55, 58.

16. For a comparison with the early development of parties in the United States, consult William N. Chambers, *Political Parties in a New Nation* (New York, 1963), and Richard Hofstadter, *The Idea of a Party System* (Berkeley, Calif., 1970). Chambers' discussion of factional politics in Chapter 1 is particularly useful.

17. *VAJ*, October 9, 1834, p. 14; October 23, 1834, pp. 53–54.

18. *The Watchman*, January 14, 1835, July 6, 1836.

19. *VAJ*, December 8, 1835, p. 164; *Supplement to The Royal Gazette*, December 5–12, 1835, Debates: December 7.

20. *VAJ*, February 2, 1836, p. 272; February 4, 1836, p. 3; W. J. Gardner, *A History of Jamaica* (London, 1873), pp. 306–307; Burn, *Emancipation and Apprenticeship*, pp. 303–304. For a discussion of the political crisis in 1838, see p. 100.

21. CO 137/211, Sligo to Glenelg, June 18, 1836, private.

22. CO 137/207, Lecesne to Aberdeen, March 27, 1835, enclosure: "Observations upon an Act to amend the Elective Franchise"; ASSP, British West Indies, Jamaica General, S22 G61, Hill to Robert Foster, April 28, 1835.

23. Burn, *Emancipation and Apprenticeship*, pp. 310–11.

24. Sligo Papers, MS 275F, Petitions from Freeholders and other inhabitants of Kingston and St. Andrew.

25. CO 137/194, Sligo to Spring Rice, December 9, 1834, no. 91.

26. *The Watchman*, January 22, 1834.

27. Ibid.

28. Ibid., June 8, 1836. See also Sligo Papers, MS 281, Private Letter Book, Sligo to Glenelg, June 18, 1836.

29. *The Watchman*, June 8, 1836.

30. Ibid., June 11, 1836.

31. Ibid., September 21, September 24, 1836.

32. Ibid., October 5, 1836.

33. Burn, *Emancipation and Apprenticeship*, p. 319.

34. CO 137/213, Smith to Glenelg, November 20, 1836, private.

35. CO 137/213, Smith to Glenelg, December 30, 1836, no. 46.

36. Ibid.

37. CO 137/220, Smith to Glenelg, October 11, 1837, no. 185; CO 137/221, Smith to Glenelg, November 13, 1837, no. 216.

38. CO 137/213, Glenelg to Smith, January 16, 1837, private.

39. For Stephen's response to the franchise act, see his minute to Sir George Grey on CO 137/213, Smith to Glenelg, December 30, 1836, no. 46 and the resulting dispatch in the same volume, Glenelg to Smith, March 30, 1837, no. 74. Stephen's more specific comment on the legislation can be found in CO 138/52, Stephen to Glenelg, February 22, 1837.

40. CO 137/226, Jordon and Osborn to Robert Stokes, December 27, 1837.
41. *VAJ*, December 15, 1837, p. 234; CO 137/226, Jordon and Osborn to Robert Stokes, December 27, 1837.
42. *VAJ*, December 7, 1837, pp. 206–207.
43. CO 137/226, Jordon and Osborn to Robert Stokes, December 27, 1837.
44. *VAJ*, October 26, 1837, p. 25; *Additional Postscript to The Royal Gazette*, October 28, 1837, Debates: October 26.
45. CO 137/226, Jordon and Osborn to Robert Stokes, December 27, 1837.
46. Joseph Sturge and Thomas Harvey, *The West Indies in 1837* (London, 1838), p. 138.
47. Howard Temperley, *British Antislavery, 1833–1870* (London, 1972), pp. 36–40.
48. Martin, *The British Colonies*, pp. 66–68; Burn, *Emancipation and Apprenticeship*, pp. 356–57.
49. *The Royal Gazette and Jamaica Times*, June 23, 1838, Debates: June 12, June 13.
50. For contrasting views on this legislation, see *The Falmouth Post*, June 20, 1838, and CO 137/228, June 25, 1838, Smith to Glenelg, confidential.
51. CO 137/228, "Protest of the Assembly of Jamaica"; Gardner, *History*, pp. 316–17.
52. *The Royal Gazette and Jamaica Times*, June 23, 1838, Debates: June 16; *The Falmouth Post*, June 27, 1838.
53. CO 138/61, Glenelg to Smith, September 13, 1837, no. 133; CO 137/226, Smith to Glenelg, January 17, 1838, no. 11 and Stephen's minute; CO 138/61, Glenelg to Smith, February 27, 1838, no. 231; CO 137/228, Smith to Glenelg, July 7, 1838, no. 138; James Spedding, *Reviews and Discussions Literary* (London, 1879), pp. 108–10.
54. *The Morning Journal*, November 6, 1838.
55. *VAJ*, October 31, 1838, p. 7; CO 137/230, Smith to Glenelg, October 13, 1838, confidential; CO 137/232, Smith to Glenelg, November 12, 1838, no. 193.
56. CO 137/230, Smith to Glenelg, December 3, 1838, confidential; *VAJ*, December 19, 1838, p. 11. Darling later served as governor of Jamaica from 1857 to 1862.
57. CO 137/230, Smith to Glenelg, December 24, 1838, confidential.
58. J. W. Pringle, *Remarks on the State and Prospects of the West Indian Colonies* (London, 1839), p. 19. See also Richard Barrett's election speech in *The Morning Journal*, December 1, 1838, and Sligo Papers, MS 281, Private Letter Book, Sligo to Stanley, May 8, 1834.
59. *The Morning Journal*, December 1, 1838.
60. *The Falmouth Post*, December 26, 1838.
61. Ibid., November 28, 1838.
62. *The Royal Gazette and Jamaica Times*, November 3, 1838, Debates: October 31.
63. Brathwaite, *Creole Society*, p. 98.
64. *The Falmouth Post*, September 18, 1839; Mavis Campbell, *The Dynamics of Change in a Slave Society* (Rutherford, N.J., 1976), p. 189; 137/238, Smith to Normanby, April 22, 1839, private.
65. *VAJ*, December 19, 1838, p. 11.

66. Burn, *Emancipation and Apprenticeship*, p. 330; The Marquis of Sligo [Peter Howe Brown], *A Letter to the Marquess of Normanby* . . . (London, 1839), pp. 30–31; CO 137/230, Smith to Glenelg, December 24, 1838, confidential.

67. Henry Taylor, *Autobiography of Henry Taylor, 1800–1875*, 2 vols. (London, 1885), 1: 248–49.

68. Cardwell papers, PRO 30/48/7/44, Taylor's memorandum, January 19, 1839.

69. CO 884/1, Confidential Print, no. 2, January, 1833, Taylor's comments on the Jamaican slave rebellion, p. 28; D. J. Murray, *The West Indies and the Development of Colonial Government, 1801–1834* (Oxford, 1965), p. 186; C. V. Gocking, "Early Constitutional History of Jamaica," *Caribbean Quarterly* 6 (May 1960): 122.

70. Gocking, "Constitutional History," p. 122; Burn, *Emancipation and Apprenticeship*, pp. 370–71.

71. Spedding, *Reviews and Discussions*, p. 119; Philip D. Curtin, *Two Jamaicas* (Cambridge, Mass., 1955), p. 97.

9

The Politics of Race: Brown Men on the Hustings, 1838–1865

The traditional accounts of the freed slaves in post-emancipation Jamaica provide little hint of their role in politics. It has been suggested that most of the freed slaves left the plantations, set up communities in the interior of the island, and had little to do with the local political institutions. Historians have therefore concluded that politics as well as the franchise were largely in the hands of the white planter class.[1] Recent research suggests that this view fails to take account of more complex developments after the abolition of slavery. Specifically, it overlooks the political role of the peasants and small farmers. It is certainly true that slaves left the plantations in large numbers after 1838. It is also true that the electorate was a tiny one; in a population of over 400,000, it never exceeded 3,000. By 1863, there were only 1,457 voters, or an average of 31 for each member of the House.[2] Yet, who were these voters, how did their composition change during the period, and what effect, if any, did they have on political life in Jamaica? If the voters were of some political significance, is there evidence that white, colored, and black politicians sought to gain their support?

It is clear that some of these voters were peasants, that is, in Douglas Hall's useful terminology, people who owned small freeholds, but who depended partly on occasional earnings from estate labor. More were probably small farmers: they were landholders who were not dependent for work on the estates and instead sometimes employed laborers themselves.[3] Since the data make it difficult to separate peasants and small farmers, they are discussed together in a group identified by their owning twenty-five acres of land or less and are referred to as small settlers or small landholders.

Elections in Jamaica were often social affairs. As in eighteenth-century Virginia, they were a source of free entertainment, with food and drink provided for those who turned out to vote. Polls were mostly held at the parish courthouse and were opened by a special returning officer. After the candidates were placed in nomination and seconded, the officer examined the eligibility of the electors. While practices varied throughout the island, it was evident that men who were not legally entitled to vote occasionally managed to do so. In one parish, the collecting constable refused to submit a list of voters who were in arrears. As a result, only three of the sixteen men who voted for the successful candidate had paid their taxes. The problem was ignored except by the opposition press. Polls usually closed early in the afternoon, although not before the custos, local officials, and the candidates themselves had a chance to appeal for support from the hustings.[4]

Politicians seeking office generally advertised their candidacy in the press. According to an unwritten rule of local politics, however, men of standing in the community did not select their own constituency but waited for an invitation to represent a parish. As factional politics in the Assembly became more intense, this practice declined. Candidates chose to run from particular parishes and organized their campaigns carefully. When an election was contested, committees were frequently formed to solicit votes and to gain support for their candidates. They canvassed voters as well as working out plans for election day.[5]

Electioneering methods included ruffianism and intimidation. Men were sometimes hired to prevent voters pledged to the opposition from reaching the polls; alternatively, they might ply the electors with drink and persuade them to vote for a particular candidate.[6] Committees also made use of the power of the disfranchised population. In the 1851 election for the seat at St. David, one candidate arrived with some thirty supporters "wearing flags, beating drums, and wearing blue ribbons," the colors of the Conservative (or member of the Country party) running for the seat. His rival was supported by a crowd of three hundred men, most of whom were nonelectors and all of whom were armed with a bludgeon. The contest was extremely close, and a riot developed when the one remaining voter pledged to the Conservative was blocked from the poll. In the ensuing tumult, the clerk of the vestry was killed. Although this was the most serious election riot during the post-emancipation period, violence characterized other elections as well.[7]

Electoral committees also sought to bribe voters. Lodging, food, and entertainment were only a part of this effort. Candidates might literally enfranchise supporters by paying the taxes of potential electors and occasionally by handing out four or five shillings to each voter. Edward Jordon denounced the practice of buying and selling votes at a meeting to back James Davidson, a white candidate running for the House in 1851. Jordon hoped that all the electors voting for Davidson would come out "free and unbought." The colored politician, George William Gordon, also supported Davidson. However, Gordon took the rather unusual public view that the people were "too depressed to part with the means of realizing something by their franchise and however sorry he was to say it, they should not be deprived of it."[8] The nature of the franchise made bribery more likely. Since the ballot was not yet secret, pressure could be applied on employees and servants to vote for particular candidates. In addition, electoral requirements had been designed during slavery to allow whites of all classes to vote. The result was that qualifications for the electorate remained relatively low before the late 1850s. Freeholders with land valued at £6 were enfranchised as were tenants and owners of rented property worth £30 per annum and taxpayers assessed at £3 a year. After abolition, the Assembly raised the minimum requirements for the vote, but the Colonial Office repeatedly disallowed the legislation. Even though the number of voters never exceeded 1 percent of the population, the small settlers who had moved off the estates made up a sizable percentage of the voters.[9]

Contemporary opinion and correlations between the voters and the amount of land they owned suggest that the small landholders could significantly influence the outcome of elections. In four selected parishes, St. Thomas in the East, Vere, St. John, and St. Thomas in the Vale,[10] landholders with less than twenty-five acres outnumbered planters who owned more than one hundred acres of land (Table 5). Since many settlers occupied land without making any legal record of their holdings, the figures are weighted in favor of the planters. Moreover, Table 5 does not take into account the shift in 1860 when a change in the franchise drastically reduced the proportion of the freehold vote.

The Falmouth Post was particularly anxious about the effect of these voters whom it described as "a low, unruly mobocracy." The paper was worried about the power of the settlers to control elections and to return agitators who were the self-proclaimed "friends of the people" and who pandered to the "un-

TABLE 5. VOTERS WITH LAND STATISTICS, 1838–1863

SAMPLE PARISH	PLANTERS OVER 500 ACRES	PLANTERS 100–499 ACRES	SMALL LANDHOLDERS 1–25 ACRES
St. Thomas in the Vale	27	23	117
Vere	24	12	51
St. John	15	21	76
St. Thomas in the East	38	14	54

SOURCES: IRO, Land Deeds; *Jamaica Almanac*, 1840, 1845; Jamaica Archives, House of Assembly Poll Books (2 vols.). See also Appendix C.

washed constituency."[11] The planters also feared that the vote of the ex-slaves would be mobilized against them, and they were concerned about two groups who sought to influence the new voters: the Baptist missionaries and the colored politicians.

Among the European missionaries, the Baptists had shown most concern for the welfare of the slaves, and after emancipation this tradition continued. Many of the missionaries counseled the ex-slaves to resist low wages and opposed much of the legislation that was directed against the emancipated population. They also urged the former slaves to purchase small freeholds and become independent producers. In the process, the missionaries believed that the new freeholders would affect the outcome of elections for parish and island-wide office. Since the Baptists were strongly opposed to the established church, they hoped to return men to the Assembly who were pledged to sever the connection between church and state in the island.[12] As their newspaper warned, "if an Assembly of whites will not give relief, men of darker colour will be found to fill their places."[13]

The Baptists made no secret of their plans. During a meeting in 1840, one of them reportedly assured the audience that "in the parish of St. Ann's we shall have 300 to 500 good and true votes and who shall we send to represent us? Shall we send Hamilton Brown and Dr. Barnett; these fornicators; these oppressors; these robbers of the people's rights and privileges?"[14] The missionaries thus encouraged the enfranchisement of the small freeholders. For example, *The Baptist Herald* noted in 1841 that the independent freeholders in Kingston had registered in large numbers, and it called on those in the country to do the same. Since *The Herald* believed that there were enough voters to return liberal assemblymen from nearly every parish, it was willing to assist any freeholder in claiming his rights.[15]

The rhetoric of the Baptists and their politics concerned local officials. Governor Charles Metcalfe observed in 1840 that they had become a political party and had great influence over the ex-slave population. Unlike other European missionaries, the Baptists were preparing for the elections and might therefore affect the results. James Stephen agreed with Metcalfe's assessment; he predicted that the Baptists would become "Masters at no very distant time of the fortunes of Jamaica." But Stephen was not worried about this development. In his view, Baptist domination of Jamaica was probably preferable to that of the planters.[16]

Despite their close ties to the emancipated population, the Baptists never succeeded in controlling island politics. In 1844, Metcalfe's successor, Lord Elgin (James Bruce), surprised them by dissolving the House a year earlier than they had expected. Although Baptist ministers had been registering large numbers of voters in anticipation of a dissolution in 1845, the new electors could not participate in the 1844 election because the island secretary's office required twelve months to register the votes. As a result, the few candidates whom the Baptists were able to sponsor did not fare well. Running as "Anti-State Church" men, they were successful in only two parishes—St. Thomas in the Vale and St. Mary. Since the returns in St. Mary were voided on the grounds of electoral corruption, the number of assemblymen who were committed to the separation of church and state was reduced to two.[17]

The death in 1845 of William Knibb and the society's declining membership during the 1840s reduced its political effectiveness. Baptist missionaries could still influence individual elections: thus, they were responsible for the return of the Trelawny coroner in 1849 and were accused of controlling the constituency.[18] Yet, by 1850, the Baptists were much less of a political force than they had been ten years earlier—not only because of their internal difficulties but also because of the opposition of the colored politicians who were appealing to the small freeholders on very different grounds from the Baptists.

The men of color in the House feared a Baptist oligarchy in control of Jamaican politics. While many people of color were dissenters, a sizable number were members of the established church. For them, the Anglican church maintained an important link with England that they were unwilling to give up; it was also preferable to the black churches which might otherwise have threatened to overwhelm an important aspect of European civilization on the island.[19] On the hustings, however, brown politicians did not debate the question of church-state relations. Instead, they concentrated on more local issues and sought to identify as closely as possible with the majority of the voters. In the process, they made use of their color to gain the support of the newly enfranchised population.

Brown politicians differentiated themselves from the whites in their speeches and in their advertisements. During a by-election in Vere, the colored candidate, Charles Jackson, told a meeting that the "whites had had their own way long enough and it was time to put them down." His supporters not only carried the usual banners and flags to the poll but also brought along sticks to prevent voters for the white candidate from expressing their preference. The election became a racial contest in which Jackson appealed to the majority on the basis of color. Jackson was successful, but one of his supporters was imprisoned for a year as a result of the riot that broke out at the poll.[20] Neither the riot nor Jackson's appeal was unique, for both were repeated during the 1851 election in St. David. The violence there prompted Governor Grey to note the increasing importance of the nonwhite electorate and their determination "to obtain influence and power."[21]

Black and colored candidates for office often directed their campaigns to attract these voters. Edward Vickars, the first black man to sit in the House, based his electioneering efforts in 1844 on the slogan "Vote for Vickars, the Black Man."[22] A brown candidate in Westmoreland, Foster Davis, chose a more subtle theme when he advertised himself as one of the "sons of Jamaica." Since Davis also noted that natives should have a greater share in the running of the island, he was clearly emphasizing his creole and colored background.[23]

While black and brown politicians sought to identify with the voters, white men seeking office were often forced to rebut claims that they had discriminated against the people of color. A banker and landowner, John V. Purrier, was accused during his election campaign of having opposed the elevation of brown men to prominent positions in the early 1830s. The report was clearly intended to persuade colored electors to vote for the opposition candidate. A few years later, a planter seeking the same seat faced a similar charge. Both accusations may well have been false; nevertheless, they reflected the continuing importance of color in elections for the House.[24]

The brown men who formed the basis of the Town party in the Assembly— or the "clique" as it was then called—made use of their color as well as other electioneering ploys to gain support. For example, Robert Osborn corresponded on behalf of brown candidates and attempted to ensure that they would be returned. In 1848, he wrote to a freeholder in St. George asking him to secure the nomination of John Nunes, a colored politician from Kingston. Osborn's arguments were interesting; he claimed that "union is strength, that Mr. N. is one of us, and a native." For Osborn, it was impossible to "help ourselves till we have a majority in the House."[25]

Although the brown politicians backed colored candidates for the Assembly, they did not always support blacks. Jordon and Osborn thus opposed the election of Edward Vickars to the House, apparently on the basis of his color. Moreover, they were not always successful in appealing to black voters. The black electorate in Kingston refused to support their candidate in a by-election in 1845.[26] As Swithin Wilmot has concluded, "the old 'aristocracy of skin,' the result of the slave experience, remained to haunt the society after emancipation, and played a more overt role in the island's elections after 1838."[27]

Brown and black politicians did not campaign solely on the basis of color. Like Osborn, they also backed issues that were designed to attract the votes of the majority. In the 1849 general election, Edward Vickars advertised his candidacy by announcing his support for universal manhood suffrage rather than one based on property. Osborn used the same method to highlight his reform record and his measure for educating the mass of the population.[28] Thus, the coloreds were appealing to the small freeholders on political as well as on racial issues. The response from the freeholders was surprisingly consistent in view of their general apathy and the pressures on them to vote differently.

Both the data from the pollbooks and contemporary opinion indicate that the freehold vote generally supported either colored candidates or men who were allied to the Town party (Table 6).[29] The evidence is difficult to collect, but the conclusion from four sample parishes suggests that small landholders voted more consistently Liberal than the planters at the other end of the scale.

TABLE 6. CONSISTENCY OF VOTING PATTERNS, 1838–1863

GROUP BY LAND-HOLDINGS	SAMPLE PARISHES	TOTAL NO. OF VOTERS WITH LAND STATISTICS	VOTERS MORE THAN ONE TIME	VOTERS MORE THAN ONE TIME CONSISTENT	PERCENT CONSISTENT VOTERS	CONSISTENT LIBERALS No.	CONSISTENT LIBERALS %	CONSISTENT CONSERVATIVES No.	CONSISTENT CONSERVATIVES %	SPLIT No.	SPLIT %
Planters 500 Acres and Up	St. Thomas in the Vale	27	13	13	100	2	15	10	77½	1	7½
	Vere	24	15	10	67	5	50	5	50	—	—
	St. John	15	2	1	50	—	—	1	50	—	—
	St. Thomas in the East	38	19	18	95	1	6	17	94	—	—
Planters 101–499 Acres	St. Thomas in the Vale	23	9	8	89	—	—	6	75	2	25
	Vere	12	6	5	83	2	40	2	40	1	20
	St. John	21	11	5	45	1	20	4	80	—	—
	St. Thomas in the East	14	5	4	80	—	—	3	75	1	25
Farmers 50–100 Acres	St. Thomas in the Vale	25	6	5	83	1	20	3	60	1	20
	Vere	6	3	3	100	—	—	3	100	—	—
	St. John	22	9	4	44	2	50	2	50	—	—
	St. Thomas in the East	11	8	5	63	1	20	4	80	—	—
Small Landholders 0–25 Acres	St. Thomas in the Vale	117	34	29	85	21	71	5	18	3	11
	Vere	51	28	20	72	16	80	4	20	—	—
	St. John	76	37	18	50	11	62	7	38	—	—
	St. Thomas in the East	54	17	11	65	4	36	7	63	—	—
Artisans Merchants With Land	St. Thomas in the Vale	24	4	2	50	2	100	—	—	—	—
	Vere	5	1	—	—	—	—	—	—	—	—
	St. John	4	1	1	100	—	—	1	100	—	—
	St. Thomas in the East	16	4	4	100	—	—	4	100	—	—
Clerks	St. Thomas in the Vale	6	—	—	—	—	—	—	—	—	—
	Vere	6	—	—	—	—	—	—	—	—	—
	St. John	1	—	—	—	—	—	—	—	—	—
	St. Thomas in the East	23	6	6	100	—	—	6	100	—	—
Artisans Merchants Without Land	St. Thomas in the Vale	16	8	7	88	4	57	2	28	1	14
	Vere	8	5	4	80	3	75	1	25	—	—
	St. John	—	—	—	—	—	—	—	—	—	—
	St. Thomas in the East	13	4	4	100	4	100	—	—	—	—
Rector Without Land	St. Thomas in the Vale	4	1	1	100	1	100	—	—	—	—
	Vere	1	—	—	—	—	—	—	—	—	—
	St. John	—	—	—	—	—	—	—	—	—	—
	St. Thomas in the East	—	—	—	—	—	—	—	—	—	—

SOURCES: IRO, Land Deeds; Jamaica Almanac, 1840, 1845; Jamaica Archives, House of Assembly Poll Books (2 vols.). See also Appendix C.

The one parish in which this did not occur, St. Thomas in the East, may have been unique. It had the heaviest concentration of planters who voted consistently Conservative and who may well have influenced their employees to vote along similar lines. St. Thomas in the East conformed to the pattern of the other constituencies, however, when the small landholders turned out in large numbers at the poll.

The relationship between the brown and black politicians and the small settler vote is highlighted more clearly by examining individual elections during the period. The most crucial election in the post-emancipation period was 1849 (Figures 3–6). Jamaican politics at that point was undergoing a major crisis: the planters in the House were intent on stopping the usual revenue bills in the hope of forcing a weak Home Government to maintain the protective duties on sugar, which the Whigs had decided to abolish. In response, the colored delegates sought to enact the annual financial legislation and thus to prevent the planters from upsetting the local economy. When the resulting legislative impasse forced Sir Charles Edward Grey to dissolve the House in 1849, the brown politicians worked hard to secure the return of assemblymen who would support the Town party and oppose the planters.[30] Although the colored faction remained a minority, it was able to bring out the settler vote in several constituencies.

This was particularly the case in St. John and in St. Thomas in the Vale. The total number of voters in both parishes for the 1849 election was the highest during the period from 1838 to 1865, and of those it was possible to trace, more than 62 percent in St. John and 63 percent in St. Thomas in the Vale were small landholders. Although the voting figures in the other two sample parishes did not reach their peak in 1849, this group had an important influence in these constituencies as well. St. Thomas in the East recorded over 49 percent of its voters in this category, while Vere reported slightly less than 46 percent for the election. The results indicated the importance of the freehold vote to the Town party. Six of the eight delegates returned in 1849 for the sample parishes became members of the colored faction; of these, four were brown, one was black, and one was a Jew. The evidence also suggests that, while bribery was probably a standard feature of almost every election, it did not determine the outcome. As in English elections during the period, the pattern in the vote reduces the significance of any electoral corruption.[31] Race, political identity, and the coloreds' pursuit of support on the hustings seemed to have been more important in attracting the small landholders than the buying of votes.

Other elections in the four parishes tended to confirm the view that the small landholding vote could swing elections to the coloreds. In St. John, 1849 proved to be an exception; in other elections between 1838 and 1865, the voters with less than twenty-five acres of land were a far smaller proportion of the electorate. The result was the return of primarily Conservative candidates. The evidence in St. Thomas in the Vale points to a similar conclusion. The

Figure 3.   ELECTIONS IN ST. THOMAS IN THE VALE, 1838–1863

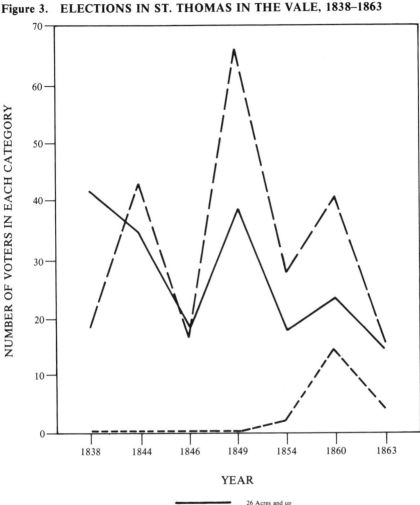

† This category for the four charts in Figure 3–6 includes rectors and artisans without land. After 1859, it also includes those earning annual salaries of £50 per annum.

SOURCES: IRO, Land Deeds; *Jamaica Almanac*, 1840, 1845; Jamaica Archives, House of Assembly Poll Books (2 vols.). The variable election dates in Figures 3–6 indicate that certain elections went unrecorded in the pollbooks as well as the existence of an occasional by-election in the parish.

only elections that recorded more than half of the 1849 small landholding vote were 1844 and 1860. In 1844, the Baptists were able to mobilize the settler vote for one of their candidates, and in 1860, the Town party was running two

Figure 4. ELECTIONS IN VERE, 1838–1860

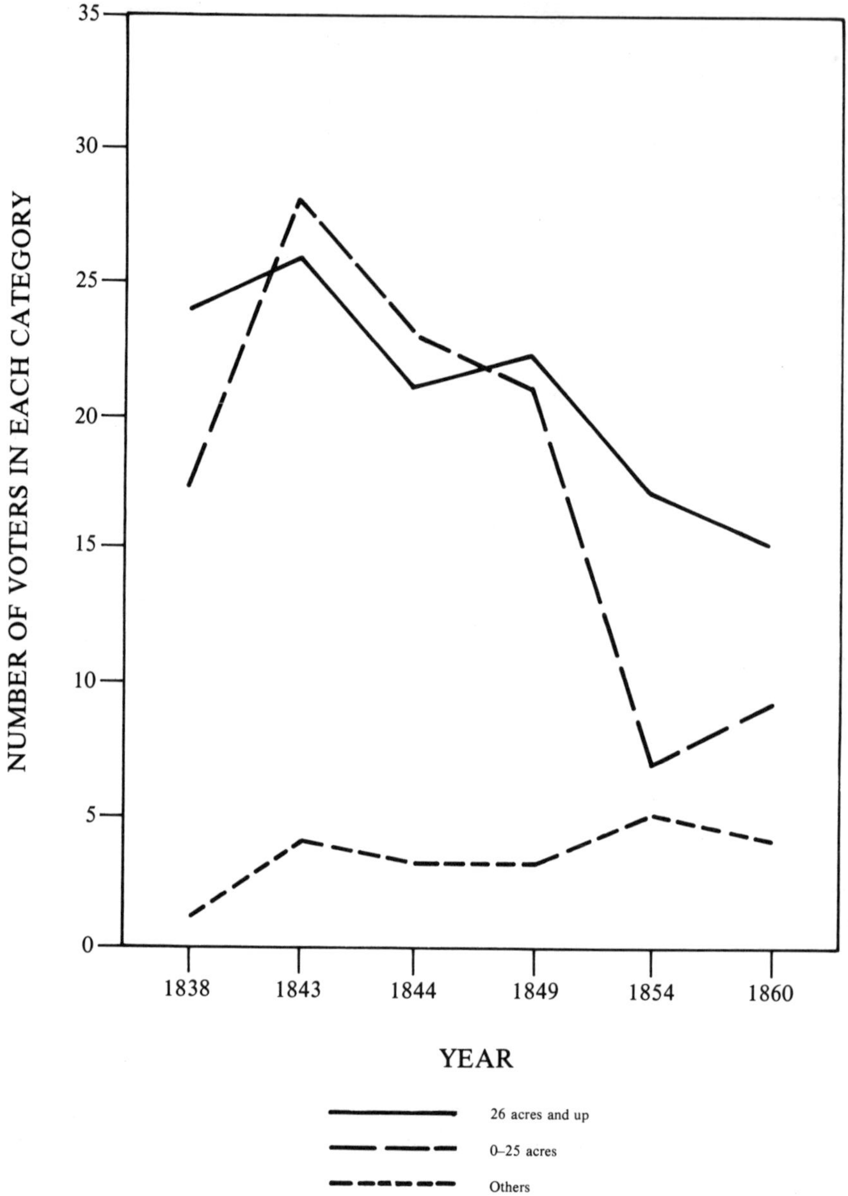

SOURCE: Same as Figure 3.

Figure 5. ELECTIONS IN ST. JOHN, 1838–1863

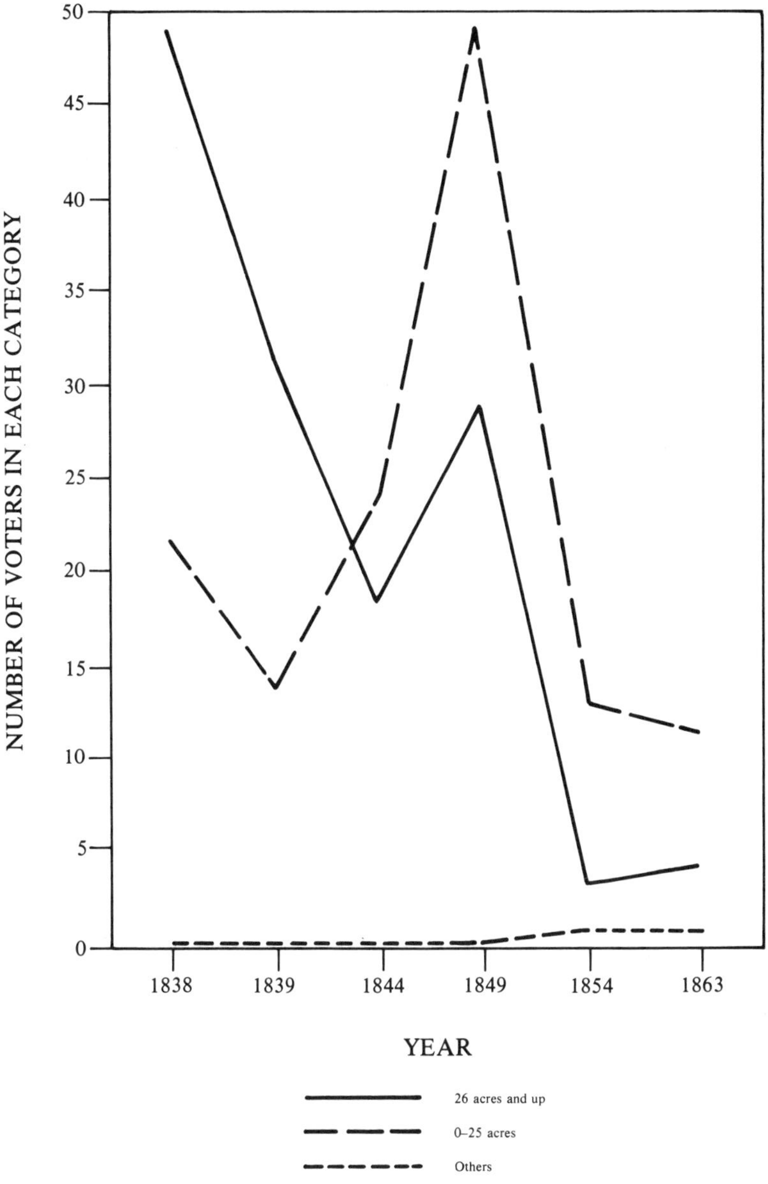

SOURCE: Same as Figure 3.

Figure 6. ELECTIONS IN ST. THOMAS IN THE EAST, 1842–1863

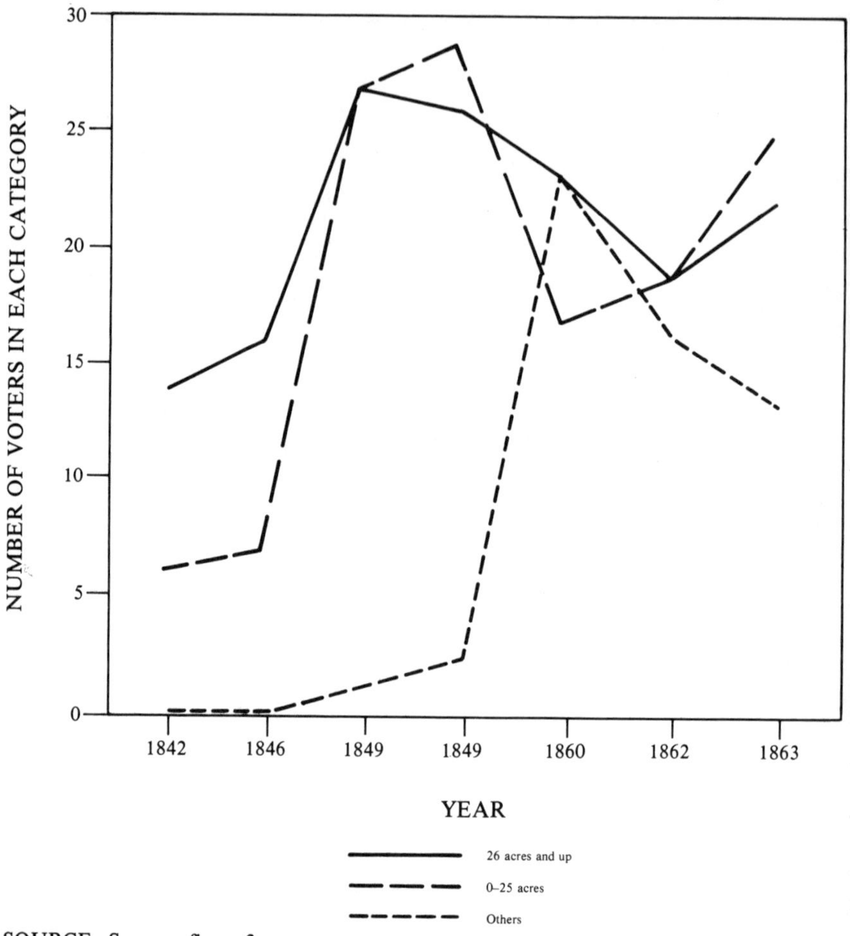

YEAR

	26 acres and up
	0–25 acres
	Others

SOURCE: Same as figure 3.

men in a heavily contested race. The figures in St. Thomas in the East show
that the only poll apart from 1849 with a roughly comparable total of the freehold vote was 1863. In that election, George William Gordon, by then the
most radical member of the House, defeated a Conservative planter with the
aid of the settler vote. Finally, in Vere, two polls in the early 1840s registered
more small landholders than in 1849, and both elections returned at least one
member of the Assembly who supported the colored faction in the House.[32]

Another group of candidates who depended on the small landholding vote
were several Jewish delegates elected to the House in the late 1840s or early
1850s. These included Aaron Salom, a shopkeeper; Moses Lyon, a tavern-
keeper; and George Lyons, a fish and provisions merchant. Lyons is an in-

teresting example of a candidate who appealed directly to the settlers. He called himself the "friend of the people" and was known to be popular among blacks. His main support came from the Baptist villages in his district, and like the other two men, Lyons was elected to office on the strength of peasant support.[33]

The brown politicians were no less aware of the importance of the settler vote. In 1847, The Morning Journal reported the disfranchisement of a large number of freeholders from St. Ann. The problem was the value of their freeholds: revising barristers had ruled that they were worth 6 percent of the assessed value and therefore less than the requirement for the vote. Since the costs of an appeal to the courts were prohibitive, The Morning Journal suggested that an organization be established to monitor the proceedings of the registration courts. The paper reported that the Liberal party would otherwise continue to suffer from disfranchisement of the poorer freeholders. The new association would prevent the loss of support which the coloreds had sought to establish among the newly enfranchised population.[34]

There were difficulties, moreover, in bringing out the settler vote. Apart from the political indifference of the overwhelming majority of the small landholders, the colored "clique" was not a party. Like similar groups in early American politics, it depended on a close coterie of personal associates rather than on a political machine.[35] The brown politicians were also limited in their geographic scope. They could not cover every constituency, and they were not always able to field candidates who could meet the rather steep qualifications for an assemblyman: a freehold worth £300 or other property valued at £3,000.[36] In addition, it became clear in the 1850s that the leading coloreds did not want a revolutionary change in the composition of the House and that the planters would do all they could to resist this development as well.

The planters therefore established political organizations to compete for the vote. Unlike the "clique," the Conservatives do not appear to have sent men around the island generating support for local candidates. Instead, the planters formed individual committees in each parish to contest the elections. The association that backed a planter for the St. James' seat in 1849, for example, worked diligently and in a highly systematic fashion. It established rural committees and listed members of the general committee in each area who were responsible for encouraging voters to support its candidate. During the same election, the "Vere Conservative Association" nominated the speaker of the House to stand for the parish.[37]

The planter organizations could not ignore the "enlarged constituencies." In many cases, the associations successfully appealed to the newly enfranchised electorate to vote for planter candidates. Robert Osborn complained that the gentry had preceded him in campaigning for the support of the £6 freeholders of St. George. Although the brown politicians also attempted to sway the small landholders, Osborn maintained that the "wealth and respectability" of the island could be more effective than the "clique" when the planters were willing to campaign among the people. The politics of deference could still swing elections in favor of white candidates, but the planters feared that deference was giving way to democracy and that the whites would no longer be able to maintain control of the island constituencies.[38]

The returns in the late 1840s and early 1850s alarmed the planters. While they still had a working majority in the House, the Conservatives enacted a new election law in 1852 to reduce the number of small freeholders on the voting lists. The measure did not alter the basic requirement for the franchise, but it included provisions restricting the vote to those who had paid their taxes.[39] The bill met with the expected opposition. In St. Mary, a public meeting concluded that the election law was directed against the poor of Jamaica. The consensus of the meeting was that the new legislation would reduce the franchise and was designed to disfranchise as many Liberals and Radicals as possible. The gathering passed resolutions against the measure and petitioned the Council and the Crown to disallow the act.[40]

Despite the implications of the legislation, the older colored politicians accepted the need for it. In their view, the new registration and the obligation to pay taxes before polling day would check the bribery and corruption that characterized many elections on the island.[41] The support of Jordon and Osborn for this aspect of the measure represented a significant shift in their point of view. It was prompted in part by the increasing violence at elections and, more importantly, by the type of candidate who was being returned to the Assembly. During the 1850s, brown political leaders became concerned about the change in the composition of the House. By then, black delegates as well as coloreds who were artisans or owned small businesses were entering the House. Although Jordon and Osborn had backed the election of some of these representatives, they feared that the House could be swamped by the new class of assemblyman. Since the whites were already threatening to abolish the House before their majority was erased, it was clear to the colored leadership that they would ultimately have to decide whether to sacrifice some of their own electoral support or the island's Constitution. Their choice was reflected in a new election law further reducing the freehold vote.[42]

The measure passed in 1859 included a provision requiring the payment of a ten shilling duty as part of the franchise. Because of this fee, there was little doubt about the intent of the legislators. Governor Charles Henry Darling wrote home that "it will practically operate as a great discouragement of the exercise of the Franchise, by the more numerous and humbler Class of Freeholders, and that it was advocated in the Assembly for no other reason."[43] The law prompted one legal authority to state that the Jamaican franchise was not only more restrictive than the English electoral requirements but also included "an actual penalty" on the exercise of the vote.[44] In addition, the bill created a new class of voters by including men with an annual salary of at least £50. This was a further boon to the planters because it meant that clerks, bookkeepers, and other salaried personnel on the estates were enfranchised, most for the first time. Since planters could usually control the votes of their supervisory staff, the measure was open to wide abuse. In one parish, for example, a wealthy proprietor and planting attorney paid the stamp duty for all his employees and was able to command a majority of the votes for the general election.[45]

The percentage of the freehold vote declined significantly as a result of the new election law (Figure 7). Whereas freeholders had made up almost 60 percent of the electorate in 1858, the percentage fell to barely 30 percent only two years later. The number of small landholders who were assessed at £6 dropped even more sharply. This category had comprised one-third of the registered voters in 1858; it was reduced to one-sixth of the total in 1860 and one-eighth by 1863.[46] Instead, taxpayers and salaried personnel dominated the polls during this period. A Baptist minister, Reverend E. B. Underhill, estimated that nearly 70 percent of the voters in the 1860s were either voting on the basis of paying taxes or receiving salaries. He concluded that the small occupiers of land were not represented in the House and that planters, attorneys, agents, clerks, and shopkeepers controlled the vote.[47]

The result of the change in the franchise was predictable: the number of colored and black representatives in the Assembly declined after reaching a peak in the early 1850s. Seventeen coloreds and three blacks had sat in the House that lasted from 1849 to 1854. The number fell to a total of seventeen for the following House and to fourteen for the 1860–1863 Assembly. When the Assembly removed the stamp duty on the vote in 1865, it was too late to have any impact on the composition of the House.[48] The planters and the leading coloreds had succeeded in reducing the threat from the small freeholders of radically altering the composition of the House of Assembly.

While the enfranchised remained a tiny fraction of the total population during this period, they were nonetheless a significant political barometer after 1838. For the first decade and a half, electoral requirements remained very much the same, largely because of a watchful Colonial Office. During that period, black and brown settlers formed a majority of the electorate and tended to favor colored candidates for the Assembly. Although planters were also able to influence the "enlarged constituencies" when they campaigned for the vote, it was the Town party politicians who worked hardest for the support of the new voters. The result was the entry of black and brown shopkeepers and artisans to an Assembly that had been dominated largely by planters, merchants, and representatives of the professional classes.

Yet, the Town party was unable to gain a majority in the House. One problem was organization. Lacking the trappings of a modern party, the "clique" could not field candidates on an island-wide basis. In addition, the factional nature of the group meant that it was unstable and subject to splits and tempo-

Figure 7. CATEGORIES OF VOTING QUALIFICATIONS, 1858–1863

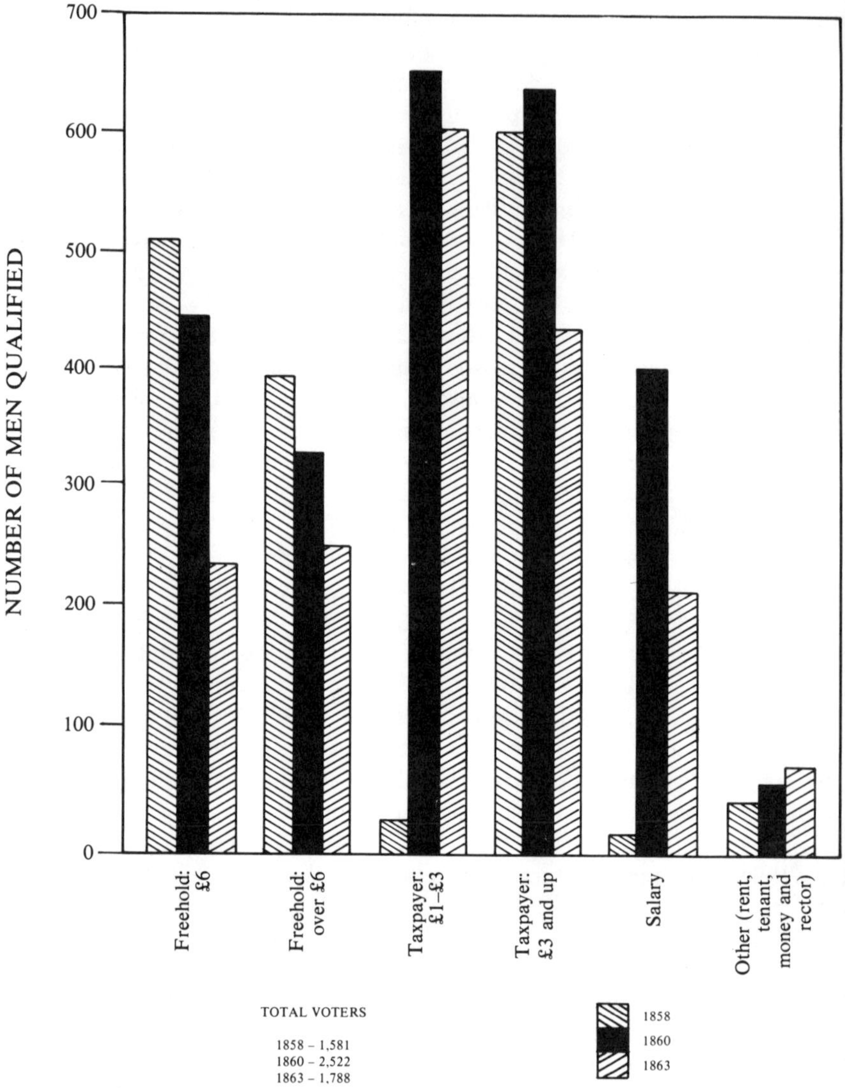
NUMBER OF MEN QUALIFIED
700
600
500
400
300
200
100
0
Freehold: £6
Freehold: over £6
Taxpayer: £1–£3
Taxpayer: £3 and up
Salary
Other (rent, tenant, money and rector)
TOTAL VOTERS
1858 – 1,581
1860 – 2,522
1863 – 1,788
1858
1860
1863

SOURCES: *VAJ*, 1859, p. 225; 1864, p. 235.

rary alliances. The nature of the society added further difficulties for the colored politicians. White planters often dominated their local areas and could control nominations and elections to the House. The strength of the plantocracy and the factional nature of the "clique" limited its political expansion. More importantly, the attitudes of the leading brown politicians ensured that nonwhites would not swamp the Assembly.

The leading coloreds frequently appealed for support to the freeholders on racial grounds, but they were unwilling to preside over a fundamental change in the representation of the island.[49] Since they feared that the whites might abolish the House because of the threat of blacks and browns, men like Jordon and Osborn attempted to strike a balance between their desire to increase the representation of the people of color and their concern for the survival of the Assembly. The change in the composition of the House in the 1840s and early 1850s thus frightened the more conservative brown politicians as well as the planters in the House. The two groups therefore raised the franchise requirement to eliminate the threatening influence of the small landholders. As in 1839, the planters were prepared to sacrifice the House of Assembly rather than allow blacks and coloreds to dominate local politics.

NOTES

1. Douglas Hall, *Free Jamaica, 1838–1865* (New Haven, Conn., 1959), p. 177. Hall has reexamined the exodus of ex-slaves from the estates after emancipation in two interesting articles: "The Flight from the Estates Reconsidered: The British West Indies, 1838–1842," *The Journal of Caribbean History* 10 and 11 (1978): 7–24; and "Fort George Pen, Jamaica: Slaves, Tenants and Labourers, 1832–1843," Paper presented to the Eleventh Conference of Caribbean Historians (1979). See also the useful treatment of this issue by Michael Craton, *Searching for the Invisible Man* (Cambridge, Mass., 1978), Chapter 12.

2. CO 137/385, Eyre to Cardwell, December 19, 1864, no. 303; Lord Olivier, *Jamaica the Blessed Island* (London, 1936), p. 184.

3. Hall, *Free Jamaica*, p. 158. See also the discussion of the peasantry in Sidney W. Mintz, *Caribbean Transformations* (Chicago, 1974), p. 148.

4. *The Cornwall Chronicle*, June 5, August 18, 1841. Charles S. Sydnor's study of politics in eighteenth-century Virginia provides an interesting comparison with electoral practices in Jamaica: *Gentlemen Freeholders* (Chapel Hill, N.C., 1952), Chapter 3.

5. The contested election for the Hanover seat in 1843 is a good example of how candidates organized their campaigns. For one candidate's advertisements, see *The Falmouth Post*, September 27, 1843; for reports of canvassing, see *The Baptist Herald*, November 22, 1843.

6. *The Baptist Herald*, November 22, 1843.

7. *The Colonial Standard*, January 29, 1851.

8. *Daily Advertiser*, November 17, 1851.

9. J. M. Ludlow, *A Quarter Century of Jamaica Legislation* (London, 1866), p. 6; Philip D. Curtin, *Two Jamaicas* (Cambridge, Mass., 1955), p. 179; CO 137/322, Barkly to Newcastle, March 22, 1854, no. 37.

10. The parishes were chosen because they were representative of the various types of population and land use in the island and because their size made them manageable. Vere was a sugar parish, St. John contained a large number of small farms, and St. Thomas in the Vale was a settler parish. St. Thomas in the East not only contained a

large number of sugar estates and a sizable black population but also was the parish in which the Morant Bay Rebellion took place.

11. *The Falmouth Post*, January 19, 1849.

12. CO 137/249, Knibb and Clarke to Russell, June 17, 1840; *The Falmouth Post*, January 19, 1849; *The Baptist Herald*, April 16, 1844.

13. *The Baptist Herald*, December 14, 1842, quoted in Swithin Wilmot, "Political Developments in Jamaica in the Post-Emancipation Period, 1838–1854" (unpublished D. Phil. thesis, Oxford University, 1977), p. 289.

14. *The Falmouth Post*, April 29, 1840. Hamilton Brown was a leader in the Colonial Church Union.

15. *The Baptist Herald*, January 27, 1841.

16. CO 137/248, Metcalfe to Russell: April 13, 1840, no. 56; April 20, 1840, no. 67, enclosure; April 30, 1840, no. 75, memo by James Stephen. The planters shared Metcalfe's view on the danger the Baptists posed. Captain E.R.W. Wingfield Yates recorded the disquiet felt by one planter in his "Journal," November 24, 1842, pp. 165–66 (MS, Institute of Jamaica).

17. CO 137/284, Elgin to Stanley, September 8, 1845, confidential; "The Elections—The Franchise," *The Jamaica Monthly Magazine* 1 (October 1844): 482–83; *The Baptist Herald*, September 24, 1844.

18. Curtin, *Two Jamaicas*, pp. 182–83; *The Falmouth Post*, January 16, January 19, 1849.

19. Elgin quoted in Theodore Walrond (ed.), *Letters and Journals of James, Eighth Earl of Elgin* (London, 1872), p. 25.

20. CO 137/285, Elgin to Stanley, December 23, 1845, no. 105.

21. CO 137/309, C. Grey to Earl Grey, February 27, 1851, no. 17.

22. "The Elections—The Franchise," pp. 482–83.

23. *The Falmouth Post*, July 24, 1849.

24. Ibid., September 27, 1843; December 22, 1848.

25. *The Morning Journal*, August 25, 1848.

26. Wilmot, "Political Developments in Jamaica," pp. 304, 306.

27. Ibid., pp. 304–305.

28. *The Morning Journal*, July 12, 1849.

29. The method used to gather and compile the information on voting patterns is described in Appendix C. Pollbooks have also recently been used to analyze elections in England. The most helpful studies are J. R. Vincent, *Pollbooks* (Cambridge, 1967); W. A. Speck and W. A. Gray, "Computer Analysis of Poll Books: An Initial Report," *Bulletin of the Institute of Historical Research* 43 (May 1970): 105–12; and T. J. Nossiter, "Voting Behaviour 1832–1872," *Political Studies* 18 (1970): 380–89. Nossiter also reviews the literature in "Recent Work on English Elections, 1832–1935," *Political Studies* 18 (1970): 525–28.

30. See Chapter 10 for a more detailed discussion of the 1849 crisis.

31. Vincent, *Pollbooks*, pp. 10–12.

32. Jamaica Archives, House of Assembly Poll Books, 2 vols. (1803–1866); IRO, Land Deeds, 1838–1865.

33. Wilmot, "Political Developments in Jamaica," pp. 273, 327.

34. *The Morning Journal*, April 26, 1847.

35. William N. Chambers, *Political Parties in a New Nation* (New York, 1963).

36. *The Baptist Herald*, January 20, 1841, pp. 20–21.

37. *The Falmouth Post*, August 3, July 27, 1849.

38. Abraham Judah and A. C. Sinclair (comps.), *Debates of the Honourable House of Assembly of Jamaica* . . . 13 vols. (Kingston and Spanish Town, 1856–1866), November 29, 1858, p. 103; *Colonial Standard and Jamaica Despatch*, January 10, 1851.

39. CO 137/313, Grey to Pakington, April 28, 1852, no. 39.

40. *Daily Advertiser*, April 20, 1852.

41. *The Morning Journal*, April 26, 1852.

42. *The Falmouth Post*, June 2, 1857; Judah and Sinclair, *Debates*, December 2, 1858, pp. 124ff.; Wilmot, "Political Developments in Jamaica," p. 325.

43. CO 137/343, Darling to Bulwer-Lytton, February 10, 1859, no. 31.

44. Ludlow, *Jamaica Legislation*, p. 7.

45. M.M.S., Matthew to Arthur, December 2, 1865.

46. *VAJ* (1859), "Return of the Qualified Voters of the several parishes. . . ," p. 225; ibid. (1865), "A Return of the Number of Registered Voters of the Island Claiming to Vote. . . ," p. 235.

47. E. B. Underhill, *The West Indies* (London, 1862), p. 215.

48. CO 137/388, Eyre to Cardwell, February 8, 1865, no. 19.

49. Judah and Sinclair, *Debates*, December 31, 1858, p. 309.

10

The Politics of Opposition: The Rise of the Brown Liberals, 1839–1853

The success of the Jamaican plantocracy against the Home Government in 1839 set an important precedent for the colony's political life. As a result, the planters in the House did not hesitate in later years and particularly after the abolition of the sugar duties to create local political crises in the hope of altering British colonial policy. Yet, during the post-emancipation period, it was not always possible for the whites to have their own way in the Assembly. The colored delegates formed an increasingly important group in the 1840s, and at the end of the decade, they tended to vote along strictly party lines in opposition to the representatives of the planters. The politics of the brown Liberals and their Town party allies were thus sharply differentiated from those of the planter class and its faction in the Assembly, the Country party.

In spite of the political turmoil in Jamaica, the man who became governor in 1839 did not have any experience in dealing with a notoriously difficult legislature. Charles Metcalfe had spent most of his life working in India; he had occupied the highest posts in the East India Company, including for a short time that of acting governor-general.[1] But Metcalfe's success as an Indian administrator was not altogether welcome in Jamaica. The West India Committee was afraid that he would abolish the constitutional forms that the planters were trying to protect.[2] It soon became clear that the committee had very little to worry about.

Metcalfe faced a formidable task. The colonial secretary, Lord John Russell, had advised him to be conciliatory to the whites and at the same time to protect the rights of the ex-slaves. Metcalfe therefore had to confront the weakness inherent in the old representative Constitution. Either he carried out

British policy and alienated the Assembly, or he supported the whites against the wishes of the Home Government. In an effort to resolve the problem, the governor chose to rely on the plantocracy to legislate effectively for the mass of the population. Since Metcalfe believed that he could entrust the planters to protect the former slaves, he was eager to reverse the critical attitude in the Colonial Office toward much of the Assembly's legislation. He also sought to gain favor with the whites by increasing their judicial powers and by gradually abolishing the stipendiary magistrates.[3]

However, the Assembly responded by enacting laws designed generally to minimize the rights of the peasantry and to limit the mobility of the ex-slaves. Although the intent of the delegates was to restrict the movement of the freed slaves away from the estates, the statutes proved ineffective. The acts alienated many of the former slaves who left the plantations to live and work elsewhere on the island. The ex-slaves were not alone in opposing the new measures. Baptist missionaries in Jamaica organized protest meetings to denounce the legislation, while officials at the Colonial Office disallowed several statutes and returned others to the island for amendment.[4] Yet, Metcalfe strongly defended the Assembly and the planters against these attacks. The governor's support of the House meant that relative calm prevailed in Spanish Town during his term of office. It also meant that Metcalfe had gained a political truce in the island by adopting almost wholeheartedly the planters' point of view. His conciliatory policy made the job of the next governor, Lord Elgin, that much easier; however, it did not come to terms with the more fundamental problems of post-emancipation Jamaica.[5]

Elgin was at a very different stage of his career than Metcalfe. When Metcalfe left Jamaica in 1842, he was already troubled by the cancerous growth that would claim his life four years later. Elgin, on the other hand, was carrying out his first governmental assignment; his biographer said that Jamaica was Elgin's "apprenticeship for a pro-consular career." After serving in the colony until 1846, Elgin became governor-general of Canada at a critical point in its history. He later acted as a special envoy to China and died while governor-general of India in 1863.[6] But in the 1840s, Elgin was still the youngest son of a Scottish peer and was described by one Jamaican as a rather needy nobleman. Since he could not afford to be as generous or as social as his predecessor, the atmosphere at King's House was very different than it had been during Metcalfe's administration.[7] The new governor nonetheless profited from the period of harmony in Jamaican politics which he found on his arrival.

A change in Colonial Office thinking and personnel also made it easier for Elgin. During the late 1830s, the emphasis in the Colonial Office had been on the emancipated population. As a result, the Colonial Office had closely scrutinized the legislation of the House for measures that were directed against the ex-slaves. By the early 1840s, there was far less agitation against the Assembly; the crucial concern now appeared to be the survival of the plantations.[8] The new colonial secretary, Lord Stanley (Edward George Geoffrey Smith Stanley), embodied this change of policy. Unlike his predecessor Russell, Stanley responded more favorably to the arguments of the West Indian planters than to the complaints of the humanitarians. What is more, he was eager to get along with the Assembly.[9]

Under Elgin, therefore, the House continued to enact legislation that primarily benefited the plantocracy. The shift in taxation away from the estates and onto the majority of the population that had begun in the early 1840s continued during Elgin's administration. With the support of the Colonial Office, the House also voted large sums of money for importing Africans and Indians to replace the labor lost because of emancipation.[10] In addition, Elgin suggested reforms in agriculture as a more permanent way of reviving the plantation economy. Arguing that the planters should modernize their methods, he sponsored a prize for the best form of cultivating cane. Furthermore, the governor encouraged the development of an industrial system of education to train the peasantry for work on the estates.[11] The House reacted by establishing a Board of Education with powers to make improvements in the Island's educational system. Although the assemblymen voted only £1,000 for the purpose, they allocated larger sums of money for the Church of England and for the reform of the judiciary.[12]

The willingness of the planters to consider this type of legislation was evidence of a growing belief in the viability of the post-emancipation plantation society.[13] The protected sugar market and reasonably good prices for sugar accounted for much of this feeling; the planters' power to legislate on their own behalf also made the transition to a free society that much easier. As in the 1830s, however, there was opposition in the House to some of the measures directed against the former slaves. Brown delegates continued to disagree with the whites about the legislative priorities facing the island.

The coloreds in the House during the period immediately after the end of apprenticeship were a small and not always unified group. There were only eight brown representatives in the House which lasted until 1844, several of whom were either inactive or did not sit for the entire term. Since they were often split among themselves, Metcalfe reported that any attempt to create a Government party would fail.[14] Yet, in spite of their lack of unity, the colored assemblymen expressed a point of view on several measures that suggested how they differed from the whites in post-emancipation Jamaica.

One of the controversial pieces of legislation that divided whites and browns during Metcalfe's administration was the bill altering the powers of the Kingston Corporation. In an abbreviated form, the history of the corporation was similar to that of the House of Assembly. When blacks and coloreds had begun to win seats on the town's Council, whites had attempted to alter the franchise and the charter of the local body. Although the Colonial Office had disallowed the franchise legislation, the white delegates sought to enact a law reducing the authority of the councillors and restricting membership of the Council to those who paid at least £20 per annum in parochial taxes. The measure prompted a colored member of the House, Charles Lake, to complain that the new bill would return the political structure of Kingston to "that system of exclusiveness, partiality, and prejudice which existed during the time of slavery, and previous to the removal of political disabilities of the Coloured and Black population."[15] Like later confrontations over the future of the Assembly, the debate on the Kingston Corporation raised the question whether blacks and coloreds would be allowed to make laws for white men.

Another important issue in the period after emancipation was the nature of the island's taxation. Since the planters were reducing their own taxes, the coloreds were worried about the increased burden on the mercantile community and on the poor. Brown assemblymen therefore sought in general to limit the rise in duties on essential foodstuffs and to retain the export duties on sugar.[16] The men of color also voted against legislation protecting the planters at the expense of the rest of the community. For example, James Taylor maintained that a duty on cattle to encourage local production would "fall very hard on the small settler." Using a similar argument, Robert Osborn opposed a planter's petition on a related issue because the House represented "all the various interests of the country" rather than simply the plantocracy.[17]

Colored opposition to the planters increased during Elgin's administration. *The Morning Journal* was particularly concerned about the effects of the militia bill, which forced the poor to attend musters at their own expense. The paper also argued against the police bill because of the high costs of keeping up the force and its fears that the police were acting as an independent standing army.[18] Since the organization was the refuge of European immigrants and sailors, the brown delegates claimed that the largely white force was unconcerned about the liberties of the predominantly black population.[19] The opposition of the brown representatives to the militia and police bills prompted the planter press to suggest that a conspiracy existed among the colored assemblymen. Thus, the *Jamaica Standard and Royal Gazette* revived old fears that Jordon, Osborn, and their political allies were subverting the defenses of the island.[20]

The brown members of the House not only attacked some of the legislation that limited the rights of the former slaves, but they also complained about the omission of measures benefiting the peasantry. Their major concern was the lack of educational facilities in the island. During a debate in 1842, William T. March observed that, although the Jamaican treasury had funds for the commercial and planting interests, there was relatively little for the church and almost none for educational purposes. Robert Russell was more specific: he proposed a bill to establish a college in Jamaica, but the House ignored the measure. Russell's proposal was similar to an act that Price Watkis had submitted nearly a decade earlier and that had met with the same indifferent response.[21]

It was not just academic education that interested the coloreds. They also sought to develop technical schools and trade training centers in metropolitan areas to deal with the urban unemployed. Men of color believed that industrial training could encourage crafts and cottage industries that would rely on local materials. Moreover, in 1844, Edward Jordon attempted to double the Government subsidy of £1,000 to the Board of Education. Yet, in spite of a slightly increased minority after the 1844 general election, the brown politicians were unable to make much headway in improving the standards of education.[22]

The coloreds faced a similar problem on the question of immigration: they did not have the votes to veto the planters' expenditures on this issue. While the colored delegates were not entirely opposed to encouraging foreign labor, they argued unsuccessfully that any scheme should be undertaken at the expense of the plantocracy. Furthermore, several brown assemblymen feared the consequences of immigration. Robert Osborn recalled the failure of importing Europeans during the 1830s, as well as the large number of destitute and dying immigrants he had seen wandering around the island.[23] Like other brown men in the Assembly, he continued to attack the House's immigration policy throughout much of the post-emancipation period.

The coloreds in the Assembly were not alone in suggesting educational reforms and opposing massive immigration. The election of 1844 returned several whites who tended to vote with the men of color, although the Town party did not act consistently together until after 1846. Two whites, Peter Harrison and A. L. Palmer, supported the brown politicians on several issues during this early period. Not much is known about Harrison. He was elected to the parish vestry of St. Dorothy and seems to have owned very little property. He also managed a savings bank but may have been illiterate.[24] Far more is known of Palmer, who was regarded in England and in Jamaica as an opponent of slavery. A Scottish doctor, he became a stipendiary magistrate during Sligo's administration and gained notoriety on the island by violating one of its important taboos: he married his Jamaican mistress who was also the mother of his children. Palmer spoke in England against the apprenticeship system and became secretary there of the Central Negro Emancipation Committee. When he returned to Jamaica after the end of apprenticeship, he published a weekly newspaper in the interests of the ex-slaves and received much abuse from the planter press.[25]

Despite the support of Palmer and Harrison, the coloreds' lack of numbers and organization in the Assembly limited their political effectiveness during the years immediately after the end of apprenticeship. Brown legislators also differed among themselves and did not always vote consistently. For example, they were generally concerned about the effects of indirect taxation, but most of them backed a capitation tax in 1842. The act taxed all male adults equally for the use of the island's roads and was described by a colored newspaper editor as a tax on the poor for the enjoyment of the rich.[26] On another issue, the leader of the people of color, Edward Jordon, voted against a measure for the repair of churches and schools, even though several brown assemblymen approved the bill.[27]

The result before 1846 was a group of brown men in the Assembly which frequently opposed the planters but which itself was capable of internal divisions. Colored assemblymen were therefore unable to provide an effective opposition to the whites. The moves toward free trade in Britain and the slowly increasing number of colored representatives changed the factional configurations in the House. The crisis after 1846 served to unite the men of color against the plantocracy and to provide further evidence of the coloreds' concern for the welfare of Jamaica.

The Whig Government's decision in 1846 to equalize the sugar duties was an economic as well as a psychological blow to the West Indian planters. Many estate owners had been able to adapt to the loss of their slaves only because of the protected price in the British market. When it became clear that free trade would replace the old system of price supports, the planters still expected that higher duties would be retained on slave-grown sugar.[28] Consequently, Lord Russell's decision to abolish this distinction violated an unwritten agreement that the planters would enjoy preferential treatment in return for having freed their slaves.

The reaction in Jamaica to these measures was immediate and hostile. Major-General Berkeley, the acting governor who had replaced Elgin and was awaiting the arrival of his successor, reported that public meetings had been held all over the island to protest against the sugar duties bill. When the Assembly met in November 1846, it concluded that the legislation would make it impossible to maintain the colony's institutions at their present level.[29] The new governor, Sir Charles Edward Grey, was thus faced with a serious crisis when he arrived on the island in December.

Grey's credentials were impressive. Educated at Oxford and a fellow of Oriel College, he had been called to the bar in 1811. Several years later, he was appointed a supreme court judge in India and eventually became chief justice for Bengal. He had also served as a commissioner to investigate the causes of Canadian discontent in 1835, had sat in the Commons for Tynemouth, and for the preceding five years had been governor of Barbados. He was a cousin of Earl Grey, the secretary of state for the colonies, and a steady supporter of the Whigs in Parliament.[30] Despite his successful career and his connections, Grey was troubled by personal difficulties. One visitor to the island reported that the governor was perpetually in debt and had therefore been forced to leave England. More importantly, Grey was never able to command the respect his immediate predecessors in Jamaica had enjoyed, and he alienated many of the coloreds in the House.[31]

The most pressing problem that confronted Grey was the planters' retrenchment legislation. These measures were designed to revise the salaries of the island's leading officials and "to make them more commensurate with the depressed state of the colony."[32] Along with the bills to lower taxes and transfer the cost of immigration to the British treasury, the retrenchment acts sought to limit public expenditure. But the laws affecting salaries clashed with the nineteenth-century view of public offices as a form of property and an index of the public faith. As a result, the governor and the council suggested less drastic, though general, reductions that would ultimately save more revenue.[33] Since the planters were unwilling to consider these proposals, the political history of the island during Grey's administration was largely a struggle between the Council and the Assembly. The colored minority in the House generally supported the Government, partly out of loyalty to the Crown and partly because of deeply held differences with the plantocracy.

The first session of the House after Grey's arrival established a recurring pattern in Jamaican politics until the end of the decade. The Assembly enacted a retrenchment bill which the Council vetoed. In return, the Country party attempted to force the upper branch of the legislature to pass the measure by threatening to stop the annual revenue bills unless the Council accepted the retrenchment act.[34] Although the Country party had a majority in the Assembly, it was rarely able to carry out its plans. The brown delegates and their allies managed in most cases to secure the island's revenue.

The votes were often very close. In February 1847, the House split evenly at eighteen votes apiece on the question of the revenue legislation. As usual, the men of color in the Assembly were at the center of the opposition to the planters. Nine of the eleven coloreds voting supported the usual money bills; among the whites who joined them were several merchants as well as two lawyers who generally voted with the men of color.[35] The differences between the coloreds and the planters over this issue tended to reflect the earlier tensions between the two groups. Although the men of color were worried about the economic decline of the plantations, Edward Jordon noted that the plantocracy had not forgotten *The Watchman* and still blamed brown men for robbing the whites of their property. The coloreds also continued to oppose any suggestion that the island's allegiance be shifted to the United States. As in the early 1830s, the men of color remained loyal to England.[36]

The severe economic crisis in 1847 dramatized the plight of the plantocracy. Several West Indian firms went bankrupt, and the Planters' Bank was forced to suspend payment in January 1848. Although the British Government sought to aid the planters, it refused to agree with a parliamentary Select Committee which recommended the maintenance of a ten shilling duty on sugar for six years. Lord Russell suggested a compromise extending protection until 1854, but not at the level recommended by the committee. The close vote on this issue in the Commons and the general weakness of the Government prompted the absentee owners and the planting attorneys to renew their efforts to stop supplies.[37]

The planters believed that they could force the Government either to maintain the sugar duties or to resign and allow the Conservatives in England to reintroduce protection. For most of the plantocracy, this was the only solution to their problem; they were unable to consider fundamental agricultural reforms that might have made West Indian sugar more competitive in the international market. According to the editor of the *New York Evening Post*, John Bigelow, the estate owners' singular dependence on protection was in character because it allowed them to do nothing. Bigelow reported that "they fold their arms under the conviction that no efforts of theirs can arrest the decay and dissolution going on about them, and that nothing but home legislation, nay, nothing but protection to their staples, can protect them from hopeless and utter ruin."[38]

This was the most important motive for bringing much of the island's economic and political life to a standstill, but it was not the only one. As in 1839, the whites were also concerned about the political success of the people of color and their growing representation in the House of Assembly. In effect, the planters were worried about the threat to their supremacy. A leading English planter, Henry Blagrove, couched the problem in different terms: he argued that the different classes and colors in the House would destroy its unity and make it impossible to legislate. Blagrove's solution was to abolish the Assembly and to initiate direct rule from London.[39]

Although the colored delegates opposed this proposal, they, like Blagrove, were prepared to cut public salaries. In part, this attitude reflected the desire of browns as well as whites to reduce the number of Europeans working in Jamaica and to open up other positions for permanent residents of the island. But since the coloreds supported the governor's more moderate measures rather than the severe cuts advocated by the Country party, they continued to vote against the planters on the issue of retrenchment. In addition, the brown representatives argued that stopping the revenue bills would not change Government policy but rather would cause a great deal of suffering in the island. The people of color maintained that they were unwilling to allow the island to be sacrificed at the whim of the West India Committee.[40]

The coloreds also disagreed with the planters about the future of the House of Assembly. Since men of every color now had places in the legislature, it was (for *The Morning Journal*) "truly a popular body."[41] However, the brown assemblymen were in favor of reforming the House: in particular, they agreed with Governor Grey's suggestion of responsible government for the colony. Robert Osborn expressed his regret that this possibility had not been considered a decade earlier, and he suggested that it would have protected Jamaica from an enormous debt and from an unwise policy of immigration.[42] Yet, the planters were opposed to any change of this kind. As a white member of the Liberals noted, the Conservatives objected to any proposal that broadened popular rights.[43]

The differences between the vying factions in the House as well as the political skill of the Liberals became more evident during a special meeting of the

Assembly called in the summer of 1848. Governor Grey had been forced to convene the House because the island treasury was bankrupt. Since the Government had just reiterated its stance on sugar duties, planters in England were advising their attorneys in Jamaica to withhold supplies and thus embarrass the Whigs. Despite their majority, the Country party was unable to carry out these orders. The Liberals managed to pack the appropriate committee of the House and were able to rescue the island from bankruptcy.[44]

An additional factor helped the pro-Government faction in 1848. In midyear, there were rumors in the island of a possible insurrection. The problem arose partly because of the political uncertainty in the island. The former slaves feared that slavery might be reintroduced if some of the whites had their way and Jamaica became part of the United States. This view was reinforced by the action of planters in western Jamaica who began to reduce wages substantially during the year. Many ex-slaves regarded this action as a first step toward the reimposition of slavery. Since the threat of unrest was serious, the governor and his supporters convinced members of the Country party that this was no time to stop supplies and to disband the police force.[45]

While the Liberals were able to make use of this crisis to get through the revenue bills, their votes in the next session indicate their unity and consistency over a wider range of issues. A Guttman scalogram[46] analysis of the votes during the session tends to confirm the staunchly pro-Government stance of the Liberals and to identify the type of measures that attracted their support (Table 7). The scale ranks in order the issues and the men who voted for them as well as each in terms of the other. The ranking is arranged in relation to the favorable votes an issue received: the most difficult to adopt is shown first in the upper left-hand corner, and the easiest in the lower right-hand corner. The assemblymen appear on the scale in terms of the number of items each endorsed, those voting positively at the top of each fourfold table, while those opposed to the measure placed at the bottom.

Table 7 groups together five votes during the sessions of the House between September 1848 and July 1849. The scalogram makes it clear that the steady core of the Liberals approved the tonnage or revenue bill, while the planters were in favor of withholding all supplies. A slightly larger minority, again made up predominantly of brown men, voted to continue meeting and to resolve the island's financial difficulties rather than plunging Jamaica into a general election. The Liberals were able to increase their numbers when they defended the Council and to defeat the Country party when it sought to reduce expenditures on road repair and to censure the speaker.[47] The votes suggest that the largely colored faction steadily pursued a policy designed to enact the normal revenue and to uphold the legislature. It was able to gain the support of members of the Country party for a measure that directly affected several Conservatives and for one that attacked the speaker, a long-standing member of the House.

The scalogram can also be used to identify the solid core of Liberal support.

TABLE 7. SCALOGRAM: VOTES IN THE HOUSE OF ASSEMBLY,
    1848–1849

		TONNAGE		ELECTION		COUNCIL		RETRENCHMENT		CENSURE	
		+	−	+	−	+	−	+	−	+	−
Tonnage Duty Bill,	+	8	0	7	0	7	0	6	0	8	0
November 8, 1848	−	0	14	0	9	0	13	3	5	7	7
Opposition to Motion for Election,	+			11	0	11	0	10	0	11	0
July 5, 1849	−			0	19	0	16	3	8	4	10
Vote of Confidence for Council,	+					15	0	12	2	15	0
February 14, 1849	−					0	24	4	11	7	12
Opposition to Retrenchment on Road Repairs,	+							18	0	14	1
February 13, 1849	−							0	13	3	8
Opposition to Censure of Speaker, December 13, 1848	+									25	0
	−									0	12

Five of the eight representatives who voted for the tonnage bill were either black or brown, as were eight of the eleven who registered their approval for continuing to sit in July 1849. The coloreds included Osborn, Jordon, Taylor, Lake, March, Gordon, and Brown; in addition, there was one black man, Vickars. Charles Jackson voted with the other men of color to defend the Council and the speaker, although he joined Moncrieffe and the Country party generally in favoring retrenchment.

As in the period before 1846, several whites joined the Liberals. The most consistent were three lawyers: John Bristowe, James Lunan, and W. W. Anderson. Lunan retired from the House after one term in 1849, and Bristowe later became a legal official in the local administration.[48] The third white, Anderson, was closely associated with the blacks and coloreds. Born in Scotland, he lived over forty years in Jamaica and served as a protector of slaves. He was a founder of the Mutual Life Assurance Society, an advocate of free colored immigration from North America, and chairman of the Kingston branch of the Anti-Slavery Society.[49]

Apart from identifying the consistent members of the Liberal faction, the scalogram suggests how the minority was often able to defeat its more numerous opponents. The Liberals generally voted together. The eleven core members of the group did not cross over to support the planters on any issue and were usually present in the House. But the planters were less regular. Of the thirteen who sought to reduce the expenditure on roads, for example, only five were in the House to block the tonnage bill. Although the Country party enjoyed a numerical superiority, it was frequently unable to capitalize on it. The members of the plantocracy were absent more of the time and were less unified than the faction dominated by the brown assemblymen.

The result was that the coloreds were able to prevent the total paralysis of the economy. They successfully pushed through several revenue bills, although the planters tacked on specific appropriations that substantially reduced the salaries of the police and other officials. The Country party also turned down a Government loan of £100,000, voted a resolution of no confidence in the Council, and forced the general election in 1849.[50] However, the planters failed to bring down the Home Government by stopping the revenue legislation. In opposing the Country party, the brown men provided further evidence that their priorities were different from those of the planter class.

The 1849 fall session of the Assembly witnessed a repetition of the voting patterns in the previous session. The "clique," while enjoying a slightly increased minority, still required a split among the planters or clever parliamentary tactics to defeat the Conservatives. The planters once again attempted to force the Council to approve a retrenchment bill, but they were unable to maintain a majority in the House for the measure. The failure of the Country party was attributable to the unity of the colored faction and the divisions among the Conservatives. In 1849, the planter delegates divided over the nature of the proposed retrenchment scheme. Since it offered compensation for the affected officeholders, the measure alienated a wing of the Country party who were opposed to the compromise. Their absence in the Conservative voting lobby and the organization of the Liberals led to the defeat of the bill.[51]

A scalogram analysis of several votes during the session and one in the following term suggests the nature of the issues that attracted the support of the Liberals (Table 8). The division on adjournment for the Jewish holidays not only identified the most consistent members of the pro-Government faction, but it also suggested that the Jews tended to vote with the planters. On the motion to pass the ordinary revenue bills for the year, the Liberal vote included the fourteen members who usually comprised the colored-dominated faction. Since it was clear by December that the major finance legislation had been passed, the Liberals gained some Conservative support for providing the governor with his salary and for allowing a minor revenue bill to pass without appropriations. In the next session, however, the "clique" was barely able to command a majority in favor of taxing property rather than incomes.[52]

The votes indicated that the Liberals continued to back the governor in providing the normal revenue. The votes also showed that the predominantly

TABLE 8. SCALOGRAM: VOTES IN THE HOUSE OF ASSEMBLY, 1849–1851

		HOLIDAYS		ORDINARY REVENUE		INCOME TAX		GOVERNOR'S SALARY		APPROPRIATIONS	
		+	−	+	−	+	−	+	−	+	−
Opposition to Adjournment for the Jewish Holidays, September 24, 1849	+	9	0	7	0	6	0	8	0	7	0
	−	0	19	0	16	3	6	4	7	5	8
For Ordinary Revenue Bills, September 6, 1849	+			14	0	8	1	10	0	12	0
	−			0	24	2	10	4	11	3	12
Opposition to Income Tax, March 28, 1851	+					16	0	9	1	11	1
	−					0	15	2	5	1	9
For Governor's Salary, December 6, 1849	+							17	0	12	2
	−							0	12	1	9
Opposition to Appropriating the Revenue, January 8, 1850	+									19	0
	−									0	14

colored faction and several Jews in the House sought to tax the estates rather than accede to a planter motion for an income tax. This was largely a matter of self-interest: men of color and Jews generally did not own large properties but earned salaries from urban occupations. Although brown politicians were concerned about the island's welfare, they were not averse to protecting their own interests as well. The black and colored vote in the House was consistently high during this period. In the 1849 session, eleven brown men and two blacks occupied places in the Assembly, and most of them voted in the divisions. Ten of the fourteen who approved the motion for normal revenues, for instance, were either black or colored, as were eleven of the nineteen who voted for the rum duty bill. Few coloreds or blacks crossed over to the Country party during the session.

As in previous sessions, a few whites tended to vote with the Liberals. In the 1849 term, two lawyers, Charles Farquharson and Samuel Jackson Dallas, were the most consistent white members of the "clique." Both were born in

Jamaica; like the coloreds, they were creoles who were more interested in the future of Jamaica than many of the Conservatives who did not regard the island as a permanent home. The two whites were also descended from among the oldest families in the island. Dallas was a grandson of the chronicler of the Maroons, a speaker of the House, and an assemblyman for over twenty-five years. His colleague, Farquharson, was a barrister and later an assistant judge of the Supreme Court.[53]

The several sessions of the House after 1850 were less divided on party lines, largely because of the disorienting effects of a severe cholera epidemic in the island. The coloreds nonetheless continued to advocate measures that reflected their concern for the local society. Many of the specific proposals were similar to those they had introduced before the retrenchment crisis had begun to dominate the legislative proceedings. Education, for example, remained high on the Liberals' list of priorities. In 1850, Robert Osborn proposed to establish schools in all parts of the island; when that failed, he sought a year later to increase the budget on education. He also joined with Alexander Heslop to introduce legislation creating local professional schools for training doctors and lawyers. All these measures met with stiff resistance. The planters were worried that an educated labor force would refuse to work on the estates. They also feared the consequences of locally educated professionals; in their view, the measure would reduce the number of trained whites from Europe practicing on the island.[54] A planter paper, *The Colonial Standard*, argued that Jamaica needed to reverse the legislation that sought "to drive out the little Anglo-Saxon blood of the country out of it."[55] As in other areas, then, the coloreds were advocating a more independent and a more creole policy than the plantocracy.

The Town party's increasing minority led to fears that it would soon dominate the House. A reporter noted that the "clique" was already regarded as the "fixed machinery of the Assembly: remove them and the mere routine of the work could scarcely be carried on."[56] The West India interest in London was disturbed not only by the turbulence of the House but also by the prospect that their representatives would be outnumbered by the opposition. The predictions of a white Liberal and manager of the island's railways, William Smith, did little to calm the absentees. Smith noted that his faction could already command half the vote when party considerations demanded it, and he claimed that the Liberals would gain an outright majority within a few years.[57]

Despite an occasional success in the House, however, the Town party was unable to alter the course of legislation dramatically during the period before 1853. It failed to defeat either the planters' immigration scheme or a change in the franchise that the Liberals opposed. Although the coloreds generally favored responsible government, they were soundly defeated on a vote to introduce it to Jamaica.[58] The coloreds' weakness in the voting lobbies reflected their minority position as well as the usual problems of a factional alliance.

Moreover, the Liberals seemed to lose their cohesion when Edward Jordon was elevated to the Council in 1852.[59] As a result, they ceased to support the Government and helped to create a serious constitutional crisis in 1853.

The problem in 1853 arose over the familiar issue of retrenchment. Planters had expected that the new Conservative Government in England would reintroduce protection. When Benjamin Disraeli's budget instead reaffirmed the policy of the Whigs on this point, the planters reacted by passing a retrenchment bill.[60] The Council vetoed the measure but the Town and Country parties united to limit expenditures and to appropriate the revenues in a manner that accomplished their goal. The Council blocked this move, and the resulting legislative crisis led to a restructuring of the factions in the House and of the Constitution as well.

The legislative standstill in 1853 highlighted the weakness of the old representative Constitution. When the two branches of the legislature were at odds with each other, the machinery of government collapsed. In the case of Jamaica, the planters' party took advantage of the Constitution in order to abolish it. They hoped to strengthen their position either by altering the composition of the Council or by destroying the House and transforming the island into a Crown Colony. Since this action would prevent blacks and coloreds from gaining a majority in the House, the absentee owners in England encouraged their agents to do away with the Assembly. As in their battle to regain protection, the plantocracy chose the path of greatest dependence on England. They were unwilling or unable to work out local solutions for their political and economic difficulties.[61]

The people of color did not share this obsessional dependence on the British Government. Brown assemblymen were indeed concerned about the loss of protection; however, they advocated measures to improve the local economy rather than to upset it in hopes of altering colonial policy.[62] Unlike the planters, brown delegates also debated the merits of immigration, proposed reforms in education, and sought to limit taxes on the small settlers. Thus, the coloreds in the House generally had a broader legislative vision than the planters: they regarded Jamaica as more than a factory for the production and export of sugar.

At the same time, the brown men in the House were politicians who sought to advance the people of color and to protect their own interests. They supported the Government, in part because of the patronage associated with it.[63] Similarly, the coloreds joined the whites in accepting the principle of retrenchment since they wanted to increase the number of positions open to natives. As a largely urban coalition, the Liberals stood to profit from avoiding an income tax. In addition, the coloreds attempted to protect the prerogatives of the House because they expected to be the majority party in it.

Governor Grey therefore concluded that the colored party sought to maintain control of nine-tenths of the revenue and generally "to make that branch of the Legislature despotic over the other two."[64] But the governor's analysis of the situation ignored the recent divisions among the coloreds. While several brown politicians sought to strengthen the House at the expense of the Council, others were leaders in the campaign for responsible government and for internal reform of the House. This group of coloreds was concerned above all about the survival of the Assembly. As Robert Osborn observed, they believed that it was the "only safeguard against the annihilation of those privileges which many of them who had been proscribed had only obtained after a long and severe struggle. Do away with the Assembly, and the colored people would sink into the insignificance from which they had risen."[65]

The 1853 crisis ended the unity of the coloreds in the House. A distinctly pro-Government group emerged, while a sizable segment of the Liberal politicians joined the planters in denouncing the Council and the Constitution.[66] The increasingly factionalized House presented serious problems for the new governor, Sir Henry Barkly. The splits among the coloreds after 1853 would also help explain why they were unable to carry out their economic and social reforms.

NOTES

1. Douglas Hall, "Sir Charles Metcalfe," *Caribbean Quarterly* 3 (1953): 90–91. More information on Metcalfe is available in Edward Thompson, *The Life of Charles, Lord Metcalfe* (London, 1938).

2. W. J. Gardner, *A History of Jamaica* (London, 1873), p. 404.

3. CO 137/248, Metcalfe to Russell, March 30, 1840, no. 50; January 12, 1840, no. 41.

4. *The Falmouth Post*, February 26, April 29, 1840.

5. CO 137/248, Metcalfe to Russell, March 30, 1840, no. 50; CO 137/251, Metcalfe to Russell, September 20, 1840, no. 116; J. L. Morison, *The Eighth Earl of Elgin* (London, 1928), p. 52.

6. Morison, *Elgin*, p. 43; *DNB*, 3: 104–106.

7. *The Falmouth Post*, September 29, 1846.

8. Herman Merivale, *Lectures on Colonization and Colonies* (London, 1861), pp. 331–32; William A. Green, *British Slave Emancipation* (Oxford, 1976), p. 175.

9. W. P. Morrell, *British Colonial Policy in the Age of Peel and Russell* (Oxford, 1930), p. 35; CO 137/256, Stanley to Metcalfe, September 27, 1841, no. 4.

10. CO 137/273, Elgin to Stanley, January 10, 1843, no. 72; CO 137/274, Elgin to Stanley, June 22, 1843, no. 131; CO 137/273, Elgin to Stanley, January 29, 1843, no. 80; CO 137/283, Elgin to Stanley, January 4, 1845, no. 2; Gardner, *History*, p. 418.

11. CO 137/275, Elgin to Stanley, November 7, 1843, no. 176; CO 137/284, Elgin to Stanley, August 5, 1845, confidential; Morison, *Elgin*, pp. 69–70.

12. CO 137/285, Elgin to Stanley, December 17, 1845, no. 3; C. V. Gocking, "Constitutional Problems in Jamaica, 1850–1866" (unpublished D. Phil. thesis, Oxford University, 1955), p. 38.

13. Douglas Hall, *Free Jamaica, 1838–1865* (New Haven, Conn., 1959), p. 23.

14. CO 137/255, Metcalfe to Russell, February 12, 1841, no. 189.

15. CO 137/253, Lake to Russell, May 14, 1840.

16. *VAJ*, December 16, 1841, p. 318; December 10, 1841, p. 298.

17. *The Morning Journal*, November 6, 1840, Debates: November 3; *Jamaica Standard and Royal Gazette*, January 3, 1842, Debates: December 30.

18. *The Morning Journal*, October 31, November 5, 1842.

19. Ibid., November 4, 1842, Debates: November 1.

20. *Jamaica Standard and Royal Gazette*, November 5, 1842.

21. *The Morning Journal*, December 2, 1843, Debates: November 29; ibid., November 16, 1843.

22. Swithin Wilmot, "Political Developments in Jamaica in the Post-Emancipation Period" (unpublished D. Phil. thesis, Oxford University, 1977), pp. 158–59; Carl Campbell, "Social and Economic Obstacles to the Development of Popular Education in Post-Emancipation Jamaica, 1834–1865," *The Journal of Caribbean History* 1 (November 1970): 71.

23. *The Baptist Herald*, November 5, 1844, Debates: October 29.

24. Glory Robertson (comp.), *Members of the Assembly of Jamaica* (mimeo, Institute of Jamaica, 1965), p. 53; Feurtado, MS notes; IRO, Will: 129–211. Harrison signed his will with a mark.

25. Robertson, *Members*, p. 56; Feurtado, MS notes; Institute of Jamaica, Biographical notes: F. L. Casserly broadcast, September 2, 1948.

26. *The Falmouth Post*, February 1, 1843.

27. *The Morning Journal*, December 2, 1843, Debates: November 29.

28. Morrell, *Colonial Policy*, p. 232.

29. CO 137/289, Berkeley to Grey: November 6, 1846, no. 41; November 21, 1846, no. 42.

30. *DNB*, 8: 622; Gardner, *History*, p. 428.

31. John Bigelow, *Jamaica in 1850* (New York, 1851), pp. 33–34; CO 137/300, Jordon to Hawes, September 7, 1848.

32. *VAJ*, November 30, 1846, p. 73.

33. *The Falmouth Post*, March 2, 1847.

34. CO 137/291, C. Grey to Earl Grey, March 9, 1847, no. 20.

35. *VAJ*, February 25, 1847, p. 246.

36. *The Morning Journal*, April 6, August 26, 1847; CO 137/294, Jordon to Lecesne, August 12, 1847.

37. Morrell, *Colonial Policy*, pp. 243–47.

38. Bigelow, *Jamaica in 1850*, p. 73.

39. *The Morning Journal*, September 30, 1848.

40. Ibid., September 30, December 26, 27, 1848.

41. Ibid., September 1, 1848.

42. Ibid., July 11, 1849, Debates: July 5.

43. Ibid., February 21, 1849, Debates: February 14.

44. CO 137/296, C. Grey to Earl Grey, June 19, 1848, no. 57; CO 137/300, Jordon to Hawes, September 7, 1848.

45. Wilmot, "Political Developments in Jamaica," pp. 203–14.

46. The use of the Guttman scalogram follows closely William O. Aydelotte's work on the House of Commons. In particular, see his article, "Voting Patterns in the British

House of Commons in the 1840's," *Comparative Studies in Society and History* 5 (January 1963): 136–38. Joel H. Sibley, *The Shrine of Party* (Pittsburgh, 1967) is also useful. A more detailed explanation of the scalogram can be found in Appendix D.

47. *VAJ*, November 8, 1848, pp. 57–59; July 5, 1849, pp. 35–36; February 14, 1849, pp. 18–19; February 13, 1849, p. 10; December 13, 1848, pp. 205–206.

48. Robertson, *Members*, pp. 50–51, 55; Feurtado, MS notes.

49. Frank Cundall, *Biographical Annals of Jamaica* (Kingston, 1904), pp. 35–36; IRO, Will: 133–384; Wilmot, "Political Developments in Jamaica," p. 94. Anderson's obituary appeared in *The Daily Gleaner*, July 7, 1877.

50. *The Morning Journal*, February 22, 1849; CO 137/298, C. Grey to Earl Grey, December 7, 1848, no. 113; *VAJ*, July 5, 1849, pp. 35–36.

51. CO 137/303, C. Grey to Earl Grey, October 22, 1849, no. 95; *The Falmouth Post*, October 30, 1849.

52. *VAJ*, September 24, 1849, p. 102; September 6, 1849, pp. 20–21; March 28, 1851, p. 323; December 6, 1849, p. 311; January 8, 1850, p. 380.

53. Robertson, *Members*, p. 52; Feurtado, MS notes; James Dallas, *The History of the Family of Dallas* (Edinburgh, 1921), p. 502. Dallas's will is in IRO, 129–110, and there is a brief description of Farquharson in Maurice O'Connor Morris, *Memini* (London, 1892), p. 89.

54. Wilmot, "Political Developments in Jamaica," p. 257; *The Colonial Standard*, May 5, 1851, Debates: May 1; *The Morning Journal*, May 5, 1851.

55. *The Colonial Standard*, March 12, 1851.

56. *Daily Advertiser*, November 4, 1851.

57. CO 137/311, C. Grey to Earl Grey, December 31, 1851, no. 115; *The Colonial Standard*, April 3, 1851, Debates: March 28.

58. CO 137/313, C. Grey to Earl Grey, March 1, 1852, no. 16; *VAJ*, January 20, 1852, p. 382; December 16, 1851, p. 253.

59. Mavis Campbell, *The Dynamics of Change in a Slave Society* (Rutherford, N.J., 1976), p. 245.

60. W. P. Morrell, *British Colonial Policy in the Mid-Victorian Age* (Oxford, 1969), p. 381.

61. CO 137/316, Grey to Newcastle, May 10, 1853, no. 40; *The Morning Journal*, August 12, 1848.

62. *The Morning Journal*, August 12, 1848.

63. *The Falmouth Post*, October 27, 1846.

64. CO 137/316, Grey to Newcastle, May 10, 1853, no. 40; *The Morning Journal*, September 29, 1853.

65. *Daily Advertiser*, May 21, 1853, Debates: May 18.

66. Ibid.

11

The Failure of
Colored Leadership,
1853–1860

The crisis in 1853 precipitated a significant alteration of the Jamaican Constitution. Faced with an enormous debt, the Assembly agreed to restrict its own privileges in return for a guaranteed loan, thereby reversing a long-standing pattern that had seen the legislature slowly erode the powers of the executive. With the House far from unanimous about these changes, the debates there highlighted the political distance between many of the white and brown politicians as well as the lack of unity among the colored representatives. This division in the colored camp—which also affected the two or three black delegates associated with the brown politicians—was a new development in Jamaican politics and sharply differentiated the period before and after 1853.

The legislative impasse also led to the disintegration of the Town party. All of the colored and black politicians present in the House supported the planters in February when the whites sought to limit expenditures for the year and to enact a sharp retrenchment measure. The ensuing clash with the Council and the threat of political and economic chaos frightened several brown representatives who retreated from these measures. They consequently voted with the Government party which sought to end the crisis. However, other brown and black assemblymen remained opposed to any accommodation with the Council and formed the Colored party. The effect of these moves was to divide the men of color and to increase the number of blocs in an already factious House.[1]

The two largely colored factions disagreed over more than immediate tactics. Thus, the brown politicians in the Government party were particularly concerned about the future of the House. William T. March maintained that those in favor of a legislative standstill were endangering the survival of the House and undermining the people's rights, while James Taylor repeated the argument he had used in opposing the planters' policy during a similar crisis in 1839. Taylor vowed that he would remain loyal to the British Government because of his debt to the Crown for securing his privileges and liberties.[2] But only a handful of brown representatives and two or three whites supported the Crown. The majority of planters, Jews, coloreds, and blacks persevered in their policy of cutting back expenditures and refusing to deal with the Council.

Charles H. Jackson was the leader of the brown and black politicians who opposed the Government. His group, the Colored party, sought to weaken the Council or possibly to get rid of it altogether because of the Council's repeated failure to pass a retrenchment scheme. Although the planters shared this view, there were important differences between them and the members of the Colored party. Whereas many of the planters hoped that the crisis would set the stage for Crown Colony government, Jackson's supporters were concerned about strengthening the House of Assembly rather than abolishing it.[3] Since the Colored party nonetheless joined the planters and the Jews, the result was a large majority for a legislative standstill but one that contained within it several potentially divisive factions.

The Assembly's refusal to enact the usual revenue legislation and to deal with an unreformed Council forced the Colonial Office to take action. One possibility was to adopt Governor Grey's suggestion that the Crown temporarily suspend the Constitution and rule through a commission. Inasmuch as a similar measure had brought down Melbourne's Government in 1839, the colonial secretary, Henry, duke of Newcastle, decided against direct imperial intervention and relied instead on the skills of a new governor, Sir Henry Barkly.[4]

It was not surprising that the Jamaican plantocracy welcomed Newcastle's choice. Unlike most of the governors appointed during this period, Barkly had close connections with the West Indies. A wealthy Scottish sugar planter and merchant, Barkly was a member of the West Indian group in the Commons, and he had just completed a successful term as governor of British Guiana. After his experience in Jamaica, Barkly served in similar posts elsewhere, first in Mauritius and then in the Cape of Good Hope.[5]

Barkly's immediate problem in Jamaica was to find a way out of the legislative crisis. His instructions in some ways simplified the task, as he was able to promise that the Government would redeem a large part of the island debt if the Assembly would undertake a reform of its procedures. The most important changes concerned the power to initiate votes; assemblymen had traditionally proposed expenditures without necessarily relating their suggestions to the amount of island revenue. Since the result had been an ever increasing debt, the Crown sought to limit this right to the executive. The Colonial Office also wanted a permanent civil list and at least one Government spokesman in the

House.[6] Yet, these suggestions for reform did not immediately end the crisis. The opposition to the revenue bill and to the Council remained united. During the early part of the regular legislative session in 1853, however, the factions within the group split, allowing a finance bill to proceed to the Council. Although Barkly privately claimed that his tactics were responsible for this success, an analysis of the votes and a report in the press several years later indicated that the deadlock was resolved on the orders of the absentee owners in England.[7]

Despite the passage of a revenue bill, the factions in the House continued to differ about the proposed constitutional reforms. The planters feared the consequences of responsible government and sought to strengthen the executive in relation to the legislature. They also insisted on transforming the Council into a largely planter body; this would guarantee them a veto in the event whites no longer dominated the Assembly.[8] The Government party, on the other hand, supported a strong executive committee that would be responsible to the House. Since the brown politicians in this faction were opposed to the planters, they asked a number of questions designed to embarrass the plantocracy:

Is it, that the intelligence of the Colony is likely to be represented by a race formerly proscribed as unfitted for any but the most menial offices? Yes or no? Is it that an old oligarchy is afraid of being overwhelmed by a liberal democracy, which would be dangerous, but for its amalgamation with a limited monarchical form of Government?[9]

Jackson's group found itself between the Government party and the planters on this issue. His Colored party therefore suggested that the executive committee act neither as a powerful policy-making body nor as a mere appendage of the governor. Instead, it should take over the Assembly's handling of the finances and meet to review the expenditures and estimates of colonial revenue. Jackson was opposed to full responsible government because he was afraid it would further divide the colony from the Crown. Although his faction was concerned about the privileges of the House, it was also worried about the effects of too much self-government.[10]

The final form of the new Constitution was a compromise. The governor therefore had to choose his executive committee from the legislature, though he retained full control over patronage. As a result, the issue of responsibility was not fully resolved; the executive committee was responsible to the governor and was also expected to retain the confidence of the Assembly. This was a serious weakness in the new system since the committee could be accountable to two different masters—the governor and the Assembly. The changes made it almost certain as well that a form of responsible government would develop, despite the view held by most of the representatives that Jamaica was unsuited for party politics.[11]

The divisions and debates in the Assembly revealed the unusual splits that had developed among the rival factions during the session. The Country party lost one of its leaders, Henry Westmorland, who also took several supporters of the party with him. However, the planters won the backing of the Colored party led by Charles Jackson. The Government party was similarly affected: it counted among its members a group of brown politicians loyal to the Crown, the representatives allied with Westmorland, and several officials sitting in the House. The result was a shifting party structure and one rather different from the factions usually associated with the Town and Country parties.[12]

The rearranged coalitions and unsteady party allegiances characterized Jamaican politics for the next decade. This had a significant effect on the colored representatives as well as the few blacks who had been united on most of the crucial issues of the day. Even though their leader, Edward Jordon, was to have a prominent place in the new government, the coloreds and blacks remained a divided minority that was increasingly less able to influence developments on its own. During the next decade, the Town party consequently changed in composition, often accommodating men like Westmorland and several Jewish representatives as well.

Despite the political divisions among the brown assemblymen, they did come together on matters that were of considerable personal importance to them. Thus, the coloreds were united on the issue of opening up government posts for natives of the island. During the previous session, for example, the men of color had unanimously joined the whites in passing legislation requiring the governor to appoint as an auditor-general a person who had lived on the island at least five years. They were also in general agreement over a bill designed to reduce judicial salaries, partly because the act would make the position less attractive to Europeans.[13] Color was accordingly a unifying factor when the possibility of positions for coloreds arose or when these jobs were endangered. Barkly noted that it was "openly avowed by Mr. Jackson that those of his colour would not allow a white Ministry to be formed. . . . Not only did Mr. Osborn and other coloured men who usually support the Government give their votes on this basis, but every official who had the slightest tinge of African blood in his veins, abandoned his usual political connexion and voted the same way."[14] Although factional politics had affected the unity of the brown representatives, they continued to vote together when it was a matter of advancing the people of color.

Parliament ratified the new administrative procedures in time for Barkly to appoint the first executive committee before the 1854 legislative session. The governor was careful about his choices since it was necessary to find men who could unite the various factions in the House. Barkly therefore asked Edward Jordon to resign his seat on the Council and move back to the Assembly. In this way, the governor expected that the administration would be able to command the support of the black and brown members of the House. The members of the executive committee did not head departments, but Jordon became responsible for measures dealing with the welfare of the peasantry. Barkly also sought to attract the planter vote by promoting Henry Westmorland to be in charge of measures concerning the economy. A senior judge in the island, Bryan Edwards, represented the Council on the committee.[15]

The governor believed that the main problem facing the new Government was the state of the island's finances. There had been an annual shortfall in the revenue, and the executive committee soon realized that the debt was increasing at an alarming rate. Barkly also commented on the steep decline in sugar exports for 1853. He noted that this drop explained and in part excused the planters' decision to create the legislative crisis that had forced the Crown to consider their plight.[16] Because of the worsening economic situation, the governor worked to steady the economy and to ensure the survival of the plantation system.

The priorities of the administration became evident during its first meeting with the legislature. One of its most important proposals was designed to right the economic balance: the bill raised duties sharply on clothing, especially on the dry goods used by the majority of the population. The minister of finance, Henry Westmorland, also sought to suspend the duty on exports that would substantially reduce the planters' costs, and he moved to organize the island's financial system on a generally more rational basis.[17] Although the legislators agreed that many of these reforms were necessary, the increased duties on clothing and the suspension of the export duties met with strong opposition in the House.

A group of black and brown politicians known as the Liberals figured prominently in the faction that opposed these measures. Earlier, several of the coloreds and blacks had supported the Government; now they voted against the administration's bills which they regarded as too strongly in favor of the planters or too markedly against the interests of the people. One of the representatives in this group, Christopher Walters, expressed his disapproval particularly about the duties on clothes. He suggested that these duties were intended to force the laborers to work on the estates at low wages. Like other Liberal assemblymen, Walters was angered about how little the planters had done for the mass of the population. He noted during a debate that instead of building bridges, parks, roads, and colleges, "all you [planters] seek is to impose fresh burdens on the people."[18]

The Liberals were vocal about their anti-planter sentiments. For example, a heated exchange arose in 1855 over the annual grant to the prince of Loando and Benquela who had been rescued from a slave ship and was reputed to be an African prince. When the usual amount awarded to the prince met with opposition, James Taylor responded that he would rather double the grant

as a peace-offering for the wrongs and injuries inflicted on the people of Africa in former days by the planters of this country. The hand of Divine Providence was in the matter, and if the planters only considered the cruelties they used formerly to inflict upon those who were the progenitors of the people from which this boy has sprung, they would not oppose the trifling grant.

Christopher Walters claimed that "they were not begging the grant, but were demanding it as a matter of right."[19]

Taylor also maintained that the planters had little justification in complaining that they could not get enough labor from the peasantry. He stated that the plantocracy had not provided education of any kind or sanitary relief for the people. The estate owners, he argued further, paid paltry wages of a shilling or less which could hardly enable the peasantry to purchase the necessities of life.[20] Since the colored and black assemblymen believed that the planters should not have reduced their taxes at the expense of the laboring population, Taylor made it clear "that there were parties within and out of the House who would warn the laborers of the injustice that was done to them and inform them of the duty they owed to themselves and their children."[21]

In the volatile atmosphere of Jamaican politics, it did not take long for the brown and black politicians to organize public meetings against the measures of the new administration. One gathering held in Kingston published resolutions condemning an act that would have made it necessary for vestries to submit estimates on their revenue and expenditure to the executive committee. Since the bill also increased the qualifications for a vestryman, those present at the meeting concluded that it was an attempt to destroy the rights of the ex-slave population. Other resolutions sought to enlist aid from the friends of the people in England, to advise the laborers of the legislation, and to pursue all constitutional means to warn the peasantry of their danger. Three Liberals, James Taylor, Foster March, and Edward Vickars, were included in the committee chosen to correspond with leading representatives of the people.[22]

The members of the Assembly who organized the meeting and several of them who led the opposition to the executive committee were also known as the Kingston Agitators. Although Jackson occasionally joined this group in the House, only a few representatives of his Colored party supported the Liberals. As in 1853, the brown and black politicians were split. Out of fifteen black and brown assemblymen who voted on the import duties bill, for instance, six opposed the administration and nine backed it. There were also several Jewish representatives, most of whom were merchants or shopkeepers, who voted with the Liberal faction. The result was a small minority made up almost entirely of coloreds, blacks, and Jews which generally was unable to defeat the measures of the executive committee.[23]

After the legislative recess at Christmas, however, it was possible for the minority to outmaneuver the committee because many of the planters remained on their estates. This was the case when the administration proposed a grant of £1,000 for education which the opposition regarded as inadequate.

James Taylor expressed his disappointment with the bill and suggested that the Jordon ministry was failing to live up to its mandate: it was not legislating for the general good. The Liberals in the Assembly were able to raise the grant to £2,000 and thus provide evidence of a group that was concerned about the problems of education.[24]

Barkly dismissed the campaign for a higher educational outlay as part of a drive for place and power by "a small knot of disappointed office-seekers." The governor noted that the minority was able to upset the Government's plans at the end of the session when there was a smaller attendance at the House. The Liberals therefore succeeded in voting grants that the administration regarded as frivolous. When the executive committee submitted its resignation as a result of these defeats, Barkly pointed out the divisions among the opposition and persuaded the members of the committee to remain in office.[25]

The governor's characterization of the minority as a group of politicians interested in office was not wholly inaccurate. Charles Jackson had expected a place on the executive committee, and James Taylor hoped to become inspector of schools.[26] Still, the evidence suggests that Barkly misunderstood the nature of the opposition. Some members of it may well have been seeking government posts, but they were also genuinely concerned about the measures the administration was proposing. Like the colored politicians who had dominated the Town party during the 1840s, these representatives were critical of bills that aided the plantocracy at the expense of the peasantry. The governor's claim that the opposition was eager to replace his executive committee is also questionable. The *Votes of the House of Assembly* indicate that most of the Liberals supported Barkly's administration on a censure motion against it.[27] Since brown men as well as blacks sought to keep Jordon in office, it would have been surprising if they had voted to unseat the executive committee.

Yet, Jordon was unable to gain the consistent backing of the colored and black assemblymen. Only Robert Osborn remained loyal to him. Others regarded Jordon's administration as having ignored the problems affecting the majority of the population. By concentrating on the financial reorganization of the colony, the executive committee lost the votes of those who were pressing for social and educational improvements. Jordon's failure to consider these changes meant that the schism among the coloreds and blacks would continue during the remainder of Barkly's term and later as well.[28]

Jordon also alienated several brown and black politicians with an election bill he submitted to the House toward the end of Barkly's stay in Jamaica. The measure was intended to abolish the variety of qualifications and to institute a single test of the elector's right to vote: each voter had to pay at least £1 in taxes per annum. Like the increase in duties on clothing, this act met with immediate opposition. The brown editor of *The Falmouth Post*, John Castello, claimed that the bill would disfranchise many of the peasantry rather than enlarge the pool of voters as the executive committee had hoped.[29] Robert Russell was also angered by the election bill. In a letter to the secretary of the Anti-Slavery Society, he described the proposed change in the franchise as a measure that "tends to deprive the present Elective body of their electoral rights." Russell asserted that the £6 freeholders who made up the bulk of the ex-slave vote usually paid between eight and twelve shillings in taxes and would therefore be denied the franchise.[30]

The vote on the act reflected the strong feelings of the Liberals. They defeated the proposal with nine of the twelve black and brown representatives present in the House opposed to the measure. As in several other controversial divisions during the period, Robert Osborn was the only colored assemblyman who regularly supported the Jordon ministry. Barkly explained this defeat by pointing out that several men of color had voted against the measure because of its potentially damaging effect on their otherwise safe seats.[31] The governor may have been right, but his allegation must be balanced against the consistent voting record of the coloreds in favor of expanding the franchise rather than narrowing it.

Barkly's view of the brown politicians may well have reflected his relative isolation from them. During his administration, he and his wife were accused of excluding people of color from the social events at King's House. When the governor finally invited one of the leading brown men in the island, Richard Hill, to a dance, the invitation was addressed to Mrs. Hill. Hill, a bachelor, pointed out the mistake, but Barkly never apologized for the error.[32] Lady Barkly also offended the coloreds when she apparently refused to dance in the same sets as the people of color who were present at King's House.[33] In the small world of Jamaican politics and society, these incidents were magnified far beyond their importance. Barkly's bias in favor of the planters thus offended many coloreds and led Russell to conclude that the governor "would have done well for the planters of a bygone era—both he and his lady take pains to make themselves unpopular."[34]

Barkly left the island in 1856. During his three years as governor, he had attempted to inaugurate the new system of government and to deal with the island's chronic financial difficulties. From an administrative point of view, he had succeeded. He was able to report an improvement in the organization of the Treasury and in the handling of business generally. Unlike the governors who had immediately preceded him, Barkly had managed to halt Jamaica's increasing deficit and even temporarily to decrease it.[35]

Although the executive committee was responsible for many of these changes, its legislative measures were less noticeably successful. The committee had failed to enact any significant reforms in education, sanitation, and other areas affecting the majority of the population. This failure was in part the result of its other priorities; for the committee and for Barkly, economic reform had to precede any radical improvements in an even rudimentary system of social services. When the administration finally submitted an important education bill in 1855, the measure easily passed the House but was blocked by the planters in the Council. Barkly therefore left a mixed legacy for his successor, Sir Charles Henry Darling, who was fortunate to inherit a relatively healthy economy but who also faced a strong opposition.[36]

Darling was well equipped to deal with the problems confronting Jamaica. A graduate of Sandhurst, he had begun his colonial career as private secretary to his uncle, Sir Ralph Darling, who was then governor of New South Wales. He acted in a similar capacity for Sir Lionel Smith in Barbados and then in Jamaica. After Smith's departure from Jamaica, Darling remained on the island to serve under Elgin as agent-general of immigration and briefly as secretary to Sir Charles Grey. In 1847, he was appointed lieutenant-governor of St. Lucia and four years later of the Cape of Good Hope. Before taking up the governorship of Jamaica, Darling had also been governor of Newfoundland, and he later occupied the same post in Victoria.[37]

Darling had several advantages over his predecessors in Jamaica. Apart from his experience elsewhere, he had worked in the administration of the island during the years immediately after emancipation, and he was briefly a member of the House of Assembly.[38] Darling was consequently aware of the problems facing the society as well as the difficulties of working with the legislature to resolve them. But despite his knowledge of the local situation, Darling made many of the same mistakes that had plagued previous governors.

Like Barkly, Darling tended to favor measures that benefited the planters at the expense of the social needs of the island. In his first speech to the Assembly, for example, Darling announced that he was unable to submit an education bill, although considerable reforms were needed in this area. The priorities of the administration were instead reflected in the bills that the executive committee submitted to the House. These included acts to reorganize various departments of government, to strengthen the powers of the predominantly planter justices of the peace, and to promote immigration.[39] The nature of the legislation did not change appreciably during the first several years of Darling's term of office. In 1859, the governor told the assemblymen that, though doctors were lacking in the rural areas, he was not prepared to suggest any act to remedy the situation. Darling also chose to overlook the need for district dispensaries in favor of providing large sums of money for a new lunatic asylum. This decision reflected the problem with much of the legislation throughout this period: it was not designed for Jamaican needs. Many of the bills were drafted in Britain to suit English requirements, and policy-makers in London too often ignored the local situation. Since public health and education were generally neglected in mid-Victorian England, these areas certainly did not receive the kind of attention they deserved in the West Indies.[40]

But the laws favoring the planters were not greeted with universal enthusiasm in the House. Some delegates opposed measures that sought to increase the powers of the planters and to limit those of the ex-slaves. While no identifiable leader emerged to head this group—again known as the Liberals—it continued to consist largely of the coloreds and blacks who had attempted to block similar acts during Barkly's administration. Although the Liberals were poorly organized and did not always vote together, they formed the only faction in the Assembly that expressed concern about the welfare of the people of the island. Darling recognized their potential strength, especially on bills relating to immigration. As a result, the governor and the executive committee were wary of proposing legistation in this field. Darling believed that the cost of importing labor should be split between the employers and the Government; however, he made certain that the administration's proposals coincided with the views of the opposition. The governor noted that the Liberals formed "a powerful party in the Assembly who consider themselves more peculiarly the Protectors of the interests of the Native population" and that they had consistently rejected proposals to spend the public funds for importing labor that would compete with the ex-slaves. The administration's bill instead made it necessary for the planters to defray the total cost of immigration.[41]

The Liberals responded in a similar way to other acts they thought infringed the rights of the peasantry. They therefore opposed a measure designed to extend the jurisdiction of the justices of the peace. In the case of larceny, this would have meant that a JP would decide a case involving the loss of twenty shillings without the consent of the accused and up to £10 with his consent. Christopher Walters pointed out his objections to the bill during a debate in the House: he maintained that it granted too much authority to men whom the peasantry already distrusted. Walters regarded the act as an example of class legislation that was directed against the "popular element."[42] When it came to a vote, the bill divided the House evenly and split the executive committee as well. Edward Jordon voted with the Liberals who won the support of ten colored and black representatives and five Jewish assemblymen. On the other hand, William Hosack, the planter representative on the executive committee, was in favor of the measure along with the Country party and five men of color who generally allied themselves with this group. The bill passed on the vote of the speaker.[43]

Like several other measures of the House, this act created widespread disaffection in the island. There had already been problems in the administration of justice because former masters had often adjudicated cases involving ex-slaves. In the post-emancipation period, the power of planter justices had increased; at the same time, the respect for the law among the majority of the population had decreased markedly. By 1860, much of the peasantry had lost faith in the magisterial courts, and many had stopped bringing their cases before them.[44] Consequently, the Liberals in the House sought to prevent a further extension in the powers of the amateur justices.

This group was also opposed to a change in the franchise which would significantly reduce the small settler vote. The election bill that the executive committee submitted in 1858 did not include any important alteration in the voting qualifications. However, the planters in the legislature vowed to defeat the act because they feared it would lead to universal suffrage.[45] When the committee responded by submitting a new bill that required each voter to pay a ten shilling duty, the Liberals vigorously objected to it. Nunes and Walters rightly pointed out that the act would tend to disfranchise the peasantry; they also argued that it was repressive and would encourage the practice of buying votes.[46] Walters, who felt strongly about the bill, maintained that he "was sent there [the House] by the £6 freeholders and [he would] not act the traitor by sacrificing those rights."[47] A large majority of the House including Jordon and several other men of color nonetheless voted with the planters in favor of the measure.[48]

The Liberals' opposition to many of the acts proposed by the administration was not confined to the legislative chamber at Spanish Town. As during Barkly's administration, the members of the faction joined other coloreds outside of the House to campaign against the offending legislation. James Taylor presided over a public meeting in Kingston which petitioned the Council to veto the bill increasing the powers of the local justices. Several Liberal assemblymen were present to hear Taylor lash out against the measure. In this instance, Taylor was exaggerating when he maintained that the bill was the most "atrocious that had ever been passed by the Assembly, and if it became law, the people would be reduced to a state worse than that of Vassalage."[49] But the rhetoric was less important than the fact that these meetings were held at all and that the colored Liberals were largely responsible for organizing them.

This was only one of several such gatherings in the late 1850s. In March 1859, George William Gordon, who would soon return to the House, chaired a meeting that was opposed to the new election law. He was joined by Robert Johnson, the editor of *The Watchman*, which was a newspaper Gordon had helped to establish in the interests of the peasantry. The result of the meeting was a series of resolutions condemning the tax on the franchise. Those present declared that the act was designed with the wrong aim in mind, as it gave the vote to men who in most cases were temporary residents of the island and deprived the £6 freeholders "who were the bones and sinews of the country." Another resolution reinforced this sentiment and concluded that the statute would perpetuate the system of class legislation that had afflicted the island.[50]

The Liberals were not the only people who organized petitions against the measures of the House. Darling reported that a group of ex-slaves as well as one describing themselves as "the sable subjects of African descent" submitted memorials attacking the franchise bill, the increased jurisdiction of the justices, and the laws generally enacted during the last six years.[51] These protests often had the active support of missionaries working in the island. One Baptist missionary, E. Hewitt, forwarded a petition alleged to represent the sentiments of 3,000 people assembled at a public meeting. The memorial complained about the burden of taxation, much of which was levied on the mass of the population through duties on food and clothing. The resolutions also opposed the recent franchise act and the enormous expenditure on immigration.[52]

Other missionaries tacitly agreed with those who protested publicly about these laws. A Methodist minister, W. Tyson, wrote home that "the whole effect of the legislation has evidently been to relieve the Planters, and to keep the people in a state of dependency." Tyson complained about the vast sums spent on immigration, though nothing was done "in the way of sanatory [sic], and other much needed enactments, to improve and increase the population which is already here."[53] E. Fraser, who was one of the first brown Methodist missionaries in Jamaica, also lamented the expenditure on immigration while public measures for the population already in the island were so few.[54] Several missionaries appealed to their home societies to lobby against specific measures. J. E. Henderson hoped that the Baptists in England or the Anti-Slavery Society could use their influence to defeat the immigration bill since the act would affect many members of his and other congregations who already found it difficult to obtain work.[55]

At the Colonial Office, Henry Taylor, who still headed the West India section, expressed similar views. He was disappointed with the planters because they had failed to provide decent educational facilities for the emancipated population. Had they made proper provisions in this field, the result would have been "an orderly and industrious" peasantry and prosperity for the plantations. Taylor was also convinced that the failure to suspend the Assembly in 1839 had doomed the prospects for the ex-slaves.[56] Although Darling reported on the development of a solid middle class and on the advancement of the peasantry, Taylor did not really believe it. His opinion was that the freed slaves were "all in a very low moral and political condition."[57] Since he maintained that the problem was a long dose of self-government, Taylor attempted to limit the prerogatives of the House and to increase the authority of the executive.[58]

In Jamaica, the public meetings and the memorials against the legislation of the House reflected a strong sense of unease in the island. This was partly a response to economic conditions. Sugar prices were generally buoyant during the period from 1855 to 1860, but peasants and rural laborers often found profits from their provision grounds declining. At the same time, taxes on a variety of necessities were rising, and the importation of foreign labor was depressing wages even further.[59] There were also two serious riots in 1859, one in Westmoreland and the other in Falmouth. The first arose over the high taxes extracted at the tollgates in the parish, and the second—in which two people were killed—was initially a dispute over a piece of land on an estate near Falmouth.

Both cases provided evidence of the deep-rooted resentment against official-dom, particularly the legal and police authorities. Moreover, the outbreak of an agricultural strike in St. Thomas in the East suggested that the laborers in the district distrusted their employers. *The Falmouth Post* reported that the workers there regarded the planters "as a set of selfish, cold-hearted, and mercenary tyrants, who care nothing for any one or anything, save when their personal interests are involved."[60]

During the late 1850s, then, there was considerable agitation in Jamaica. Much of it was directed against the legislation of the House and was a result of the increasing economic difficulties many people were facing. Against the background of these protests, the riots in 1859 frightened the whites. These fears were heightened by rumors that demonstrators at Falmouth had warned of another Haiti. The American vice-consul, R. A. Harrison, reported on the increasing antagonism between blacks and whites, and was afraid that these feelings might lead to the expulsion of the whites.[61] Despite these forebodings, the Assembly seemed oblivious to events around it. Apart from the Liberals, few members of the House were apparently concerned about the expressions of dissatisfaction in the colony. Instead, the Assembly involved itself in constitutional wrangles that eventually brought down Jordon's ministry and replaced it with a wholly planter administration.

The constitutional problem that arose during the 1859 legislative session involved the right of assemblymen to recommend grants of money on their own or to increase an expenditure proposed by the administration. This issue had been at the heart of the constitutional changes in 1854 and highlighted the dissatisfaction of many members with the loss of their most valued privilege. In addition, several representatives complained about the growing power of the executive committee and the consequent decline in the importance of the Assembly.[62] Charles Jackson was responsible for raising the question about the rights of assemblymen, and he also led the opposition to Darling during a special session of the House held in March 1860. The brown representative claimed that Darling had committed a breach of the Assembly's privileges when he proposed a specific clause for a bill concerning the Post Office. With the support of the Country party and against the united opposition of the other coloreds in attendance, Jackson succeeded in passing a resolution against the governor.[63]

Darling was thus faced in 1860 with an increasingly recalcitrant House. At the same time, he had to deal with a problem caused by his executive committee. It had advised him to draw extra funds for main road expenditures from the general revenue but denied any responsibility to the legislature for his advice. The governor was therefore confronted with the prospect of being censured by a committee of the House for mishandling funds. In order to forestall criticism against himself and to prevent representatives from attempting to regain their old privileges, Darling suggested that the administration should be conducted on the principle of responsible government.[64]

The executive committee disagreed with Darling's interpretation of the Constitution. It argued that the House had established a committee to assist the governor, who alone would be responsible for the conduct of public affairs. The three members of the administration, Edward Jordon, William Hosack, and George Price, also feared that responsible government would lead to a ruinous system of party politics.[65] They were joined by Benjamin Vickers, a planter with a seat on the Legislative Council, who was prepared to sell his estates and leave the island because he was afraid the new system would lead to "a war of races." The West India Committee was also opposed to this development and lobbied the Colonial Office in support of the executive committee's point of view.[66]

The debate over responsibility resulted in the resignation of the executive committee. Although the coloreds and blacks in the House almost unanimously backed the committee, their numbers had fallen in the general election held before the 1860 legislative session. On the other hand, Henry Westmorland won the votes of a strengthened Country party for a compromise resolution that fell between Darling's position and that of the outgoing administration. It made the governor responsible to the colony and maintained the inherent right of the House to declare a lack of confidence in the executive committee.[67] Since the new administration was comprised wholly of planters and did not include any men of color, the period of colored leadership had ended. Jordon and several of his political allies became part of the opposition.

During the six years after the inauguration of the new Constitution in 1854, successive governors had recognized the importance of the coloreds in the House. Edward Jordon had therefore enjoyed a prominent place on the executive committee and was responsible for what could have been its most significant legislation: the measures on behalf of the emancipated population. As part of the administration, Jordon was also able to influence the awarding of contracts and the appointments to government jobs. The colored and black politicians associated with Jordon thus gained positions and promotions more easily when he was in office.

Jordon's role in the government helps to explain why black and brown representatives supported his administration on crucial votes, despite their disagreements with him over matters of policy. Soon after Jordon came to office, for example, the blacks and browns united to defeat a censure motion against the executive committee. In 1860, they opposed Darling's move toward responsible government, at least partly because this meant a change in the composition of the committee. Like Jordon, several coloreds opposed the idea of ministerial government on principle; others backed Jordon "in the hope of retaining him in office, as the Representative of their class and no other ground."[68] Apart from times of crisis, however, Jordon was unable to rely on the consistent support of blacks or men of color in the House. Jordon's difficulties with the Liberals stemmed from a different outlook on the problems affecting Jamaica. While Jordon was concerned primarily with the economic and administrative reorganization of the colony, the Liberals were worried about the condition of the emancipated population. Jordon's proposals also seemed to limit the rights of the people which the largely brown opposition was seeking to protect. The leader of the coloreds thus alienated many of his former supporters by submitting a restrictive election bill in 1856 and by voting for a measure in 1859 that was directed against the small settlers. In addition, Jordon's administration produced little in the way of education or sanitation legislation, even though it was his job to submit measures to aid the peasantry. The Liberals were therefore angered and frustrated by Jordon's *laissez-faire* attitude and by his increasingly pro-planter sympathies.

The divisions among the coloreds suggest in part why the number of non-white representatives declined in 1860. Their failure to unite allowed the planters to enact franchise legislation that significantly reduced the traditional vote of the colored and black politicians. When Jordon got back into office three years later, there were fewer black and brown assemblymen and even less scope to bring about the changes he had sought earlier in his career.

NOTES

1. *VAJ*, February 2, 1853, p. 240; Newcastle Papers, NeC 9553, Barkly to Newcastle, December 10, 1853, private. In reviewing these developments, W. P. Morrell is correct in assuming that the Government party consisted of officials, but he is unaware of the brown representatives who also were members of the faction. See his *British Colonial Policy in the Mid-Victorian Age* (Oxford, 1969), p. 384.

2. *The Morning Journal*, May 23, 1853, Debates: May 18; *Daily Advertiser*, May 21, 1853, Debates: May 18.

3. *The Morning Journal*, May 21, 1853, Debates: May 18; CO 137/316, Grey to Newcastle, May 10, 1853, no. 40.

4. Morrell, *Mid-Victorian Age*, p. 383.

5. Arthur N. Birch and William Robinson (comps.), *The Colonial Office List for 1865* (London, 1865), p. 171; William Law Mathieson, *The Sugar Colonies and Governor Eyre, 1849–1866* (London, 1936), pp. 67, 130.

6. Morrell, *Mid-Victorian Age*, p. 383.

7. *VAJ*, November 10, 1853, p. 111; *The Falmouth Post*, May 2, 1856. Barkly discusses the success of the measure in the Newcastle Papers, NeC 9553: Barkly to Newcastle, November 10, 1853, private; Barkly to Roberts, November 26, 1853, private.

8. *The Morning Journal*, December 5, 1853, Debates: November 30.

9. Ibid., December 2, 1853.

10. Ibid., December 5, 1853, Debates: November 30.

11. C. V. Gocking, "Constitutional Problems in Jamaica, 1850–1866" (unpublished D. Phil. thesis, Oxford University, 1955), p. 133. For a detailed discussion of Barkly's skill in steering the new Constitution through the Assembly and the Council, see Swithin Wilmot, "Political Developments in Jamaica in the Post-Emancipation Period, 1838–1854" (unpublished D. Phil. thesis, Oxford University, 1977), pp. 343–48.

12. Gocking, "Constitutional Problems," pp. 95–96; The Morning Journal, December 5, 1853.

13. The Morning Journal, October 1, 1853; VAJ, March 28, 1854, p. 477.

14. Newcastle Papers, NeC 9553, Barkly to Roberts, December 10, 1853, private.

15. CO 137/324, Barkly to Grey, October 19, 1854, no. 107. Edwards was replaced two years later by George Price, a planter and a later critic of Governor Eyre.

16. CO 137/324, Barkly to Grey, December 30, 1854, no. 130; CO 137/323, Barkly to Newcastle, May 30, 1854, no. 70.

17. CO 137/324, Barkly to Grey, December 30, 1854, no. 130; The Morning Journal, December 15, 1854, Debates: December 12; CO 137/326, Barkly to Russell, April 30, 1855, no. 46.

18. The Morning Journal, December 15, 1854, Debates: December 12.

19. The Falmouth Post, March 20, 1855, Debates: March 13.

20. Daily Advertiser, February 25, 1855, Debates: February 15.

21. The Morning Journal, December 15, 1854, Debates: December 12.

22. The Falmouth Post, January 23, 1855.

23. Ibid.; [Augustus C. Sinclair], The Political Life of the Hon. Charles Hamilton Jackson . . . (Kingston, n.d., circa 1878), pp. 14–20; VAJ, December 19, 1854, pp. 137–38.

24. The Morning Journal, December 15, 1854, Debates: December 12; VAJ, March 13, 1855, p. 381.

25. CO 137/326, Barkly to Russell, May 18, 1855, confidential. William Hosack, a planter and an agent for several absentee owners, replaced Westmorland as minister of finance at this point.

26. [Sinclair], Jackson, pp. 14–20; The Falmouth Post, May 23, 1856; ASSP, Jamaica, 1850–1859, G63, Russell to Chamerovzow, January 9, 1857.

27. VAJ, February 15, 1855, p. 291.

28. CO 137/377, Darling to Newcastle, January 27, 1863, confidential.

29. The Falmouth Post, December 7, 1855.

30. ASSP, British West Indies—Jamaica General, 1850–1859, S22 G63, Russell to Chamerovzow, December 24, 1855.

31. VAJ, February 7, 1856, p. 281; CO 137/331, Barkly to Labouchere, April 9, 1856, confidential.

32. ASSP, Jamaica, 1850–1859, G63, Russell to Chamerovzow, January 26, 1856, private.

33. The Falmouth Post, June 22, October 2, 1855. Barkly's not altogether convincing defense on this general issue is in the Newcastle Papers, NeC 9553, Barkly to Roberts, March 10, 1854, private.

34. ASSP, Jamaica, 1850–1859, G63, Russell to Chamerovzow, March 1, 1856.

35. CO 137/331, Barkly to Labouchere: April 9, 1856, confidential; March 16, 1856, no. 44.

36. CO 137/331, Barkly to Labouchere, April 9, 1856, confidential.

37. Birch and Robinson, *The Colonial Office List*, p. 182.

38. Glory Robertson (comp.), *Members of the Assembly of Jamaica* (mimeo, Institute of Jamaica, 1965), p. 52.

39. CO 137/335, Darling to Labouchere, November 10, 1857, no. 37; November 26, 1857, no. 43.

40. CO 137/346, Darling to Newcastle, November 8, 1859, no. 131; Philip D. Curtin, *Two Jamaicas* (Cambridge, Mass., 1955), p. 206.

41. CO 137/336, Darling to Labouchere, February 8, 1858, no. 14.

42. Abraham Judah and A. C. Sinclair (comps.), *Debates of the Honourable House of Assembly of Jamaica . . .*, 13 vols. (Kingston and Spanish Town, 1856–1866): November 25, 1858, p. 68; November 22, 1858, p. 44.

43. *VAJ*, November 30, 1858, pp. 63–64.

44. Curtin, *Two Jamaicas*, pp. 193–95.

45. CO 137/343, Darling to Bulwer-Lytton, February 10, 1858, no. 31; Judah and Sinclair, *Debates*, November 29, 1858, p. 100.

46. Judah and Sinclair, *Debates*, December 9, 1858, pp. 181–83.

47. Ibid., p. 187.

48. *VAJ*, December 9, 1858, p. 113.

49. *The Falmouth Post*, December 3, 1858.

50. CO 137/344, Darling to Bulwer-Lytton, March 12, 1859, no. 48. *The Watchman* took its title from the newspaper Jordon and Osborn had founded in 1829 to campaign for the rights of the free coloreds. Robert Russell commented favorably on the paper in a letter to the secretary of the Anti-Slavery Society. See ASSP, Jamaica, 1850–1859, G63, Russell to Chamerovzow, March 1, 1856, private.

51. CO 137/345, Darling to Bulwer-Lytton, June 9, 1859, no. 74; CO 137/343, Darling to Bulwer-Lytton, February 24, 1859, no. 34.

52. CO 137/346, Darling to Newcastle, October 10, 1859, no. 123.

53. M.M.S., Tyson to the General Secretary, March 1858.

54. Ibid., Fraser to the Secretary of the Anti-Slavery Society, March 1858.

55. Institute of Jamaica, Henderson Papers, Henderson to Underhill, April 8, 1859.

56. CO 137/322, Barkly to Newcastle, February 21, 1854, no. 24, Taylor's minute on stipendiary magistrates' reports, April 16, 1854.

57. CO 137/349, Darling to Newcastle, March 28, 1860, no. 49, Taylor's minute.

58. CO 137/334, Bell to Labouchere, March 24, 1857, no. 24, enclosure, Taylor's minute.

59. Douglas Hall, *Free Jamaica, 1838–1865* (New Haven, Conn., 1959), pp. 173, 236.

60. Ibid., pp. 248–49; *The Falmouth Post*, May 21, 1858.

61. *The Falmouth Post*, May 21, 1858; National Archives, Washington, D.C., Dispatches from the United States Consul in Kingston to the Secretary of State, Harrison to Cass, March 24, 1859.

62. Judah and Sinclair, *Debates*, December 6, 1859, pp. 122–57.

63. CO 137/348, Darling to Newcastle, January 10, 1860, no. 3; *VAJ*, March 27, 1860, p. 7.

64. CO 137/351, Darling to Newcastle, November 23, 1860, no. 156; CO 137/353, Darling to Newcastle, April 30, 1861, no. 58; March 1, 1861, no. 31.

65. CO 137/351, Darling to Newcastle, November 23, 1860, no. 156, executive committee minute, September 25, 1860; CO 137/352, executive committee to Newcastle, December 6, 1860; Judah and Sinclair, *Debates*, November 9, 1860, pp. 22–23.

66. CO 137/351, Vickers to Thomson, Hankey & Co., November 24, 1860; West India Committee Minutes, 1860–1863, Cave to Hosack, January 1, 1861, pp. 66–67.

67. CO 137/351, Darling to Newcastle, November 24, 1860, confidential; Judah and Sinclair, *Debates*, November 21, 1860, p. 152. The one colored representative who voted with the Country party was Wellesley Bourke.

68. CO 137/351, Darling to Newcastle, November 24, 1860, confidential.

12

The Decline of the Colored Creoles, 1860–1865

Since planters dominated the executive committee formed in 1860, colored and black politicians provided part of the opposition to it. Brown and black delegates continued to press for measures favoring small settlers, particularly in the fields of taxation and the franchise. Yet, successive governors helped to weaken the colored faction in the Assembly, even after Edward Jordon had returned to the executive committee in 1863. They were aided by officials at the Colonial Office who, fearing the development of party government in Jamaica, sought to undermine the prerogatives of the House of Assembly. As the number of black and brown representatives declined during the early 1860s, it was far less possible for them to defend the House and to remain a significant political force in the island.

The immediate problems for the new administration were not wholly political; the executive committee was also confronted with a steadily worsening economy and serious problems for the plantations. After a period of relatively high cane prices, the sugar market underwent one of its periodic slumps. Prices fell sharply during the 1860s, and at the same time, the outbreak of the American Civil War led to a substantial rise in the cost of importing food and clothing. Toward the end of 1860, the island also witnessed a great religious revival. Large numbers of laborers refused to work on the estates and ignored their provision grounds, preferring instead to participate in the revival. Although the outbreak of religious fervor was over by 1862, its effects on Jamaica's economy were considerable. With the price of necessities already high, the scarcity of food and the decreased output of sugar threatened an already shaky economic structure.[1] In this situation, the executive committee required politicians with more experience and more expertise than those appointed by Governor Darling to replace Edward Jordon and his colleagues.

All the men on the new committee were associated with the sugar estates and represented an increasingly important wing of the plantocracy. As one West Indian historian has described them, they were "a home-grown aristocracy."[2] Raynes Waite Smith, for example, was a member of an old Jamaican family and an important resident proprietor. He had been an assemblyman from 1843 to 1853 and had returned to the House again in 1860. While Smith's colleagues on the committee did not share his Jamaican pedigree, they had all been in the colony long enough to be classified as locals. George Solomon had emigrated from England to Jamaica at the age of nineteen and had succeeded as a merchant and sugar planter; he was also one of the few prominent Jews who had not been born in the colony. When Solomon retired after a year on the executive committee, Hugh Whitelocke, an estate owner from Westmoreland, took his place. Whitelocke had lived in Jamaica since 1821 and served in the House off and on for nearly a decade. The third member of the administration, Baron von Ketelhodt, occupied a seat on the Legislative Council. He was born in Germany but had settled in Jamaica during the 1830s and remained after having married a wealthy widow with considerable property in the island.[3]

Since planters controlled the administration, it was not surprising that they promoted measures designed to aid the plantations. Unlike the previous executive committee, they were in favor of increasing the flow of indentured laborers and paying for them out of the general revenue. The planters also continued to raise import duties on necessities and approved legislation extending the jurisdiction of local justices which tended to augment the power of the plantocracy over the peasantry.[4] Yet, despite its majority in the House, the executive committee was unable to enact all of its legislative program. As in the period before 1853, colored and black politicians were among the leaders of the opposition and occasionally could outmaneuver the Government.

The colored and black delegates in the Assembly managed to thwart some of the administration's proposals, though their numbers had dropped sharply by 1860.[5] During the session that lasted from 1860 to 1863, they made up less than a quarter of the total membership of the House. In addition, the coloreds and blacks did not all vote together. Two of the brown assemblymen, Wellesley Bourke and Stephen Mais, were consistent supporters of the Country party. Several other brown and black representatives were reluctant to join Edward Jordon who had often deserted the Liberals in the 1850s. Nevertheless, the men of color as well as the blacks were more united than they had been while Jordon had held office. As in most political factions, it was easier to maintain a semblance of harmony when the group was in opposition. The coloreds were also joined by other blocs in the Assembly: Henry Westmorland and his allies voted with them as well as a few Jews who departed from their traditional association with the Country party.[6] The result was a loosely organized party that opposed much of the administration's legislation, especially in the fields of immigration, taxation, and representation. As usual, Robert Osborn had a prominent part in the debates on these issues. On the question of immigration, for example, he complained that the cost of importing laborers would fall heavily on the poor. Furthermore, the small settlers who could use a few immigrants would be unlikely to receive them since indentured workers were generally placed on the larger estates. Osborn was joined in the debate by A. H. Lewis, a Jewish member of the Town party, who argued that the immigration act was like the other measures sponsored by the executive committee: it was intended solely "to promote the interests of the sugar plantations." Despite the efforts of the Town party, the administration carried the bill with a comfortable majority. Like the division on a proposed change in the franchise, the pro-planter lobby included several colored representatives.[7]

Osborn also led the campaign against the ten shilling duty on the franchise, partly because the cost of casting a ballot had reduced the small settler vote and consequently the number of brown and black men in the House. When Osborn submitted a motion against the voting tax, he was backed by most of the colored and black Liberals in the Assembly. However, Edward Jordon joined the Jews and the planters in opposing Osborn's motion.[8] Jordon's attitude on this issue highlighted the continuing splits among the coloreds as well as the difficulty of unifying them even when they were in opposition.

There were other bills which the Liberals regarded as class legislation. John Nunes argued that an executive committee proposal to import molasses would hurt the small settlers since it would reduce the price of this commodity even further. Christopher Walters made the same point about coffee: he stated that most of it was grown by ex-slaves who would suffer if the duty were substantially reduced. The members of the Town party also complained about the firearms registration act because the settler population was strongly opposed to it.[9] Similarly, representatives of the faction pointed to the consequences of increasing the number of houses subject to tax. Edward Jordon noted that the very poor urban dweller would be affected by the measure, and A. H. Lewis warned that the poor were already taxed too heavily: "they were taxed on their bread, their salt, their lucifers, their clothes, and everything else they used. . . . If this new impost was passed it would have the effect of creating not revivals, but something worse, which would be regretted."[10]

Although the coloreds and their allies continued to express their concern about the small settlers, they were also worried about maintaining the privileges of the House. Osborn was therefore relieved when the executive committee withdrew a bill that sought to exclude government officials from sitting in the Assembly. The colored representative regarded the measure as "a monstrous proposition" that was "only the commencement of a system; and no one can tell what may be the next attack on our privileges, if the House do not at once make a stand."[11] On a similar note, the Town party narrowly defeated an act that would have deprived assemblymen of their immunity from arrest.[12] As during the rest of the post-emancipation period, brown and black representatives were eager to protect the rights of members and the prerogatives of the House. This proved to be particularly difficult in the 1860s when successive governors and the Colonial Office were moving in the opposite direction.

Yet, on several issues that arose after 1860, coloreds found themselves supporting rival factions. In one instance, Wellesley Bourke criticized Jordon's administration, while Robert Osborn vehemently defended it. Osborn asserted that the blacks and coloreds in the colony had supported the former executive committee and that the small minority of whites who may have applauded its resignation was numerically insignificant. He also observed that Bourke had no right to attack Jordon who had risked his life so that men like Bourke could enjoy their full civil rights. Bourke was therefore a "bastard brown man" because he could never really understand what was "in the hearts of coloured and black men, which none can touch but coloured men, and that the genuine kind too."[13] Osborn's unparliamentary language reflected his strong feelings and also provided a clue about his position in the colony's political hierarchy. He was unpopular among the local establishment and could never assume the leadership of the coloreds. On the other hand, Osborn was a useful complement to Jordon who was a calmer and more dispassionate politician.[14]

Darling deplored Osborn's speech in the House and dismissed the opposition to the planter executive committee. The governor wrote home that Jordon had attempted to form a party based on color while in office and that he was continuing to act in the same way after his resignation. Since *The Morning Journal* kept up its attack against the new administration and against Darling personally, the governor fired the paper's owners, Osborn and Jordon, from their posts on the Privy Council. Darling was justified in taking this step because the newspaper's tone bordered repeatedly on the verge of libel.[15] But the strained relations between the governor and the leading brown politicians were symptomatic of more serious political problems during the remainder of Darling's term in the colony.

The difficulties between Darling and the coloreds also reflected the governor's inability to deal with criticism. The colonial secretary, the duke of Newcastle, was aware of this aspect of Darling's personality. A couple of years earlier, he had noted that the governor was "intolerant of difference of opinion" and capable of showing "no scruple as to the tools he uses to undermine an enemy."[16] Darling thus appears to have distorted Jordon's position as a result of the 1860 crisis over responsible government. Since Jordon had disagreed with Darling, the governor's response had been to label the brown leader as a party man who sought to make color an organizing principle. The charge was not true: Jordon had resigned from the administration rather than base his appeal on party and on race. Jordon's alliance with Westmorland re-

volved around a similar point. The two men believed that the governor should
be at the constitutional center of local government, and both feared the development of racial parties. Like the man who succeeded him, however, Darling
drew an incomplete and inaccurate picture of Jordon and of the coloreds in
general.[17]

Despite Darling's hostility to the men of color, they remained an influence in
Jamaican politics. In November 1861, the Assembly voted Jordon speaker
pro tem of the House to replace Charles Morales, who was too ill to take up his
duties. Jordon defeated the executive committee's candidate, Henry Westmorland, because of the nearly unanimous support of the colored and black
representatives as well as the votes of the Jews who joined them in the crucial
divisions.[18]

During the remainder of the session, the Liberals and the other members of
the Town party continued to express their concern about the rights of the
smaller settlers. George Henderson, a white newspaper editor, not only complained about executive committee measures which he believed interfered in
the people's rights, he also made a prophetic speech in the Assembly on the
importance of considering the needs of the ex-slave community. He argued
that the House could not

ignore these people: they must have a voice in the legislation, and it is very unwise so to
restrict them in their rights, as to prevent their exercising the franchise freely. . . . I maintain, that those who look forward and see the coming storm, and do not provide against
it, by wisely legislating for the people of this country are not performing their duty to the
people.[19]

The addition of men like Henderson to the Town party helped to revive it. In
the meantime, the executive committee was running into trouble. Its legislation
proved to be partial; the administration's vision was limited to increasing indirect taxes, extending the prerogative of predominantly planter justices, and
attempting to aid the owners of estates at the cost of any significant social measures. The committee was also more unpopular and less capable of admin-
istering the colony than its predecessor. Just before Darling went on leave in
1862, it compounded the problems. Together with the governor, the executive
committee approved the beginning of a tramway scheme that ultimately led to
a scandal and to its forced resignation a year later.[20] In the midst of a difficult
political situation and a deepening economic crisis, Lieutenant-Governor
Edward John Eyre arrived in the island to replace Darling for one year. His
term of office—which was extended to four years—witnessed the end of the
representative system in Jamaica and with it the political hopes of the coloreds.

The son of a Yorkshire vicar, Eyre had emigrated to Australia in 1832 as a
settler when he was seventeen years old. He prospered as a sheep farmer and

an overlander, bringing cattle and sheep from Sydney to South Australia. Challenged by the mostly unknown areas of central and Western Australia, Eyre explored large tracts of the country's hinterland, and in 1841 he made the extremely difficult journey across Australia between Adelaide and Albany. He was feted as a hero and was given the job of protector of the aborigines at Moorundie in South Australia. Before he was thirty, Eyre had thus become known as an explorer, had been praised for his work with the aborigines, and had found the means to earn a substantial living.[21]

Eyre's later career was less successful. Although he served as lieutenant-governor under Sir George Grey in New Zealand between 1846 and 1853, Eyre found himself in opposition to the governor whom he had grown to dislike.[22] He also faced problems in his next appointment as lieutenant-governor of St. Vincent and temporarily as governor of the Leeward Islands. His most recent biographer, Geoffrey Dutton, blames some of Eyre's difficulties on his personality: he was "shy, poor, and solitary." Since colonists tended to think of him as a sheep driver who was socially of little consequence, Eyre never had the self-confidence governors so badly needed.[23] A harsher critic who has closely examined Eyre's work in St. Vincent and in Antigua regards him as self-seeking and anxious to further his own career even at the expense of others. Despite some question about his ability to deal with the Assembly in Jamaica, the Colonial Office appointed him to act in Darling's place while the governor was on leave.[24]

Eyre almost immediately ran into trouble with the most outspoken colored politician in the island, George William Gordon. Gordon had grown increasingly concerned with the problems of the poor, at about the same time he was becoming interested in the Native Baptists. As a magistrate in Morant Bay, he had complained to Darling about the state of the jail in the parish. When Eyre arrived in Jamaica, Gordon reported that the rector had sent an ill and poor man to the prison where the man had subsequently died. Gordon complained about the rector's illegal imprisonment of the man and about the filthy condition of the lockup. Eyre's rather impulsive response was to censure Gordon and remove him from the magistracy.[25] Although Henry Taylor supported the lieutenant-governor's action, the Colonial Office official also applauded Gordon's attempt to improve conditions at the jail and chided Eyre for not carefully examining the evidence.[26] Yet, Eyre made the same mistake when the Morant Bay Rebellion broke out in 1865 and over the construction of a tramway across the island.

The building of the tramway appeared to be a straightforward proposition. The island government promised to provide three-quarters of the initial cost, with the tramway company putting up the remainder of the capital. Problems developed because the island engineer, who was responsible for checking the estimates, was himself involved in developing the scheme. It later became clear that the estimates for the work were fraudulent and that the total cost of the project would not exceed the Government's contribution. A former member of the executive committee, George Price, had warned Eyre about the lack of proper specifications and details. The lieutenant-governor, however, ignored the objections.[27]

Eyre and his executive committee ran into other serious difficulties. Apart from the tramway, the committee ineptly handled the general management of the main roads. As a result of their lack of supervision, toll rents went unpaid, and the secretary of the department was implicated in embezzling the funds and eventually absconded from the island. These irregularities did not go unnoticed in the House of Assembly. The Town party attacked the administration and accused it of failing to invest funds for the return of immigrants and of violating other legal responsibilities regarding the finances.[28]

The nature of the opposition was similar to the previous two sessions. It was in a minority at the beginning of the term and failed to carry Westmorland's motion of censure against the executive committee's handling of the finances. As details of the frauds became known, more representatives were unwilling to entrust any further revenue to the administration. Recalling the session, George Price noted that the Town party was able to block much of the proposed legislation. In eight important divisions, the Government measures received 127 votes, three less than the opposition.[29]

Eyre nevertheless retained his executive committee in office and characterized the moves in the House as "an attempt to work the Constitution of Jamaica by party Government." He pointed out his own difficulty as lieutenant-governor and his desire not to embarrass Darling by appointing men who had expressed their personal and political animosity toward the governor.[30] Eyre's remarks were designed to improve his own standing at the Colonial Office and to cover up his responsibility in the maladministration of the finances. Like Darling, he chose to attack the leadership of the Town party for making use of party politics. The lieutenant-governor ignored Jordon's opposition to responsible or party government, and failed to report the many grievances which the colored leader and his political allies had raised against the executive committee. Although Eyre also presented a false picture of the problems Darling would face in Jamaica, he convinced the Colonial Office that the governor's return to the island would only complicate the situation.[31]

As a result of the legislative impasse between the parties in the House, Eyre dissolved the Assembly. He was encouraged to do so by his executive committee which confidently predicted that the opposition would be decimated in the ensuing general election. But the outcome was very different. The number of planters in the House declined, while several men of color who had voted with the Country party were either defeated or did not run. They were replaced by brown men who generally supported Edward Jordon, including the man Eyre had removed from the magistracy, George William Gordon. The Smith-Whitelocke ministry resigned after its first defeat in the House, and

Eyre reluctantly appointed Jordon, Westmorland, and, for a brief time, G. L. Phillips, a wealthy Jewish merchant from Montego Bay, to form a new executive committee.[32]

Eyre was in an unenviable situation. He had expected Darling's return to the island before the end of the elections and certainly before the new session of the House. Yet, Darling's appointment as governor of Victoria did not fundamentally change Eyre's precarious position. Eyre was subject to immediate recall, and he as well as the island's politicians expected each succeeding mail to announce the name of his successor. In the meantime, Eyre had to work with an executive committee whom he had secretly and unfairly stigmatized in his dispatches and with an Assembly in which the Town party had gained a tiny majority.[33]

The lieutenant-governor's response to the situation was to curry favor with the Colonial Office at the expense of the Assembly and his new administration. Since Henry Taylor was interested in reducing the powers of the House, Eyre painted a picture of local politics which coincided with Taylor's views. Eyre also gradually undermined the position of his executive committee and made it impossible for Jordon and his colleagues to retain their majority. As a first step, he almost certainly would have supported a motion in the House from a member of the Country party, Wellesley Bourke, to alter the island's Constitution.[34]

Bourke, a colored clerk of the peace from St. James, had consistently voted with the planters. Soon after the change in administration, he submitted a proposal to establish a unicameral legislature that would consist of representatives nominated by the governor and elected members. Bourke's plan reflected the anxiety of Country party members about their political future and, more immediately, about the return of Jordon to the executive committee and the nomination of Charles Jackson as speaker.[35] It was clear from the debates that many of the whites were also very worried about the changing composition of the House.

The outgoing members of the administration and Eyre's closest allies, Raynes Waite Smith and Hugh Whitelocke, were strongly in favor of a unicameral House. Recalling a golden past when the whites had easily dominated island politics, Whitelocke observed that "the people have sunk into a state of barbarism: therefore there can be no harm in substituting a patriarchal despotism for popular representation." Smith made a similar point. He found the existing state of things intolerable and warned that there could "be no mistake as to the class of men who will find their way into the House: and it cannot be expected that he and others like him, will stifle their aristocratic feelings, and associate, even politically, with the legislative mushrooms of yesterday's growth." Not for the first time were the representatives of the home-grown aristocracy frightened that they would be swamped by blacks and coloreds.[36]

On the other hand, Jordon and the other brown assemblymen (apart from

Bourke) who voted in the division were united against the proposal. George William Gordon described it as a restriction rather than as an expansion of popular rights, and Jordon spoke about the importance "of maintaining amicable relations with those classes of the population who are rapidly acquiring influence."[37] It was not surprising that the colored representatives attacked Bourke's motion. As the proposed change in the Constitution included a higher qualification for the vote, it would have further reduced the number of colored and black representatives in the House. While the men of color predictably opposed the measure, they also gained the support of Henry Westmorland, Jordon's ally on the executive committee and an important member of the plantocracy.

Unlike Smith and Whitelocke, Westmorland believed that the planters should "live on friendly terms with those who are rapidly rising into power and importance." Since the white population was declining, Westmorland felt it was useless to struggle against what he described as "that march of civilization which is making such strides in the country." He warned "that the influence of the class to which I belong would diminish immensely, were it known that we desire to do away with popular rights and the House of Assembly."[38] In light of how Westmorland and his supporters voted after the Morant Bay Rebellion, this may well have been a largely political speech rather than an honest declaration of principles. Still, Westmorland joined the coloreds to defeat Bourke's motion, thereby sparing the Assembly for another two years before it underwent drastic surgery.[39] During that time, Lieutenant-Governor and then Governor Eyre moved in other directions to limit the prerogatives of the House and to undermine the colored politicians who were in the vanguard of its defense.

Eyre had the knack of creating unnecessary problems which magnified in importance as he stubbornly maintained his point of view. The controversy over Peter Espeut, a government official, illustrates the lieutenant-governor's obstinacy and his unwillingness to take the advice of his new executive committee. Soon after the administration had taken office, Eyre informed them that he was seeking the resignation of Espeut and another official, William T. March. The two men, who were delegates to the House, had angered Eyre by voting against the Whitelocke-Smith ministry. They therefore had the choice of giving up their seats in the Assembly or their government posts in a colony where such jobs were at a premium. March vacated his place in the House, but Espeut resigned under protest and began a protracted struggle against the lieutenant-governor's decision.[40]

As in the case of Gordon and in the tramway affair, Eyre was taking what Frederick Rogers at the Colonial Office later described as "a rash step." In the first place, Eyre ignored his executive committee which pointed out that he was disregarding the law that protected Espeut's position. George Price, who had replaced G. L. Phillips in the administration, claimed that the lieutenant-governor refused to look at the relevant law and instead responded that "he did not care for the island law and that the Colonial Secretary was his law." Since Price was writing in a strongly partisan tone against Eyre, this conversation may have been apocryphal. It did, however, coincide with Eyre's behavior over this issue and throughout his term of office in the island.[41]

Apart from the local statute which he was prepared to ignore, Eyre was also setting a precedent with his executive committee. Espeut and March were staunch supporters of the Jordon-Westmorland administration in a situation where the executive committee needed all the votes it could command. Eyre was thus making it difficult for his leading officers to retain their majority. He was also attacking a principle which the people of color had defended: the right of the Jamaican electorate to return whomever they wished to the Assembly.[42] Although the members of the executive committee were oppsed to Eyre on this matter, they did not resign, apparently because they expected the lieutenant-governor to be relieved of his post at any moment. The issue was resolved when the law officers in England ruled that Espeut was legally entitled to sit in the House despite his votes against the Government.[43]

While the Espeut case was under consideration, Eyre suspended two other officials in a move that was bound to create further difficulties. The men, David Ewart and Solomon Lindo, were subagents of immigration who were responsible for the welfare of immigrants in their districts. While there was some question about the way Ewart and Lindo had handled their jobs, there was more discussion about the manner in which Eyre had removed them from office. Lindo appeared before the Privy Council, the traditional arbiter in situations of this kind, which found that he was guilty of neglect, though it did not favor his suspension. Ewart never even came before the Council. As in the controversy over Espeut, Eyre chose to override the local ruling and wrote home to the Colonial Office for another decision. In the meantime, he suspended the two immigration officers.[44] Since many politicians were already worried about the increasing tendency of the Crown to interfere in local affairs, Eyre's action only inflamed them further.

The matter was complicated by the religious and racial background of the two men: Ewart was a man of color and Lindo a Jew. Moreover, Lindo's father, who was a custos of St. Mary and a delegate to the Assembly, had cast the deciding vote in the decision that had forced the planter executive committee to resign. Consequently, he was an important convert to the Town party. Inasmuch as the majority of this party were either Jewish or colored and were known to be concerned about advancing members of their own group, Eyre was again in conflict with the party that supported his executive committee.[45]

Because of these recurring problems, a small handful of assemblymen moved to censure Eyre. The representatives not only complained about Eyre's arbitrary behavior; they were also unhappy about the lieutenant-governor's opening speech of the 1863 session in which he had described the past year as one of "average prosperity." Since the price of foodstuffs had rocketed as a

result of the American Civil War and the sugar market had suffered a significant decline, members objected to this comment. Eyre's strongest critic in the
House, George William Gordon, declared in October that Jamaica could
never improve until Eyre was relieved. Gordon added that "the only thing for
us to do is to tell [Newcastle] that we are not satisfied, that there will be no
progress, no improvement, so long as Lieutenant-Governor Eyre is here, and
governs as he has governed during the last eighteen months."[46] When Gordon
returned to the same theme in the following January, he could not persuade the
few members who remained in the House to second several resolutions against
Eyre. Yet, a month later, a significant minority of the Assembly passed a similar motion.[47]

The change occurred because Eyre would not allow Ewart to discuss his
removal from office when the subagent appeared before a special committee of
the House. Thirteen assemblymen, who called themselves the "patriots" and
were members of the Town party, regarded this action as an abuse of their
rights. Although the group had not supported Gordon's earlier motion against
Eyre, a leading colored representative, S. C. Burke, maintained that they could
not ignore Ewart's heavy-handed dismissal and his enforced silence before the
House. They therefore voted in a small House largely empty of Country party
delegates to censure Eyre and to refuse doing business with him.[48]

The representatives from the Town party were particularly displeased about
what they viewed as Eyre's attempt to rule directly through the colonial secretary. Robert Osborn complained about the secrecy that surrounded the lieutenant-governor's dispatches. It was un-English, he said, and had not been
done that way by other governors in the past. Furthermore, Osborn believed
that the colonies should be left to run themselves: "we are better able to
manage our affairs than any Colonial Secretary five thousand miles away . . .
and I want to know if he is to be permitted to put aside our constitution . . . and
rule the country by despatches from the Colonial Office?"[49] The thirteen
"patriots" hoped their action would result in Eyre's removal from office. Like
the planters who had halted the proceedings of the legislature at other points in
the post-emancipation period, they were attempting to influence the decisions
taken at the Colonial Office.[50]

Eyre's response to the moves in the House against him was to belittle the
opposition and minimize their grievances. He wrote home that the Jews and
coloreds had formed a party because they felt aggrieved about his having fired
a man of color and a Jew from their posts. The lieutenant-governor also raised
a constitutional point which he knew would be well received at the Colonial
Office—the need for the Crown to resist the Assembly's demands. Eyre
argued that the House wanted the right to review Government appointments
and dismissals and that the executive committee had its eye on the control of
patronage. Since, in Eyre's view, this was tantamount to responsible government, he was strongly opposed to it.[51]

As in earlier dispatches, Eyre was unfairly portraying his opposition. Although he was correct in suggesting that the coloreds and Jews were anxious to protect Ewart and Lindo and that both groups eagerly sought Government places and contracts, there were other reasons why they acted together. By glossing over the issues that served to unite the members of the Town party, Eyre was making the same mistake he had made throughout his stay in Jamaica: he was ignoring the most important elements of the situation and was providing a very one-sided view of local politics.

Several Jews had already begun to vote with the Town party before Eyre's arrival in 1862. They shared some of the same assumptions as the coloreds and were opposed to the planters' administration of the island. On a different level, coloreds and Jews were almost all creoles, which differentiated them from many of the planting attorneys and estate owners. They therefore sought to protect local institutions such as the Assembly from the encroachment of the Crown. But Eyre was wrong to suggest that the Town party wanted to increase the powers of the House by usurping the functions of the executive. As a constitutional historian has observed, the House was not seeking the control of patronage; it was instead "denying the right of the Crown to set itself above its own rules and regulations."[52]

Despite the unity of the faction opposed to Eyre, their refusal to work with the lieutenant-governor had precisely the opposite effect than they had intended. Faced with what it perceived as a challenge to its prerogative, the Colonial Office moved to bolster the executive. Newcastle promoted Eyre to be governor and expressed his approval of the way in which the lieutenant-governor had dealt with the problems he had confronted. When this news reached the island, the opposition to Eyre collapsed, and a special session of the House held in June 1864 to deal with leftover business went smoothly and without any apparent difficulty.[53]

The turmoil in the House for much of its session meant that the Assembly did not produce any legislation of great importance. In part, this was a consequence of the executive committee's position between Eyre and the Assembly. It was responsible to the lieutenant-governor as well as to its own supporters who had censured Eyre. Apart from George Price who secretly sponsored a motion to censure Eyre, the members of the administration seemed prepared to serve the lieutenant-governor. As a result, one of their allies in the House found it difficult to distinguish them from their predecessors, and claimed that they were pursuing the same policy as the previous members of the executive committee.[54]

The loyalty of the Jordon-Westmorland ministry to Eyre had a damaging effect on the unity of the Town party. Linked with the promotion of the lieutenant-governor and the failure of the faction's censure motion, it led to a split in the party. During the 1864–1865 session, the brown representatives and the Jews no longer tended to vote together and now could be found on each side of nearly every issue.[55] The men of color in the House faced other political problems as well. First, Edward Jordon resigned from the executive committee and the Assembly in October 1864 to assume the post of acting receiver-general. As in 1852, when Jordon had become a member of the Legislative Council, his departure left the brown politicians without a leader. Second, several brown and black men who had been elected to the House in 1863 were no longer sitting there by 1864. March had relinquished his seat, Jackson was speaker, and Walters was ill; out of twelve colored and black representatives, only eight brown delegates remained, including Bourke and Mais who voted with the Country party. Since a planter, William Hosack, replaced Jordon on the executive committee, the administration was again dominated entirely by planters, although of a significantly higher caliber than the Whitelocke-Smith ministry.[56]

The legislation for the 1864–1865 session therefore reflected the traditional pattern of high import duties on necessities and little substantial attention to the very serious difficulties affecting the colony. The administration dealt with the problem of agricultural larceny, for example, by considerably increasing the sanctions against it. Though this action came at a time when food was prohibitively expensive and a drought had reduced local production, the Government sponsored a bill embodying corporal punishment and long jail sentences for minor offenses. The executive committee also submitted a measure for the construction of an expensive dock scheme to be funded from public revenues.[57]

George William Gordon provided the most consistent opposition to these acts. He noted that the bill inflicting corporal punishment was an example of class legislation, aimed only at the lower classes. In his view, the dock was a commercial enterprise which the people's taxes should not have had to support.[58] Gordon's attacks on Eyre also continued unabated. In a letter to the secretary of the Anti-Slavery Society, Gordon wrote that "the session has come to a most unsatisfactory conclusion and if Mr. Eyre is to remain here the sequel will be Rebellion in the Island."[59] Gordon was not alone in voting against most of the Government measures; he was often joined by three other men of color, S. C. Burke, Daniel Nathan, and John Nunes.[60] Since the Country party again enjoyed a majority in the House, these representatives were unable to round up enough support to defeat the measures they opposed.

Apart from Gordon, there were men outside of the House who attacked much of the Assembly's legislation. In a letter to the colonial secretary, E. B. Underhill, the secretary of the Baptist Missionary Society, expressed his concern about developments in Jamaica. Underhill called for "a searching inquiry" into the acts of the House and warned that the people in the island were starving as a result of the drought and the difficulty of finding work. When Eyre circulated the letter in Jamaica, many of his respondents concurred in Underhill's views. Meetings were also held across the island to support the allegations Underhill had made.[61]

Eyre did not discount the reports of distress in the island, but he suggested that the blame for many of the problems rested with the people.[62] When a deputation from one of the most affected parishes presented him with a petition on the condition of the laboring classes, Eyre indicated that he did not approve of the resolutions. In the governor's view and for the Colonial Office as well, "any man who was willing to labor could make a comfortable living."[63] This attitude, in the face of substantial evidence to the contrary, was largely responsible for the outbreak of the Morant Bay Rebellion later in the year.

By the spring of 1865, the mood of the island was grim. *The Falmouth Post* reported that the colony was facing economic ruin; at the same time, there were fears of local riots as a result of the Underhill meetings. Some observers believed that the Assembly was to blame for many of the problems confronting the colony. They claimed that the House had ignored the social needs of the people and had devoted itself primarily to keeping up the production of sugar.[64]

Officials at the Colonial Office shared this point of view and were prepared to consider changes in the Constitution. By 1863, the Colonial Office had decided not simply to resist party government but also to exploit party divisions that might lead to a reform of the House. Two years later, Henry Taylor noted that differences among the factions in the Assembly could result in its abolition.[65] When the Colonial Office received a resolution attacking the House in July 1865, Taylor's minute on it became the basis for a dispatch welcoming any action in this direction: "if the majority of the Assembly could be induced to pass enactments in amendment of its own constitution, HM's Government would be ready to give those enactments its most attentive and favourable consideration."[66]

Like Taylor, a large number of assemblymen hoped for significant changes in the island's Constitution. One faction associated with the absentees and the West India Committee sought to abolish the Assembly and to establish a Crown Colony form of government in its place. Another group representing the local resident plantocracy envisioned strengthening the oligarchical nature of the House. These delegates wanted a unicameral House with a high franchise requirement to ensure it would be dominated almost entirely by white planters. The third clique, consisting largely of coloreds and several Jews, worked to maintain the representative system and to uphold the prerogatives of the House. The men of color in particular were concerned about any changes in the Constitution that would exclude them from participating in the political life of the island.[67] The colored politicians also expressed the most concern for the ex-slave population, but they gained little support from the two governors who served in Jamaica during the 1860s.

Darling and Eyre instead helped to undermine this faction. When the coloreds were in opposition, the two governors had portrayed them as party politicians who were interested only in office. The Jordon-Westmorland ministry suffered a similar fate. Eyre ignored it much of the time and made it impossible for the executive committee to maintain its majority in the House. Since Eyre had advocated a unicameral legislature and was eager to abolish the Assembly altogether, it was not surprising that he helped to weaken the one group in the House that consistently upheld its prerogatives. When the Morant Bay Rebellion broke out, the coloreds were in no position to prevent the majority from handing over the responsibility for the island to the Crown.

NOTES

1. Douglas Hall, *Free Jamaica, 1838–1865* (New Haven, Conn., 1959), pp. 237–40; Philip D. Curtin, *Two Jamaicas* (Cambridge, Mass., 1955), pp. 170–72.

2. C. V. Gocking, "Constitutional Problems in Jamaica, 1850–1866" (unpublished D. Phil. thesis, Oxford University, 1955), p. 431.

3. Apart from Solomon, these politicians are mentioned in Feurtado, MS notes, and are all listed in Glory Robertson (comp.), *Members of the Assembly of Jamaica* (mimeo, Institute of Jamaica, 1965), pp. 57–58. Darling discussed Smith and Solomon in a dispatch to Newcastle: CO 137/351, Darling to Newcastle, November 24, 1860, confidential. More on Smith is available in the IRO, Will: 132–207 and in the biographical files, Institute of Jamaica. These files also contain some information on Solomon, as does CO 137/380, Eyre to Newcastle, March 9, 1864, confidential. Background on Hugh Whitelocke is available in CO 137/356, Darling to Newcastle, July 24, 1861, no. 116 and in IRO, Inventory: 161–67. Ketelhodt's inventory is preserved in IRO, Inventory: 160–165, and he is mentioned in most studies of the Morant Bay Rebellion.

4. CO 137/354, Darling to Newcastle: May 7, 1861, no. 63; May 6, 1861, no. 62; CO 137/353, Darling to Newcastle, March 9, 1861, no. 38.

5. There were two black delegates in the Assembly which sat from 1860 to 1863, only one of whom remained there after 1863. Figure 2, p. 65, charts the decline of the coloreds and blacks in the House during this period.

6. Gocking, "Constitutional Problems," pp. 431–32.

7. Abraham Judah and A. C. Sinclair (comps.), *Debates of the Honourable House of Assembly of Jamaica* . . . , 13 vols. (Kingston and Spanish Town, 1856–1866): February 14, 1861, pp. 399–400; March 4, 1861, p. 507; *VAJ*, February 14, 1861, p. 231.

8. Judah and Sinclair, *Debates*, December 5, 1860, pp. 206–18; *VAJ*, December 5, 1860, p. 134.

9. Judah and Sinclair, *Debates*, February 19, 1861, p. 437; February 18, 1861, p. 432; December 11, 1860, pp. 238–40.

10. Ibid., February 20, 1861, pp. 447–48.

11. Ibid., November 27, 1860, p. 155.

12. *VAJ*, November 20, 1860, pp. 120–21.

13. Judah and Sinclair, *Debates*, November 27, 1860, p. 161.

14. *The Jamaica Guardian*, February 27, 1861.

15. CO 137/353, Darling to Newcastle, February 22, 1861, separate; CO

137/356, Darling to Newcastle: September 3, 1861, no. 126; September 17, 1861, no. 130, enclosure: *The Morning Journal*, September 9, 1861.

16. CO 137/345, Darling to Bulwer-Lytton, July 9, 1859, no. 87, Newcastle's note: October 3, 1859.

17. CO 137/353, Darling to Newcastle, February 22, 1861, separate; Gocking, "Constitutional Problems," p. 431.

18. Judah and Sinclair, *Debates*, November 12, 1861, p. 4.

19. Ibid., December 18, 1861, pp. 210–11.

20. Ansell Hart, *The Life of George William Gordon* (Kingston, 1972), p. 49. Gordon's stinging attack on the executive committee is included in Hart's biography, pp. 53–55.

21. Eyre's early career in Australia is best treated in Geoffrey Dutton, *The Hero as Murderer* (London, 1967), pp. 16–166. See also William Law Mathieson, *The Sugar Colonies and Governor Eyre* (London, 1936), p. 148, and for a strongly partisan view against Eyre, see Lord Olivier, *The Myth of Governor Eyre* (London, 1933).

22. Dutton, *The Hero*, p. 196.

23. Ibid., pp. 175–76.

24. Gocking, "Constitutional Problems," pp. 442, 436. See also Arthur N. Birch and William Robinson (comps.), *The Colonial Office List for 1865* (London, 1865), p. 187.

25. CO 137/367, Eyre to Newcastle, July 8, 1862, no. 41, enclosures; *The Falmouth Post*, August 15, 1862; Henry Bleby, *The Reign of Terror* (London, 1868), p. 25.

26. CO 137/367, Eyre to Newcastle, July 24, 1862, no. 52, Taylor's minute.

27. Hart, *Gordon*, pp. 48–51; Olivier, *Eyre*, pp. 62–66; George Price, *Jamaica and the Colonial Office* (London, 1866), pp. 40–43.

28. Price, *Jamaica and the Colonial Office*, p. 52; Olivier, *Eyre*, p. 66; Judah and Sinclair, *Debates*, November 25, 1862, pp. 73–81.

29. *VAJ*, November 25, 1862, p. 121; Price, *Jamaica and the Colonial Office*, pp. 30–31.

30. CO 137/368, Eyre to Newcastle, December 23, 1862, confidential. The executive committee rebutted Eyre's allegations when it learned a year later how he had characterized its actions. See CO 137/379, Eyre to Newcastle, February 20, 1864, no. 59, enclosures: executive committee minute.

31. Gocking, "Constitutional Problems," pp. 496–97, 516–17.

32. CO 137/370, Eyre to Newcastle, January 31, 1863, no. 63, enclosure: minute of the executive committee; CO 137/371, Eyre to Newcastle, April 18, 1863, confidential. Information on Phillips is available in Feurtado, MS notes; Robertson, *Members*, p. 56; A.P.M. Andrade, *A Record of the Jews in Jamaica* (Kingston, 1941), p. 167.

33. Price, *Jamaica and the Colonial Office*, p. 37; CO 137/375, Eyre to Newcastle, November 23, 1863, confidential.

34. Price, *Jamaica and the Colonial Office*, p. 33; Gocking, "Constitutional Problems," p. 484.

35. *The Falmouth Post*, May 8, 1863.

36. Ibid.

37. Judah and Sinclair, *Debates*, April 22, 1863, pp. 193–94, 202–204.

38. Ibid., p. 201.
39. *VAJ*, April 22, 1863, p. 94.
40. CO 137/372, Eyre to Newcastle, May 9, 1863, no. 105; CO 137/373, Eyre to Newcastle, July 24, 1863, no. 181. Espeut's quite interesting defense of his position is enclosed in the latter dispatch.
41. CO 137/376, Eyre to Newcastle, December 7, 1863, no. 281, note by Frederick Rogers; Price, *Jamaica and the Colonial Office*, p. 51.
42. Gocking, "Constitutional Problems," p. 484; Price, *Jamaica and the Colonial Office*, p. 51.
43. CO 138/75, Newcastle to Eyre, February 26, 1864, no. 765.
44. CO 137/374, Eyre to Newcastle, September 23, 1863, no. 226; CO 137/375, Eyre to Newcastle, October 20, 1863, no. 338.
45. CO 137/379, Eyre to Newcastle, February 8, 1864, no. 54; CO 137/375, Eyre to Newcastle, November 24, 1863, confidential; *VAJ*, March 31, 1863, p. 19. The elder Lindo, Alexander Joseph Lindo, is discussed by Feurtado, MS notes, and Robertson, *Members*, p. 55. He owned an estate in St. Mary, was associated with the planting interest, and later held office as inspector and director of the Public Hospital. His will is available in IRO, Will: 130–208. See also the *Daily Advertiser*, November 19, 1851.
46. CO 137/375, Eyre to Newcastle, November 4, 1863, no. 260; Judah and Sinclair, *Debates*, October 28, 1863, p. 25.
47. CO 137/378, Eyre to Newcastle, January 18, 1864, no. 13, enclosure: *The Jamaica Watchman and People's Free Press*, January 21, 1864; Judah and Sinclair, *Debates*, January 21, 1864, pp. 61–63.
48. CO 137/379, Eyre to Newcastle, February 9, 1864, confidential; Judah and Sinclair, *Debates*, June 13, 1864, pp. 436–42; *VAJ*, February 8, 1864, p. 383.
49. Judah and Sinclair, *Debates*, May 31, 1864, p. 351.
50. CO 137/382, Eyre to Newcastle, May 4, 1864, no. 140.
51. CO 137/379, Eyre to Newcastle: February 8, 1864, no. 54; February 9, 1864, confidential; February 22, 1864, no. 62.
52. Gocking, "Constitutional Problems," p. 545.
53. CO 137/380, Newcastle to Eyre, April 1, 1864, no. 79; April 6, 1864, no. 794; *VAJ*, June 6, 1864, pp. 13–15.
54. CO 137/382, Eyre to Cardwell, May 23, 1864, no. 157; Judah and Sinclair, *Debates*, June 13, 1864, p. 424.
55. For example, *VAJ*, November 21, 1864, p. 104; February 9, 1865, pp. 335–36.
56. The Jordon appointment led to a further dispute between the Colonial Office and the Assembly which is summarized in CO 137/391, Eyre to Cardwell, May 3, 1865, no. 121. Jordon eventually served as island secretary rather than as receiver-general.
57. CO 137/388, Eyre to Cardwell, March 22, 1865, no. 38. The legislation of the House is more generally reviewed in J. M. Ludlow, *A Quarter Century of Jamaica Legislation* (London, 1866), but in particular see pp. 18–19.
58. CO 137/390, Eyre to Cardwell, April 15, 1865, no. 89, enclosure: Gordon to Cardwell, March 24, 1865.
59. *ASSP*, British West Indies-Jamaica General, 1860–1869, S22 G64, Gordon to Chamerovzow, February 25, 1865.
60. For example, *VAJ*, February 2, 1865, p. 322; February 9, 1865, pp. 335–36.

61. CO 137/390, Eyre to Cardwell, April 19, 1865, no. 90; CO 137/391, Eyre to Cardwell, May 17, 1865, no. 132. Although Underhill may have overstated the degree of suffering in the island, W. L. Mathieson understated it in his discussion of the problem. See Mathieson, *Governor Eyre*, p. 175, and also the response of the Baptist ministers in Jamaica to Underhill's letter in Edward B. Underhill, *A Letter Addressed to the Rt. Honourable E. Cardwell* (London, 1865), pp. 37–38.

62. CO 137/391, Eyre to Cardwell, May 6, 1865, no. 128.

63. *The Falmouth Post*, July 18, 1865. The Colonial Office view was expressed by Henry Taylor in "The Queen's Advice," which was a response to a petition from "certain poor people" in St. Ann. See CO 137/190: Eyre to Cardwell, April 25, 1865, no. 115, enclosure and Taylor's minute; Cardwell to Eyre, June 14, 1865, no. 222.

64. *The Falmouth Post*, May 23, 1865; Hall Pringle, *The Fall of the Sugar Planters of Jamaica* (London, 1869), p. 19.

65. Gocking, "Constitutional Problems," p. 294; CO 137/390, Eyre to Cardwell, April 19, 1865, no. 90, Taylor's minute.

66. CO 137/391, Eyre to Cardwell, June 6, 1865, no. 137, Taylor's minute. Taylor's comments became the basis for the dispatch which is recorded in the same volume: Cardwell to Eyre, July 7, 1865, no. 236.

67. Curtin, *Two Jamaicas*, p. 210.

The Legacy of
Morant Bay

On October 11, 1865, a mob consisting of several hundred people marched into Morant Bay. Its first objective was to break into the police station and obtain additional arms; the crowd then approached the courthouse where a meeting of the vestry was taking place. Warned of the danger, the custos, Baron von Ketelhodt, had deployed a group of volunteer militia men to protect the officials. The volunteers were heavily outnumbered and could not prevent the people from continuing to surge forward and bombard them with stones and bottles. When the demonstrators still did not disperse after Ketelhodt had read the Riot Act, the captain of the militia gave the order to fire. As a result, several people were killed and the angry mob rushed the defenders. Some of the volunteers and vestrymen escaped, and others retreated into the courthouse, which the attackers set on fire. Eventually, the rioters killed eighteen people and wounded thirty-one others, including the custos and several members of the vestry. In the days immediately after the event, roving bands of men murdered four more persons and wounded another three.

The response to the outbreak was swift and cruel. Eyre mobilized the army and gained the support of the Maroons against the rebels, who put up almost no resistance. Official figures showed that 439 people lost their lives to the Government forces, often without any trial at all. In addition, 600 men and women were flogged and nearly 1,000 homes were destroyed. The riot also had other consequences. Since the frightened representatives of the House were convinced that a stronger form of government was necessary to deal with events of this magnitude, they abolished the Assembly. A Royal Commission which investigated the riot criticized the severe measures taken by the governor, and

Eyre resigned to face the threat of prosecution for murder at home. Although he ultimately retired peacefully to Devon, Eyre left a sad legacy for the colony, especially for the people of color.[1]

The riot at Morant Bay occurred at a time when conditions were especially difficult in the colony. Economic distress had affected the island generally, and the meetings to discuss the Underhill letter had broadcast the people's grievances over a wide audience. Reports of possible trouble were circulating during the summer, and *The Falmouth Post* reported just before the outbreak that agitators were urging the people to resist payment of their taxes, by force if necessary.[2]

The situation in St. Thomas in the East was more acute than elsewhere in the island. The parish had a history of poor relations between employers and their workers; in addition, the local vestry was dominated by a corrupt plantocracy and a pro-planter rector, Reverend Victor Herschell. In 1862, Herschell and Ketelhodt had helped to engineer the dismissal of George William Gordon from the vestry, though he was one of the few representatives who spoke for the small settlers. Two years later, the vestrymen convinced Governor Eyre to remove a popular colored stipendiary magistrate, T. Witter Jackson, from the parish. Jackson's departure made it less likely that the settlers would get a fair hearing from the courts, a problem that was felt throughout the rest of Jamaica as well.[3]

During the summer of 1865, Gordon—who was the delegate to the Assembly for St. Thomas in the East—traveled extensively throughout the island and among his constituents. He spoke at meetings on behalf of the peasantry and used language that was often ambiguous: it was possible to interpret his speeches as a call to action against the oppression of the planters. Gordon's political agent in St. Thomas in the East, Paul Bogle, seems to have regarded the statements in this light.[4] A small landowner and a native Baptist preacher, Bogle organized an informal army of his own and developed a rhetoric aimed at uniting the blacks behind him. He gained the backing of many settlers who felt thwarted by the existing political and legal system in the district.[5]

The immediate causes of the outbreak were two court cases in which Bogle and his men intervened to protect the defendants. When the police attempted to serve warrants on Bogle, his supporters forcibly extracted a promise from the constables "to join their colour" and "cleave to the black." The leaders of the campaign then drafted a petition to Eyre expressing their loyalty and seeking his protection against the local justices. When Eyre ignored the letter, Bogle carried out the threat in it "to put our shoulders to the wheel" and led his forces to confront the militia at Morant Bay.[6]

The events preceding the outbreak suggest that there was no island-wide plot to destroy the government. The riot grew out of the settlers' frustration over disputes about land as well as the difficulty of obtaining a fair trial in the parish.

Since one of the most prominent black men in the island, Charles Price, was murdered at the courthouse and other blacks and coloreds also lost their lives there, the outbreak was not solely a conflict between blacks and whites. Eyre could not comprehend any of this; he regarded it as a direct threat to British rule and as a conspiracy to overthrow the whites.[7]

The retribution was therefore savage. Not all of it could be blamed on Eyre, however, as other men had direct control over the soldiers in the field. Nevertheless, the governor approved the army's actions and took steps on his own that also violated the law. Since he believed that Gordon was responsible for the riot, Eyre had him arrested in Kingston and brought to Morant Bay where martial law was in force. Gordon was tried and hanged, though not before the presiding officer had gained Eyre's sanction for the death penalty. When the Royal Commission investigated the case, it could find no evidence of Gordon's complicity in the outbreak. Eyre had unjustly condemned a political opponent and had taken advantage of the situation to do so.[8]

The governor moved in the same way against the House of Assembly. He had earlier expressed his hope that the Assembly could be abolished and replaced by a nominated unicameral legislature. When he addressed the House less than a month after the events at Morant Bay, Eyre counseled the delegates to create a strong government of this type. Although several representatives were prepared to accept the governor's proposal, members of the Country party still wanted to retain their place in local politics. As a result, they sought to amend the scheme, and they eventually agreed to a compromise—a twenty-four man body in which half of the membership would be elected and half nominated. The franchise would exclude most of the black and colored population, and the requirements for a seat on the new Council would keep it almost entirely in the hands of the plantocracy. Not surprisingly, the opposition to these changes came from a small group of Jewish and colored representatives. The brown assemblymen were considerably reduced in numbers and divided as well. Those who argued against the proposals were nonetheless carrying on the political tradition of the coloreds which had continued for more than thirty years.[9]

Robert Osborn and S. C. Burke were the most outspoken critics of the plan to alter the Constitution. Osborn maintained that the white representatives had held secret meetings to organize large majorities in favor of betraying the country. Their rationale was that the elements of self-government were not present in the colony; in other words, there were fewer whites left in Jamaica. Yet, Osborn noted that the planters had nothing to complain about, for they were still dominant and were able to have everything their own way. He concluded that "the colored people have never sought to prevent their [the plantocracy] having the largest share in the government of the country. They only sought to prevent its being exclusive."[10]

Osborn stressed the coloreds' moderation in other ways as well. He had claimed earlier that the coloreds could have secured the return of an over-whelming majority of nonwhite delegates to the House. However, they had not done so because Osborn and most of the other brown representatives believed that the transfer of power should occur only gradually.[11] Osborn saw no reason to change his attitude as a result of the riot at Morant Bay. The people of color were still "a peaceable, forbearing, and loyal people" who did not deserve to lose their rights. Although Osborn declared that he would not live to see the results of the constitutional changes, he was worried about the effects on his children and grandchildren. "At present, they have little to clamour for, but take away the constitution; send them back into political degradation and slavery, and tell me if you think this will render them and ourselves more con-tented than we are now."[12]

Osborn's colleague, S. C. Burke, argued along similar lines. In his view, there were no grounds for disfranchising the coloreds.

Is it because of the wicked insurrection by the negroes of St. Thomas in the East that a class of men, who have ever been most loyal and conservative—who have done good service to the state—who have by their honest industry acquired property equal in pro-portion to their white fellow subjects, considering the period since they have enjoyed political privileges and power—who have educated their children so as to fit them to be good and useful citizens—and who have the greatest possible interest in maintaining peace and good order in the community—should be deprived of the right of electing their representatives?[13]

Burke also claimed that Jamaica was not suited for Crown Colony govern-ment. There were too many educated coloreds and whites in the island who were accustomed to representative institutions. Moreover, Burke blamed the planters for many of Jamaica's difficulties. They had carried on interminable battles with the Colonial Office to the detriment of the colony, and they had not improved the condition of the ex-slaves. The irony for Burke was that the situa-tion had now changed; a middle class had developed which could resist class legislation. Since the whites could no longer monopolize political power, they were making use of the riot as a pretext to give up the Assembly. In its place, Burke maintained that the planters wanted to establish a scheme that would enable them to dominate the Government once again.[14]

The arguments had little effect on the House. Apart from a group of about ten coloreds and Jews who opposed the alterations in the Constitution, the ma-jority of assemblymen approved of a unicameral legislature. Since several members remained concerned about the possibility of factions developing within the new body, they welcomed a dispatch from the Colonial Office indi-cating that the Crown was willing to take full responsibility for the colony. This meant Crown Colony government on the Trinidadian model, a system in which the governor worked with a nominated Council composed of six officials and three unofficial members. Henry Taylor was satisfied with these changes because he believed they would allow the Government to retain the upper hand and still provide an opportunity for a degree of local opinion.[15] There was no room, however, for the continued advance of the coloreds.

Crown Colony government initially brought in its wake some important reforms for the colony. The finances were improved as was the island's legal system. Although there was little progress regarding education, there were advances in the public health. Yet, on balance, direct rule from London was not a success: it widened the gap between the coloreds and the whites and made Jamaica even more dependent on England. Despite the defects of the Assembly, it had gradually accommodated different groups in the society, at least until the 1850s. Crown Colony government cut short this important political and social development.[16]

The colored delegates, foreseeing these problems in 1865, had sought to retain the representative system. Their arguments in its favor were not new; they were reiterating the general principles they had been expressing throughout the period before and after emancipation. As during the campaign for civil liberties in the 1820s, then, the people of color did not wish to upset the hierarchical framework of the society. The coloreds had profited from their position on the white, brown, and black pecking order. Although they were often scorned by the whites, the browns were not at the bottom of the ladder. At the same time, the men of color did not totally forget their responsibility to the blacks. Relations between browns and blacks were not always harmonious, but colored assemblymen with the support of a few blacks were the only representatives who consistently advocated legislation in favor of the emancipated population. In part, this reflected the coloreds' vision of the future: they rightly maintained that blacks and browns would one day control the island. Yet the coloreds were in no hurry to speed this development along. Haiti stood as a reminder of the consequences of rapid social change in the Caribbean. Moreover, brown men did not wish to see the departure of the whites whom they regarded as a civilizing force in the society. The coloreds criticized the planters, but they found it difficult to envision life without the estates.

The planters did not view the people of color in the same light. As during slavery, the coloreds remained a threat to the supremacy of the plantocracy. The influx of brown assemblymen and their unity during the late 1840s persuaded the planters to consider changes in the Constitution; Crown Colony government was a further move to retain power for the white minority. Similarly, the Colonial Office did not make use of the coloreds in helping to enact Crown policy. While officials in the 1830s recognized the pro-British stance of the brown representatives, they did not show the same interest in the coloreds after emancipation.

Faced with the planters' hostility and the indifference of the Colonial Office, the coloreds were unable to remain united. Although they had provided an opposition to the plantocracy and a different set of solutions to the problems affecting the society, they split among themselves when they developed into a significant political force. During the 1850s, their leader, Edward Jordon, became concerned about the number and character of the black and brown assemblymen entering the House. He was worried that the whites would abolish representative government to safeguard their dominant position. Nonetheless, other coloreds continued to express an interest in the welfare of the population and in measures that reduced the planters' powers over the ex-slaves. The political divisions and subsequent weakness of the coloreds made it possible for the plantocracy to opt for a colonial solution to their problems. The brown politicians who had sought to preserve the most important creole institution in the island knew what this meant for their own future as well as for the island.

NOTES

1. W. P. Morrell, *British Colonial Policy in the Mid-Victorian Age* (Oxford, 1969), pp. 411–12; Douglas Hall, *Free Jamaica, 1838–1865* (New Haven, Conn., 1959), pp. 247–48; PP, 1866, [3683], xxx, Report of the Jamaica Royal Commission (hereafter Royal Commission), pp. 12–41. Bernard Semmel has examined the controversy over the handling of the events at Morant Bay in *The Governor Eyre Controversy* (London, 1962).

2. CO 137/393, Eyre to Cardwell, August 7, 1865, no. 198; *The Falmouth Post*, October 3, 1865.

3. Henry Bleby, *The Reign of Terror* (London, 1868), p. 19; Hall, *Free Jamaica*, p. 252, n. 3.

4. Royal Commission, p. 37.

5. CO 884/2, Confidential Print, no. 2, Papers relating to the Insurrection in Jamaica, October 1865.

6. Thomas Harvey and William Brewin, *Jamaica in 1866* (London, 1867), p. 22; Royal Commission, p. 10; Philip D. Curtin, *Two Jamaicas* (Cambridge, Mass., 1955), p. 197.

7. Hall, *Free Jamaica*, pp. 250–52; CO 137/394, Eyre to Cardwell, November 2, 1865, no. 262. Eyre's first dispatch about the outbreak is also useful. See CO 137/393, Eyre to Cardwell, October 20, 1865, no. 251.

8. Bleby, *Terror*, pp. 103–104; Royal Commission, p. 38.

9. CO 137/394, Eyre to Cardwell, November 8, 1865, no. 284; C. V. Gocking, "Constitutional Problems in Jamaica, 1850–1866" (unpublished D. Phil. thesis, Oxford University, 1955), pp. 588–91.

10. Abraham Judah and A. C. Sinclair (comps.), *Debates of the Honourable House of Assembly of Jamaica* . . . , 13 vols. (Kingston and Spanish Town, 1856–1866), December 5, 1865, p. 135.

11. Ibid., December 31, 1858, p. 309.

12. Ibid., December 5, 1865, p. 135; November 21, 1865, pp. 75–76.

13. Ibid., November 16, 1865, pp. 43–44.

14. Ibid., pp. 46–47; CO 137/403, Storks to Cardwell, March 31, 1866, no. 79, enclosure.

15. CO 137/403, Storks to Cardwell, March 31, 1866, no. 79, enclosure; CO 137/406, Storks to Cardwell, June 23, 1866, no. 138, Taylor's minute: July 15, 1866.

16. Morrell, *Mid-Victorian Age*, pp. 428–30; Gocking, "Constitutional Problems," p. 626. For an alternative view, at least in the first decade of Crown Colony rule, see Vincent John Marsala, *Sir John Peter Grant* (Institute of Jamaica, 1972).

APPENDIX A

In *The Dynamics of Change in a Slave Society*, Mavis Campbell discusses the free coloreds in nineteenth-century Jamaica. Since her account differs substantially from the one presented here, it seems useful to set out some of the major differences in interpretation and some of the principal problems I have encountered with this book.

It is in Campbell's discussion of the period after 1830 that our differences are greatest. In her view, the coloreds wanted above all else "to be identified with the whites and to cooperate with them in all respects" (p. 145). She maintains that the leader of the coloreds, Edward Jordon, was the outstanding example of this type of behavior. His aim after 1838, she argues, was to be recognized as a gentleman and to acquire offices for himself and his brown friends (p. 189). Moreover, Jordon's newspaper, *The Watchman*, "was solidly behind the planters" on the question of emancipation (p. 212). Yet, the situation immediately before and after emancipation was far more complex than Campbell suggests. While some free coloreds were opposed to emancipating the slaves, Jordon and his political allies supported the abolitionists and protected the dissenting missionaries whom the whites regarded as their enemies. Coloreds were prepared to fight against the whites in the 1830s rather than allow the planters to secede from the empire. In addition, Jordon's close connections with the Anti-Slavery Society in the 1830s and his general opposition to the plantocracy in the Assembly until the early 1850s hardly suggest that he was prepared to cooperate fully with the whites.

Campbell comes to other conclusions which seem unwarranted. For her, the coloreds' political party, the Town party, had no policies: "indeed, it is no mere cynicism to suggest that if the mulatto men of the island were not so sedulously snubbed by the whites then there would probably be no Town Party" (p. 212). This position fails to take account of the coloreds' activities in the House where they opposed expensive immigration schemes, they pursued educational and medical improvements in the island, and they fought against planter plans for retrenchment which might have ruined the local economy. Campbell cites little evidence to substantiate such assertions, and since she has failed to identify most of the colored representatives and has not studied their votes in the Assembly, her book is filled with errors that undermine her argument. Thus, she misinterprets the coloreds' voting records when she argues that Robert Osborn joined the other coloreds in supporting "all the claims of the planters" until the 1860s (pp. 263–64). The evidence suggests just the opposite. Osborn as well as nearly all the men of color had a long history of opposing the planters in the Assembly. Campbell also denigrates the few coloreds she can identify. She finds that Robert Russell's only qualifications for a job were his color and his background as a copying clerk (p. 201). But

Russell was a barrister who later became registrar in chancery and had a considerable correspondence with the Anti-Slavery Society.

There are many other errors of fact. For example, John Campbell was not the second man of color to sit in the House (p. 84)—he was the third. Not all the brown assembly-men opposed the bill to establish a unicameral legislature in 1863 (p. 292). Indeed, the delegate who sponsored the measure was a man of color. Campbell's statement that "it cannot be overemphasized that he [George William Gordon] was the only member of the Town Party who made concrete criticisms of some of the governor's measures" (p. 299) is incorrect. I have demonstrated in Chapter 12 that many coloreds voiced strong opposition to Eyre's policies. George Solomon was not "on the periphery of the Town Party" (p. 306); on the contrary, he was part of the Country party administration which was established in 1860. George William Gordon and Richard Hill were not the only coloreds in public life who were concerned with the problem of education (p. 321), as Robert Osborn was widely known as a leading reformer in this field. In addition, other colored members of the House, including William Thomas March, Robert Russell, James Taylor, and Price Watkis, sought to expand the educational facilities in the island. Several brown representatives, and not just S. C. Burke, opposed the abolition of the Constitution in 1865 (p. 361).

It is not simply a question of factual errors. I take issue with an interpretation that denounces most of the coloreds yet ignores the reality of a creole group with its own values and attitudes. Despite opening up this field of research and also providing some useful background material, Campbell's book suffers from a singular bias against the coloreds as well as a tendency to stereotype them. This bias may derive from a failure to make use of the archives and libraries in Jamaica. It is also possible that Campbell allowed her indignation at the twentieth-century behavior of the coloreds to cloud her treatment of the group a century earlier.

APPENDIX B

A variety of sources were used to identify the black, colored, and Jewish members of the House. All of the assemblymen during the period are listed in Glory Robertson (comp.), *Members of the Assembly of Jamaica* (mimeo, Institute of Jamaica, 1965). This work carries further an earlier volume which included all the representatives to the House up to 1830: John Roby, *Members of the Assembly of Jamaica from the Institution of That Branch of the Legislature to the Present Time* (Montego Bay, 1831). Other biographical aids include Captain James H. Lawrence-Archer, *Monumental Inscriptions of the British West Indies* . . . (London, 1875) and a more recent work on Jamaica, Philip Wright (comp.), *Monumental Inscriptions of Jamaica* (London, 1966). For information on the men who attended Oxford, the manuscript by William Cowper, "A Catalogue of Men Born in the Island of Jamaica who matriculated at at Oxford 1689-1885 . . ." is useful and for the Jews, Jacob A.P.M. Andrade, *A Record of the Jews in Jamaica* . . . (Kingston, 1941) is essential. W. A. Feurtado's "MS notes on official and other personages in Jamaica" include information on most of the members of the Assembly.

The problem of identifying men of color in the Assembly is particularly difficult after emancipation. Since distinctions of color were generally avoided after 1834, only the most prominent brown politicians have been previously identified. Hence, the most useful sources for the purpose are the incidental comments in the island press and the occasional references in the *Votes of the House of Assembly*, the debates reported in the newspapers, and the collected *Debates* for the later period. In addition, the jury listings, the biographical notes in the West India Reference Library, and the advice of two local historians, H. P. Jacobs and Ansell Hart, were invaluable. When available, the wills, inventories, and land records stored in the Island Record Office were helpful. The secondary literature also provided a few clues. In England, the Colonial Office correspondence contained some otherwise unobtainable personal information on members of the Assembly. Again, the newspapers available in England often supply hints that other sources do not provide.

APPENDIX C

The attempt to correlate voting and landowning patterns involved sources available only in Jamaica. The first step was to select four sample parishes (see Chapter 9, note 10) and to compile a list of all the voters in these districts for the Assembly elections after 1838, making use of the House of Assembly pollbooks.

The next step was to find out how much land each voter owned. The *Jamaica Almanac*, 1840 and 1845, includes lists of proprietors and their holdings for these two dates but nothing for the next twenty years. Since the only sources that provide this information for the whole period are the Land Deeds at the Island Record Office, all the transfers of land among the voters in the sample parishes from 1838 to 1865 were examined. Although this was a laborious task, it soon became clear that the lists in the *Almanacs* were far from complete.

This method had its problems. For example, transfers of land do not necessarily indicate the amount of land an individual owned. A more serious difficulty was the absence of land records for many of the voters; they simply did not turn up either in the *Almanacs* or in the deeds. It is likely that the missing records generally belonged to the smaller landholders, largely because planters were more likely to record their transactions than settlers owning a few acres. Our figures also indicate that the voters for whom there were no land records tended to vote in the pattern of smaller freeholders. In addition, it was possible to obtain additional background on some of the voters by examining the militia and jury lists and other records in *The Royal Gazette*. Unfortunately, Jamaican electoral data did not follow the English example of listing occupations, and this information is therefore obtainable only in a small number of cases. The available data on the voters were punched on cards and run through a computer to sort the landholders into groups.

In order to determine if there was some consistency to the vote, it was necessary to describe the political affiliations of the candidates for the Assembly in the four parishes. In a faction-ridden House, this presented some difficulties. The *Votes*, however, provide a basis for making judgments about the successful candidates for office, and many of the losers ran elsewhere and eventually sat in the House. Members were also generally allied to the Town or Country parties or, in broader terms, to the Liberal or Conservative groupings in the House. Brown politicians formed the basis of the Liberal faction in the 1840s and early 1850s and with some important exceptions continued to support the Town party in the later period as well. It was therefore possible to assess the voters' choices in most cases.

A computer program was then designed to find out if there was a correlation between the landholding patterns of the voters and their choices for assemblymen. Since many electors voted only once, their votes were not useful for our purposes because we wanted to determine the consistency of the vote. Despite these problems, the figures that emerged provided a pattern suggesting that the largely black and brown small landholders tended to support colored candidates and those allied to the Town party.

APPENDIX D

The basis of the scalogram can perhaps best be understood by examining the first two votes in Table 7. In the first division, the hardcore Liberals support the passage of the tonnage bill. They can therefore be arranged on a chart as follows:

Roll Call

	1
W. W. Anderson	+
Lake	+
Taylor	+
Jordon	+
Osborn	+
Hitchins	+
Vickars	+
Bristow	+

On a later vote to proceed with the session of the House, a slightly larger minority can be identified, nearly all of whom voted for the first issue as well:

Roll Call

	1	2
W. W. Anderson	+	+
Lake	+	+
Taylor	+	+
Jordon	+	+
Osborn	+	+
Hitchins	+	
Vickars	+	+
Bristow	+	+
March		+
G. W. Gordon		+
Lunan		+
Brown		+

By examining a whole series of votes during a session, it is possible to produce a cumulative pattern and thereby reveal a relationship between different issues and the factions that supported them.

The ten fourfold tables compress that information into a manageable unit. The figures in the upper left-hand corner of the top row indicate that of the eight assembly-men who voted positively on the first issue, seven in two cases, six in one case, and all eight again on the last issue stayed together. The 0 in the upper right-hand corner makes it clear that none of them crossed over to the opposition.

In the next division on the motion to oppose an election, the pattern is much the same. The Liberals again stuck together; in only one vote was there an absentee. Similarly, seven of the eleven who voted to support the tonnage bill can be identified. The scale can thus be read across as well as up and down in order to analyze the support for each issue. Although the Liberals are of most interest in this study, the negative vote of the planters' party can also be examined in the same way.

Bibliography

West Indian material is increasingly well served by bibliographies and by guides to the important archives. In the latter category, most British and Jamaican repositories have published lists of their own holdings. Other guides that have proved useful include Arthur E. Gropp, *Guide to Libraries and Archives in Central America and the West Indies*. . . (New Orleans, Middle American Research Institute, Tulane University of Louisiana, 1941) and Herbert C. Bell and David W. Parker, *Guide to British West Indian Archive Materials, in London and in the Islands, for the History of the United States* (Washington, D.C., Carnegie Institute of Washington, 1926). More recently, Kenneth E. Ingram, *Sources of Jamaican History, 1655–1838: A Bibliographical Survey with Particular Reference to Manuscript Sources*, 2 vols. (Zug, Switzerland, Inter Documentation Co., 1976), has uncovered fresh material. The same author has produced another guide: *Manuscripts Relating to Commonwealth Caribbean Countries in U.S. and Canadian Repositories* (Barbados, Caribbean Universities Press, 1975).

There are also a variety of bibliographical aids. Two early studies are still valuable: Frank Cundall, *Bibliographica Jamaicensis* (Kingston, Institute of Jamaica [1908]) and Lowell J. Ragatz, *A Guide for the Study of British Caribbean History, 1763–1834* (Washington, D.C., U.S. Govt. Printing Office, 1932). Ragatz has published two checklists of parliamentary sessional papers relating to the British West Indies and the slave trade. A massive bibliography, Lambros Comitas, *Caribbeana 1900–1965, A Topical Bibliography* (Seattle, Wash., University of Washington Press, 1968) and the same author's updated *The Complete Caribbeana, 1900–1975: A Bibliographic Guide to the Scholarly Literature*, 4 vols. (Millwood, N.Y., KTO Press, 1977), has superseded many smaller works. In addition, the published catalogues of libraries with important West Indian collections are helpful. These include the Schomburg Collection, the Colonial Office Library (now the Foreign and Commonwealth Office Library), the library of the West India Committee, the Royal Empire Society Library (now the Royal Commonwealth Society), and the Boston College Library.

OFFICIAL PAPERS

Although the official sources remain largely in England, collections in Jamaica offer an opportunity to examine the period from another perspective. This is particularly important for those seeking to get away from a total reliance on the official correspondence or from a wholly metropolitan outlook. The Archives of Jamaica are the major source of this kind. While they have an incomplete set of the correspondence between local officials and the Colonial Office, the Archives contain much local material. The wills and the inventories, for example, provide some valuable hints about the free coloreds. The House of Assembly Poll Books, 2 vols., 1803–1866, make it possible to study the effects of changes in the franchise as well as in the electorate. The Archives also house the vestry minutes of several parishes and the Journals of the Council.

Two neighboring offices, the Island Record Office and the Registrar General's Department, are also useful depositories. Unlike the Archives, they are not well equipped to deal with scholars; however, it is possible to make use of the collections in both offices. The Island Record Office contains nearly a thousand volumes of land deeds, which record the transfers of land in the island. This source is important in attempting to assess the wealth of individual politicians as well as the landholding patterns of the electorate. The records of births, baptisms, marriages, and deaths are stored in the Registrar General's Department.

The materials in Jamaica are significant, but the records at the Public Record Office in London remain the major collection of official papers. The Colonial Office 137 series, the governor's outgoing correspondence, is a vital source, and the documents for the period run to several hundred volumes. Other related series include 138, the dispatches from the colonial secretary; 139, the acts of the Jamaican Legislature; and 140, the sessional papers of the Assembly and the Council. These are the most essential records specifically on Jamaica, but there are others in various categories. The 323 series, for example, contains the Law Reports on the acts of the legislature. The 318 series includes the material on the Lecesne and Escoffery case as well as an invaluable collection of the memorials and grievances of the free coloreds in the West Indies during the 1820s. The Confidential Print in 884 has important memoranda on Jamaica, including papers on the Morant Bay Rebellion. The Cardwell Papers contain Henry Taylor's crucial memorandum on the Assembly in 1839 and correspondence that could be considered under the heading of private papers.

Relevant material in the United States is not of great consequence. Nonetheless, the dispatches from the U.S. consuls in Kingston proved of interest, partly because a staunchly proslavery official reported developments during most of the post-emancipation period. The correspondence was read on microfilm; the originals are in the National Archives, Washington, D.C.

PRIVATE PAPERS

The collection of private papers at the West India Reference Library (now the National Library of Jamaica), Institute of Jamaica, is a well-organized and important source. The institute contains rare printed books and pamphlets as well as an extensive biographical file that was of considerable use in preparing this work. Other biographical aids in manuscript include W. A. Feutado's "MS Notes on official and other personages in Jamaica" and William Cowper's "A Catalogue of Men Born in the Island of Jamaica who matriculated at Oxford 1699–1855. . . ."

Some valuable diaries and correspondence are also in the collection. Richard Hill's notebooks and his diary of travels to Cuba, America, and Canada are available. More voluminous are the Sligo papers, which include official and private correspondence and the estate records of the governor's properties in Jamaica. The eight volumes of public and private letters were particularly useful for information on political developments during Sligo's administration in Jamaica. Two planters who sat in the House, Henry John Blagrove and H. A. Whitelocke, have left diaries or letterbooks, as have two military men stationed in the island, E.R.W. Wingfield Yates and Robert Knight Heaven. The Casserly collection contains rough notes and typescripts on the case of Lecesne and Escoffery, on Kingston generally, and on Edward Jordon.

Other sources in Jamaica include the congregation diaries and other accounts of the Moravian missionaries who served in Jamaica. These records are kept in the Archives at Spanish Town. Also at the Archives is the journal of a brown stipendiary magistrate, T. Witter Jackson.

In England, there are a variety of outstanding collections. At the British Museum, the Ripon papers (Add. MSS 40,862–3) contain private letters between Mulgrave and Goderich, while the Lord Holland papers (Add. MSS 51, 816–9) include correspondence from Sligo and other officials in the island. The West India Committee library, with its collection of minute books covering the meetings of the West India Committee throughout the period under review and its minutes of separate meetings of the West India merchants and of various standing and general committees, is now located at the Institute of Commonwealth Studies, University of London. The Newcastle papers at the University of Nottingham contain some valuable private correspondence from Governor Henry Barkly; this correspondence was read on microfilm.

The holdings of the Methodist Missionary Society are especially useful. The library contains the correspondence of missionaries who were in Jamaica from the 1830s, and their letters often shed light on the free coloreds, many of whom were Methodists. In addition, there are various antislavery pamphlets, material on the problem of relicensing preachers in Jamaica, and files of miscellaneous West Indian newspapers.

At Oxford, the antislavery papers in Rhodes House contain some of the most valuable items for this study. The collection provides a rare opportunity to examine correspondence from free colored politicians. In this case, the letters are to British humanitarians. A careful search among the S22 G61–64 files yielded letters from Robert Russell, Richard Hill, Robert Johnson, Charles Lake, and George William Gordon. These files also contain correspondence from a liberal white member of the Assembly, W. W. Anderson. In addition, they house some letters and papers of Dr. R. R. Madden, who served as a stipendiary magistrate in Jamaica and who had close connections with the British and Foreign Anti-Slavery Society.

The Henry Taylor papers are at the Bodleian Library at Oxford. While far from complete, they are the only known papers of a man who dominated Colonial Office thinking on the West Indies for nearly fifty years. Several of his literary manuscripts and notebooks are also at the Bodleian.

PRINTED MATERIALS

Nearly all of the books, pamphlets, newspapers, and articles listed below were consulted at the Institute of Jamaica, the British Museum, the Public Record Office, the Foreign and Commonwealth Office Library, and the library of the Royal Commonwealth Society. Much of the secondary literature was available at one of three university libraries: Yale, the University of the West Indies (Mona), and the University of London. The Caribbeana Collection at the Boston College Library offered some additional material as did the American Antiquarian Society, Worcester, Massachusetts.

Newspapers and Magazines

Newspapers were among the most valuable sources for this book, partly because three of the major papers during the period were edited by men of color. The newspapers were the only source for the debates in the House of Assembly until 1856, when a local version of *Hansard* was published. Although the Institute of Jamaica contains the most important collection of nineteenth-century Jamaican papers, many have been withdrawn from use and have not as yet been microfilmed. Fortunately, it was possible to examine several papers before they were finally withdrawn.

The institute has an incomplete run of *The Watchman and Jamaica Free Press* (later *The Jamaica Watchman*), which was begun in 1829 and edited by Edward Jordon and Robert Osborn. Its successor, *The Morning Journal*, began publication in 1838; a more complete collection is available in England (see below). Another brown man, John Castello, edited *The Falmouth Post* which is available throughout the postemancipation period, apart from some withdrawn and missing issues. There were other less known colored-run newspapers, most of which have not survived. Nonetheless, it was possible to look at copies of *The Struggler*, 1829, a free colored paper published in Montego Bay, and *The Watchman and Kingston Free Press*, 1859, which was owned and edited by two leading brown politicians, George William Gordon and Robert Johnson. Other papers published on behalf of the emancipated slaves included the *West Indian and Jamaica Gazette*, 1838, whose editor was a stipendiary magistrate, and *The Baptist Herald*, 1841, 1843–1845.

The planter press, however, dominated the island. Those consulted include *The St. Jago Gazette*, 1813–1816; *The Kingston Chronicle*, 1821–1823; *The Cornwall Chronicle*, 1841; *Jamaica Standard and Royal Gazette*, 1841–1846; *The Colonial Standard and Jamaica Despatch*, 1851; *Daily Advertiser (and Lawton's Commercial Gazette)*, 1851–1855, 1857; *The Jamaica Guardian*, 1861, 1863; and *The Jamaica Tribune and Daily Advertiser*, 1862–1863.

Local magazines also proved helpful and attested to the existence of a diverse reading public. The most useful were *The Baptist and Literary Herald*, 1836; *The Jamaica Journal of Arts, Sciences, and Literature*, 1837; *The Jamaica Monthly Magazine*, 1844–1848; *The Jamaica Quarterly Journal of Literature, Science, and Arts*, 1861; and *The West India Quarterly Magazine*, 1861–1862.

The Public Record Office also contains a significant collection of Jamaican newspapers. Its Colonial Office 141 series includes *The Royal Gazette*, 1794, 1813–1838; and 142 contains *The Watchman*, 1830–1836 (incomplete), *The Kingston Chronicle*, 1835–1837, and *The Morning Journal*, 1838–1854.

Parliamentary Materials

Parliamentary Papers [PP], 1825, (74) 25, 133–68, Accounts and Papers: Further Papers, being Return to an Address for copy of any Information respecting the apprehension of two free men of colour named Lecesne and Escoffery.

PP 1826–1827 (127), 18, 433, Accounts and Papers; West India Colonies, Coloured Population, Return of the Coloured Population in each of the West India Colonies.

PP 1830 (582), 21, 621, A Return from all the Slave Colonies belonging to the Crown . . . of the population, distinguished into White, Free Black, and Coloured, and Slaves . . . from 1st January 1825.

PP 1830–1831 (280), 6, 343–47, Estimates and Accounts: An estimate of the sum required to be granted to make good the losses sustained by Louis Celeste Lecesne and John Escoffery, in consequence of their removal from Jamaica in the year 1823. . . .

PP 1831–1832 (365) 47, 321, Jamaica Slave Manumissions, 1825–1830.

PP 1831–1832 (59), 31, 275, Accounts and Papers: Laws Passed for the Relief of the Catholics, Jews, and Free Persons of Colour in Jamaica.

PP 1866 (3683), 30, 12–41, Report of the Jamaica Royal Commission.

Hansard's Parliamentary Debates [Hansard], New Series, 9, 11, 13, 17.

Hansard, 3d Series, 3.

Official and Semi-Official Documents

Acts of the Assembly, passed in the Island of Jamaica from 1681 to 1737, inclusive (London, 1738–1739).

Acts of Assembly, passed in the Island of Jamaica from the year 1681 to the year 1769, inclusive, 2 vols. (Kingston, 1787).

Curran, Hon. C. Ribton. *The Statutes and Laws of the Island of Jamaica, 1681–1888*, rev. ed., 12 vols. (Kingston, 1889).

Journals of the Assembly of Jamaica, 1663–1826, 14 vols. (Jamaica, 1811–1829).

Judah, Abraham and Sinclair, A. C. (comps.). *Debates of the Honourable House of Assembly of Jamaica, Commencing from the Fourth Session of the First General Assembly under the New Constitution*, 13 vols. (Kingston and Spanish Town, 1856–1866).

Laws of Jamaica, 1681–1837, 9 vols. (St. Jago de la Vega, 1837).

Votes of the Assembly of Jamaica, 36 vols. (Jamaica, 1830–1866).

Biographical Aids and Registers

Andrade, Jacob A.P.M. *A Record of the Jews in Jamaica from the English Conquest to the Present Time* (Kingston, The Jamaica Times Ltd., 1941).

Birch, Arthur N. and Robinson, William (comps.). *The Colonial Office List for 1865* (London, 1865).

Cundall, Frank. *Biographical Annals of Jamaica* (Kingston, Institute of Jamaica, 1904).

Dallas, James. *The History of the Family of Dallas* (Edinburgh, T. and A. Constable, Ltd., 1921).

Feurtado, W. A. *Official and Other Personages of Jamaica from 1655 to 1790* (Kingston, 1896).

Ives, R. H. *Jamaica Directory* (Kingston, 1878).

Jamaica Almanac (Kingston, 1840, 1845).

Lawrence-Archer, James H. *Monumental Inscriptions of the British West Indies* (London, 1875).

Oliver, Vere Langford. *Caribbeana: Being Miscellaneous Papers Relating to the History, Genealogy, Topography, and Antiquities of the British West Indies*, 6 vols. (London, Mitchell Hughes & Clarke, 1910).

Robertson, Glory (comp.). *Members of the Assembly of Jamaica from the General Election of 1830 to the Final Session January 1866* (mimeo, Kingston, Institute of Jamaica, 1965).

Roby, John. *Members of the Assembly of Jamaica from the Institution of That Branch of the Legislature to the Present Time* (Montego Bay, 1831).

Stephen, Sir Leslie and Lee, Sir Sydney (eds.). *The Dictionary of National Biography* (London, Oxford University Press, 1959–1960).

Wright, Philip (comp.). *Monumental Inscriptions of Jamaica* (London, Society of Genealogists, 1966).

Contemporary Works

Abbott, Thomas F. *Narrative of Certain Events Connected with the Late Disturbances in Jamaica and the Charges Preferred Against the Baptist Missionaries in that Island* (London, 1832).

Adams, John Quincy. *Letter Read on the Occasion of the West India Emancipation in Bangor, Maine, May 27, 1843* (Boston, 1843).

Anderson, W. W. *A Description and History of the Island of Jamaica* (Kingston, 1851).

Baird, Robert. *Impressions and Experiences of the West Indies and North America in 1849*, 2 vols. (London, 1850).

Barclay, Alexander. *A Practical View of the Present State of Slavery in the West Indies* (London, 1828).

―――. *Remarks on Emigration to Jamaica: Addressed to the Coloured Class of the United States* (London, 1840).

[Barrett, Richard]. *A Reply to the Speech of Dr. Lushington in the House of Commons on the 12th June, 1827 on the Condition of the Free-Coloured People of Jamaica* (London, 1828).

Beckford, William. *A Descriptive Account of the Island of Jamaica*, 2 vols. (London, 1790).

Belisario, I. M. *Sketches of Character in Illustration of the Habits, Occupation and Costume of the Negro Population in the Island of Jamaica* (Kingston, 1837).

Bickell, Reverend R. *The West Indies as They Are; or a Real Picture of Slavery: but More Particularly As It Exists in the Island of Jamaica* (London, 1825).

Bigelow, John. *Jamaica in 1850: or, the Effects of Sixteen Years of Freedom on a Slave Colony* (New York, 1851).

Bleby, Henry. *Death Struggles of Slavery: Being a Narrative of Facts and Incidents which Occurred in a British Colony during the Two Years Immediately Preceding Negro Emancipation* (London, 1853).

——. *The Reign of Terror: A Narrative of Facts Concerning Ex-Governor Eyre, George William Gordon and the Jamaica Atrocities* (London, 1868).

——. *Scenes in the Caribbean Sea: Being Sketches from a Missionary's Note-Book* (London, 1854).

Bridges, Reverend George W. *The Annals of Jamaica*, 2 vols. (London, 1828).

——. *Emancipation Unmask'd in a letter to the Right Honourable the Earl of Aberdeen* (London, 1835).

Brown, Reverend J. T. and Underhill, E. B. *Emancipation in the West Indies* (London, 1861).

Buchner, J. H. *The Moravians in Jamaica* (London, 1854).

Burchell, William F. *Memoir of Thomas Burchell* (London, 1849).

Burge, William. *A Letter to the Right Honorable Sir George Murray, G.C.B., His Majesty's Principal Secretary of State for the Colonies, Relative to the Deportation of Lecesne and Escoffery from Jamaica* (London, 1829).

——. *A Reply to the Letter by the Marquis of Sligo to the Marquis of Normanby, Relative to the Present State of Jamaica* (London, 1839).

——. *The Speech of W. Burge, Esq., Q.C., at the Bar of the House of Commons against the Bill entitled "An Act to make temporary provision for the Government of Jamaica," 22 April 1839* (London, 1839).

Buxton, Charles. *Slavery and Freedom in the British West Indies* (London, 1860).

——. (ed.). *Memoirs of Sir Thomas Fowell Buxton, with an Inquiry into the Results of Emancipation* (London, 1860).

Caldecott, A. *The Church in the West Indies* (London, 1898).

Campbell, Mrs. [née Bourne]. *The British West India Colonies in connection with Slavery, Emancipation, etc. By a Resident in the West Indies for Thirteen Years* (London, 1853).

——. *Suggestions relative to the Improvement of The British West India Colonies . . .* (London, 1853).

Candler, John. *Extracts from the Journal of John Candler Whilst Travelling in Jamaica* (London, 1840).

[Carlile, Edward]. *Thirty-Eight Years' Mission Life in Jamaica—A Brief Sketch of The Rev. Warrand Carlile* (London, 1884).

[Carlyle, Thomas]. "Occasional Discourse on the Negro Question," *Fraser's Magazine* 40 (December 1849): 670–79.

Case of the British West Indies Stated by the West India Association of Glasgow (Glasgow, 1852).

Castello, John. *"Tracts for the Times" or Voluntaryism Exposed* (Falmouth, Jamaica, 1844).

Clark, John. *A Brief Account of the Settlements of the Emancipated Peasantry* (Birmingham, 1852).

Clarke, John. *Memoir of Richard Merrick, Missionary in Jamaica* (London, 1850).

——. *Memorials of Baptist Missionaries in Jamaica* (London, 1869).

Clarkson, Thomas. *Not a Labourer Wanted for Jamaica* (London, 1842).

Coleridge, Henry Nelson. *Six Months in the West Indies in 1825* (London, 1826).

Cust, Sir Edward. *Reflections on West India Affairs, After a Recent Visit to the Colonies. Addressed to the Consideration of the Colonial Office* (London, 1839).

Dallas, R. C. *The History of the Maroons*, 2 vols. (London, 1803).

D'Aubree, Paul. *Colonists and Manufacturers in the West Indies* (London, 1844).

Davy, John. *The West Indies, Before and Since Emancipation* (London, 1854).

Day, Charles William. *Five Years' Residence in the West Indies*, 2 vols. (London, 1852).

De la Beche, H. T. *Notes on the Present Condition of the Negroes in Jamaica* (London, 1825).

Dowden, Edward (ed.). *Correspondence of Henry Taylor* (London, 1888).

Duncan, Henry. *Presbyter's Letters on the West India Question* (London, 1830).

Duncan, Reverend Peter. *A Narrative of the Wesleyan Mission to Jamaica; with Occasional Remarks on the State of Society in that Colony* (London, 1849).

Duperly, Adolph. *Daguerrian Excursions in Jamaica* (Paris, 1844).

Edwards, Bryan. *The History, Civil and Commercial, of the British Colonies in the West Indies*, 2 vols. (London, 1793).

———. *The Proceedings of the Governor and Assembly of Jamaica in Regard to the Maroon Negroes* (London, 1796).

Eight Practical Treatises on the Cultivation of the Sugar Cane—written in consequence of His Excellency the Earl of Elgin's offer of a Prize of One Hundred Pounds (Spanish Town, 1843).

"The Elections—The Franchise," *The Jamaica Monthly Magazine* 1 (October 1844): 481–92.

Feurtado, W. A. *A Forty-Five Years' Reminiscence of the Characteristics and Characters of Spanish Town* (Kingston, 1890).

The Florence Hall Controversy and the Falmouth Riots (Falmouth, Jamaica, 1859).

Foster, H. B. (comp.). *Memoirs of Mrs. Eliza Ann Foster* (London, 1844).

Foulks, Theodore. *Eighteen Months in Jamaica, with Recollections of the Late Rebellion* (London, 1833).

Gardner, William James. *A History of Jamaica from Its Discovery by Christopher Columbus to the Year 1872* (London, 1873).

Grey, Henry George, 3d Earl. *The Colonial Policy of Lord John Russell's Administration*, 2 vols. (London, 1853).

Gurney, Joseph John. *A Winter in the West Indies* (London, 1840).

Hakewill, James. *A Picturesque Tour of the Island of Jamaica* (London, 1825).

Harcourt, Henry. *The Adventures of a Sugar Plantation* (London, 1836).

Harvey, Thomas and Brewin, William. *Jamaica in 1866. A Narrative of a Tour Through the Island with Remarks on Its Social, Educational and Industrial Condition* (London, 1867).

Hill, Richard. *Lights and Shadows of Jamaica History; Being Three Lectures Delivered in Aid of the Mission Schools of the Colony* (Kingston, 1859).

———. *A Week at Port Royal* (Montego Bay, 1855).

Hincks, Francis. *The Results of Negro Emancipation* (London, 1859).

Hinton, John Howard. *Memoir of William Knibb* (London, 1847).

History and Adventures of OBI or Three Fingered Jack (London, n.d.).

Hodgson, Captain Studholme. *Truths from the West Indies* (London, 1838).

Horsford, Reverend John. *A Voice from the West Indies: Being a Review of the Character and Results of Missionary Efforts in the British and Other Colonies in the Charibbean Sea* (London, 1856).

Hovey, Sylvester. *Letters from the West Indies* (New York, 1838).

Innes, John. *Letter to the Lord Glenelg on Negro Apprenticeship* (London, 1838).

———. *Thoughts on the Present State of the British West India Colonies* (London, 1840).

Jamaica and Its Governor during the Last Six Years (London, 1871).

Jamaica and the Recent Insurrection There, by a Late Resident in the Island [1866].

Jelly, Thomas. *A Brief Inquiry into the Condition of Jamaica* (London, 1847).

Kaye, John William. *Selections from the Papers of Lord Metcalfe* (London, 1847).

Kelly, James. *Voyage to Jamaica and Seventeen Years' Residence in That Island* (Belfast, 1838).

King, Reverend David. *The State and Prospects of Jamaica* (London, 1850).

[Knibb, William]. *Facts and Documents Connected with the Late Insurrection in Jamaica* (London, 1832).

———. *Speech of the Rev. William Knibb Before the Baptist Missionary Society in Exeter Hall, April 28, 1842* (London, 1842).

Knibb, Reverend William and Borthwick, P. *Colonial Slavery, Defense of the Baptist Missionaries from the Charge of Inciting the Late Rebellion in Jamaica in a Discussion between Knibb and Borthwick* [in Bath, December 15, 1832] (London, 1833).

Leslie, Charles. *A New and Exact Account of Jamaica* (Edinburgh, 1739).

Levien, Sidney. *A Chronicle of the Rebellion in Jamaica* (n.p., n.d.).

Lewis, Matthew Gregory. *Journal of a West India Proprietor, 1815–17*, edited with an introduction by Mona Wilson (London, 1929).

Lindo, Abraham. *Dr. Underhill's Testimony on the Wrongs of the Negro in Jamaica Examined in a Letter to the Editor of The Times* (London, 1866).

Lloyd, William. *Letters from the West Indies during a Visit in the Autumn of MDCCCXXXVI and the Spring of MDCCCXXXVII* (London, 1838).

Logan, James. *Notes of a Journey through Canada, the United States of America, and the West Indies* (Edinburgh, 1838).

Long, Edward. *The History of Jamaica*, 3 vols. (London, 1774).

[Luckock, Benjamin]. *Jamaica: Enslaved and Free* (London, [1846]).

Ludlow, J. M. *A Quarter Century of Jamaica Legislation* (London, 1866).

Madden, Richard Robert. *Twelve Months' Residence in the West Indies During the Transition from Slavery to Apprenticeship*, 2 vols. (London, 1835).

Madden, Thomas More (ed.). *The Memoirs of Richard Robert Madden* (London, 1891).

Marindin, George Eden (ed.). *Letters of Frederick, Lord Blachford* (London, 1896).

Marly; or, The Life of a Planter in Jamaica, 2d edition (Glasgow, 1828).

Marsden, Peter. *An Account of the Island of Jamaica* (Newcastle, 1788).

Martin, R. Montgomery. *The British Colonies: Their History, Extent, Condition, and Resources*, 4 vols. (London, 1854).

Maxwell, James. *Remarks on Present State of Jamaica, with a Proposal of Measures for the Resuscitation of Our West Indian Colonies* (London, 1848).

A Memorial from the Association of Jamaica Proprietors to the Right Hon. the Viscount Melbourne and the Marquis of Normanby (London, 1839).

Merivale, Herman. *Lectures on Colonization and Colonies* (London, 1861).

Middleditch, Reverend T. *The Youthful Female Missionary: A Memoir of Mary Ann*

Hutchins (London, 1840).

Moister, Reverend William. *The West Indies, Enslaved and Free* (London, 1883).

Morris, M. O'Connor. *Memini; or, A Mingled Yarn* (London, 1892).

Morson, Henry. *The Present Condition of the British West Indies; Their Wants and the Remedy for These* (London, 1841).

Mozley, Geraldine (ed.). *Letters to Jane from Jamaica, 1788–1796* (London, 1938).

Noel, Baptist Wriothesley. *The Case of George William Gordon, Esq., of Jamaica* (London, 1866).

Nugent, Maria. *Lady Nugent's Journal of Her Residence in Jamaica from 1801 to 1805*, edited by Philip Wright (Kingston, 1966).

Oughton, Samuel. *Jamaica: Why It Is Poor and How It May Become Rich* (Kingston, 1866).

Phillippo, James M. *Jamaica: Its Past and Present State* (London, 1843).

Price, George. *Jamaica and the Colonial Office* (London, 1866).

Pringle, Hall. *The Fall of the Sugar Planters of Jamaica* (London, 1869).

Pringle, J. W. *Remarks on the State and Prospects of the West Indian Colonies* (London, 1839).

Renny, Robert. *An History of Jamaica* (London, 1807).

Report of the Standing Committee of the Chamber of Commerce, Jamaica, upon the Present Condition of that Colony . . . (London, 1847).

Roundell, Charles Savile. *England and Her Subject Races with Special Reference to Jamaica* (London, 1866).

Samuel, Reverend Peter. *The Wesleyan-Methodist Missions in Jamaica and Honduras Delineated* (London, 1850).

Scotland, George. *A Statement of Facts Relating to the Case of George Scotland, Esq., late Collecting Constable of the Parish of Metcalfe* (Spanish Town, 1862).

Scott, Michael. *Tom Cringle's Log* (Paris, 1836).

[Senior, Bernard Martin]. *Jamaica, as It Was, as It Is, and as It May Be . . .* (London, 1835).

Sewell, William G. *The Ordeal of Free Labor in the British West Indies* (New York, 1861).

Shaw, John. *A Ramble Through the United States, Canada, and the West Indies* (London, 1856).

Shore, Joseph and Stewart, John (eds.). *In Old St. James, A Book of Parish Chronicles* (Kingston, 1911).

[Sinclair, Augustus Constantine]. *The Political Life of the Hon. Charles Hamilton Jackson, A Sketch of the Political History of Jamaica for the Past Thirty Years* (Kingston, n.d., circa 1878).

Sligo, the Marquis of [Browne, Peter Howe]. *A Letter to the Marquess of Normanby Relative to the Present State of Jamaica* (London, 1839).

Solomon, George. *Population and Prosperity; or, Free vs. Slave Production* (Kingston, 1859).

Southey, Thomas. *Chronological History of the West Indies*, 3 vols. (London, 1827).

Spedding, James. *Reviews and Discussions Literary, Political, and Historical not relating to Bacon* (London, 1879).

BIBLIOGRAPHY   215

Statement of the Proceedings of the People of Colour of Jamaica in an Intended Appeal to the House of Assembly of 1823, for the Removal of Their Political Disabilities (1823).

Stephen, Sir George. *Anti-Slavery Recollections in a Series of Letters Addressed to Mrs. Beecher Stowe* (London, 1854).

Sterne, Henry. *A Statement of Facts* . . . (London, 1837).

[Stewart, J.] *An Account of Jamaica and Its Inhabitants* (London, 1808).

Stewart, John. *A View of the Past and Present State of the Island of Jamaica* (Edinburgh, 1823).

Sturge, Joseph and Harvey, Thomas. *The West Indies in 1837* (London, 1838).

Taylor, Henry. *Autobiography of Henry Taylor, 1800–1875*, 2 vols. (London, 1885).

——. *The Statesman*, with an introd. by Harold J. Laski (London, 1927).

Thome, James A. and Kimball, Horace J. *Emancipation in the West Indies* (New York, 1838).

Trollope, Anthony. *The West Indies and the Spanish Main*, 2d ed. (London, 1860).

Turnbull, David (ed.). *The Jamaica Movement for Promoting the Enforcement of the Slave-Trade Treaties and the Suppression of the Slave Trade* . . . (London, 1850).

Underhill, Edward Bean. *A Letter Addressed to the Rt. Honourable E. Cardwell, with Illustrative Documents on the Condition of Jamaica and an Explanatory Statement* (London, 1865).

——. *The West Indies: Their Social and Religious Condition* (London, 1862).

Waddell, Reverend Hope Masterton. *Twenty-Nine Years in the West Indies and Central Africa: Review of Missionary Work and Adventure, 1829–1858* (London, 1863).

Walrond, Theodore (ed.). *Letters and Journals of James, Eighth Earl of Elgin* (London, 1872).

Whiteley, Henry. *Three Months in Jamaica in 1832: Comprising a Residence of Seven Weeks on a Sugar Plantation* (London, 1833).

Williams, Cynric R. *A Tour Through the Island of Jamaica from the Western to the Eastern End in the Year 1823* (London, 1826).

Williams, James. *Narrative of Events Since the 1st of August, 1834. By an Apprenticed Labourer in Jamaica* (London, 1837).

Secondary Sources

Anstey, Roger. *The Atlantic Slave Trade and British Abolition, 1760–1810* (London, The Macmillan Press Ltd., 1975).

Bennett, J. Harry, Jr. *Bondsmen and Bishops: Slavery and Apprenticeship on the Codrington Plantations of Barbados, 1710–1838* (Berkeley, Calif., University of California Press, 1958).

Berlin, Ira. *Slaves Without Masters: The Free Negro in the Antebellum South* (New York, Pantheon Books, 1974).

Boxer, C. R. *Race Relations in the Portuguese Colonial Empire, 1415–1825* (Oxford, Clarendon Press, 1965).

Brathwaite, Edward. *The Development of Creole Society in Jamaica, 1770–1820* (Oxford, Clarendon Press, 1971).

Bridenbaugh, Carl and Roberta. *No Peace Beyond the Line: The English in the Caribbean, 1624–1690* (New York, Oxford University Press, 1972).

Buckley, Roger Norman. *Slaves in Red Coats: The British West Indian Regiments, 1795–1815* (New Haven, Conn., Yale University Press, 1979).

Burn, W. L. *The British West Indies* (London, Hutchinson, 1951).

————. *Emancipation and Apprenticeship in the British West Indies* (London, Jonathan Cape, 1937).

Burroughs, Peter. *The Canadian Crisis and British Colonial Policy, 1828–1841* (London, Edward Arnold, 1972).

Campbell, Mavis. *The Dynamics of Change in a Slave Society: A Sociopolitical History of the Free Coloreds of Jamaica, 1800–1865* (Rutherford, N.J., Fairleigh Dickinson University Press, 1976).

Cell, John W. *British Colonial Administration in the Mid-Nineteenth Century: The Policy-Making Process* (New Haven, Conn., Yale University Press, 1970).

Chambers, William N. *Political Parties in a New Nation: The American Experience, 1776–1809* (New York, Oxford University Press, 1963).

Clarke, Colin G. *Kingston, Jamaica: Urban Development and Social Change, 1692–1962* (Berkeley, Calif., University of California Press, 1975).

Clarke, Edith. *My Mother Who Fathered Me: A Study of the Family in Three Selected Communities in Jamaica* (London, George Allen and Unwin, 1957).

Cohen, David W. and Greene, Jack P. (eds.). *Neither Slave Nor Free: The Freedmen of African Descent in the Slave Societies of the New World* (Baltimore, The Johns Hopkins University Press, 1972).

Coupland, Sir Reginald. *The British Anti-Slavery Movement*, with an introd. by J. D. Fage, reprinted (London, Frank Cass and Co., 1964).

Craton, Michael. *Searching for the Invisible Man: Slaves and Plantation Life in Jamaica* (Cambridge, Mass., Harvard University Press, 1978).

Craton, Michael, and Walvin, James. *A Jamaican Plantation: The History of Worthy Park, 1670–1970* (London, W. H. Allen, 1970).

Cundall, Frank. *Historic Jamaica* (London, West India Committee, 1915).

Curtin, Philip D. *The Image of Africa: British Ideas and Action, 1780–1850* (Madison, Wis., The University of Wisconsin Press, 1964).

————. *Two Jamaicas: The Role of Ideas in a Tropical Colony, 1830–1865* (Cambridge, Mass., Harvard University Press, 1955).

Davis, David Brion. *The Problem of Slavery in Western Culture* (Ithaca, N.Y., Cornell University Press, 1966).

Deerr, Noel. *The History of Sugar*, 2 vols. (London, Chapman and Hall, Ltd., 1949).

Degler, Carl N. *Neither Black Nor White: Slavery and Race Relations in Brazil and the United States* (New York, The Macmillan Co., 1971).

Dickie-Clark, H. F. *The Marginal Situation: A Sociological Study of a Coloured Group* (London, Routledge & Kegan Paul, 1966).

Drescher, Seymour. *Econocide: British Slavery in the Era of Abolition* (Pittsburgh, University of Pittsburgh Press, 1977).

Dunn, Richard S. *Sugar and Slaves: The Rise of the Planter Class in the English West Indies, 1624–1713* (Chapel Hill, N.C., The University of North Carolina Press, 1972).

Dutton, Geoffrey. *The Hero as Murderer: The Life of Edward John Eyre* (London, Collins, 1967).

Eisner, Gisela. *Jamaica, 1830–1930: A Study in Economic Growth* (Manchester, Manchester University Press, 1961).

Goveia, Elsa. *Slave Society in the British Leeward Islands at the End of the Eighteenth Century* (New Haven, Conn., Yale University Press, 1965).

———. *A Study on the Historiography of the British West Indies to the End of the Nineteenth Century* (Mexico, Instituto Panamericano de Geografiá e Historia, 1956).

Green, William A. *British Slave Emancipation: The Sugar Colonies and the Great Experiment, 1830–1865* (Oxford, Clarendon Press, 1976).

Hall, Douglas. *A Brief History of the West India Committee* (Barbados, Caribbean Universities Press, 1971).

———. *Free Jamaica, 1838–1865: An Economic History* (New Haven, Conn., Yale University Press, 1959).

Hall, Henry. *The Colonial Office, A History* (London, Longmans, Green & Co., 1937).

Handler, Jerome S. *The Unappropriated People: Freedmen in the Slave Society of Barbados* (Baltimore, The Johns Hopkins University Press, 1974).

Hart, Ansell. *The Life of George William Gordon* (Kingston, Institute of Jamaica, 1972).

Henriques, Fernando. *Family and Colour in Jamaica* (London, Eyre and Spottiswood, 1953).

Higman, B. W. *Slave Population and Economy in Jamaica, 1807–1834* (Cambridge, Cambridge University Press, 1976).

Hofstadter, Richard. *The Idea of a Party System: The Rise of Legitimate Opposition in the United States, 1780–1840* (Berkeley, Calif., University of California Press, 1970).

Jacobs, H. P. *Sixty Years of Change, 1806–1866: Progress and Reaction in Kingston and the Countryside* (Institute of Jamaica, 1973).

James, C.L.R. *The Black Jacobins*, 2d ed. (New York, Alfred A. Knopf, Inc., 1963).

Jordan, Winthrop D. *White Over Black: American Attitudes Toward the Negro, 1550–1812* (Chapel Hill, N.C., The University of North Carolina Press, 1968).

Klingberg, Frank J. *The Anti-Slavery Movement in England: A Study in English Humanitarianism* (New Haven, Conn., Yale University Press, 1926).

Kloosterboer, W. *Involuntary Labour Since the Abolition of Slavery: A Survey of Compulsory Labour Throughout the World* (Leiden, E. J. Brill, 1960).

Knaplund, Paul. *James Stephen and the British Colonial System* (Madison, Wis., University of Wisconsin Press, 1953).

Knutsford, Viscountess [Holland, M. J.]. *Life and Letters of Zachary Macaulay* (London, Edward Arnold, 1900).

Leyburn, James. *The Haitian People*, rev. ed. (New Haven, Conn., Yale University Press, 1966).

Livingstone, W. P. *Black Jamaica: A Study in Evolution* (London, Sampson, Low, Marston & Co., 1899).

Long, Anton V. *Jamaica and the New Order, 1822–47* (Kingston, Institute of Social and Economic Research, 1956).

Lowenthal, David. *West Indian Societies* (New York, Oxford University Press, 1972).

McCulloch, Samuel Clyde (ed.). *British Humanitarianism: Essays Honoring Frank L. Klingberg* (Philadelphia, The Church Historical Society, 1950).

Manning, Helen Taft. *British Colonial Government After the American Revolution* (New Haven, Conn., Yale University Press, 1933).

Marsala, Vincent John. *Sir John Peter Grant, Governor of Jamaica, 1866–1874* (Institute of Jamaica, 1972).

Mason, Philip. *Patterns of Dominance* (London, Oxford University Press, 1970).

Mathieson, William Law. *The Sugar Colonies and Governor Eyre, 1849–1866* (London, Green & Co., 1936).

Mellor, George R. *British Imperial Trusteeship, 1783–1850* (London, Faber & Faber, 1951).

Metcalfe, George. *Royal Government and Political Conflict in Jamaica, 1729–1783* (London, Longmans, Green & Co., 1965).

Mintz, Sidney. *Caribbean Transformations* (Chicago, Aldine Publishing Co., 1974).

Morison, J. L. *The Eighth Earl of Elgin: A Chapter in Nineteenth Century Imperial History* (London, Hodder & Stoughton, 1928).

Morrell, W. P. *British Colonial Policy in the Age of Peel and Russell* (Oxford, Clarendon Press, 1930).

———. *British Colonial Policy in the Mid-Victorian Age* (Oxford, Clarendon Press, 1969).

Murray, D. J. *The West Indies and the Development of Colonial Government, 1801–1834* (Oxford, Clarendon Press, 1965).

Olivier, Margaret (ed.). *Sydney Olivier, Letters and Selected Writings* (London, George Allen & Unwin, 1948).

Olivier, Lord [Haldane, Sydney]. *Jamaica the Blessed Island* (London, Faber & Faber, 1936).

———. *The Myth of Governor Eyre* (London, The Hogarth Press, 1933).

Pares, Richard. *A West India Fortune* (London, Longmans, Green & Co., 1950).

Parry, J. H., and Sherlock, Philip M. *A Short History of the West Indies* (London, The Macmillan Press Ltd., 1956).

Patterson, Orlando. *The Sociology of Slavery: An Analysis of the Origins, Development and Structure of Negro Slave Society in Jamaica* (London, MacGibbon & Kee, 1967).

Penson, Lillian. *The Colonial Agents of the British West Indies* (London, University of London Press, 1924).

Pitman, F. W. *The Development of the British West Indies, 1700–1763* (New Haven, Conn., Yale University Press, 1917).

Ragatz, Lowell J. *The Fall of the Planter Class in the British Caribbean, 1763–1833: A Study in Social and Economic History* (New York, Century Co., 1928).

Roberts, George W. *The Population of Jamaica* (Cambridge, Cambridge University Press, 1957).

Roberts, W. Adolphe. *Six Great Jamaicans* (Kingston, The Pioneer Press, 1952).

Robinson, Carey. *The Fighting Maroons of Jamaica* ([London], William Collins and Sangster (Jamaica) Ltd., 1969).

Rose, J. Holland, et al. *The Cambridge History of the British Empire*, 8 vols. (Cambridge, Cambridge University Press, 1940), Vol. 2: *The Growth of the New Empire, 1783–1870.*

Semmel, Bernard. *The Governor Eyre Controversy* (London, MacGibbon & Kee, 1962).

Sibley, Joel H. *The Shrine of Party: Congressional Voting Behavior, 1841–1852* (Pittsburgh, University of Pittsburgh Press, 1967).

Smith, M. G. *The Plural Society in the British West Indies* (Berkeley, University of California Press, 1965).

Spurdle, F. G. *Early West Indian Government* (Palmerston North, New Zealand, Frederick G. Spurdle [1962]).

Swinfen, D. B. *Imperial Control of Colonial Legislation, 1813–1865* (Oxford, Clarendon Press, 1970).

Taylor, S.A.G. *The Western Design* (Kingston, Institute of Jamaica, 1965).

Temperley, Howard. *British Antislavery, 1833–1870* (London, Longman, 1972).

Thompson, Edward. *The Life of Charles, Lord Metcalfe* (London, Faber & Faber, 1938).

Vincent, J. R. *Pollbooks: How Victorians Voted* (Cambridge, Cambridge University Press, 1967).

Waddell, D.A.G. *The West Indies and the Guianas* (Englewood Cliffs, N.J., Prentice-Hall, Inc., 1967).

Weber, Max. *From Max Weber*, edited by H. H. Gerth and C. Wright Mills (London, Routledge & Kegan Paul, 1970).

Williams, Eric. *Capitalism and Slavery*, rev. ed. (London, André Deutsch, 1964).

Winks, Robin W. *The Blacks in Canada, A History* (New Haven, Conn., Yale University Press, 1971).

Wood, Donald. *Trinidad in Transition: The Years After Slavery* (London, Oxford University Press, 1968).

Wright, Philip. *Knibb 'the Notorious' Slaves' Missionary, 1803–1845* (London, Sidgwick & Jackson, 1973).

Wrong, Hume. *Government of the West Indies* (Oxford, Clarendon Press, 1923).

Young, D. M. *The Colonial Office in the Early Nineteenth Century* (London, Longmans, 1961).

Articles

Aydelotte, William O. "Voting Patterns in the British House of Commons in the 1840's," *Comparative Studies in Society and History* 5 (January 1963): 134–66.

Beaglehole, J. C. "The Colonial Office, 1782–1854," *Historical Studies, Australia and New Zealand* 1 (1941): 170–89.

Braithwaite, Lloyd. "Social Stratification in Trinidad: A Preliminary Analysis," *Social and Economic Studies* 2 & 3 (1954): 5–175.

Brathwaite, Edward. "Jamaican Slave Society, A Review," *Race* 11 (1968): 331–42.

Campbell, Carl. "Social and Economic Obstacles to the Development of Popular Education in Post-Emancipation Jamaica, 1834–1865," *The Journal of Caribbean History* 1 (November 1970): 57–88.

Cundall, Frank. "Richard Hill," *The Journal of Negro History* 5 (1920): 37–44.

Davis, David B. "James Cropper and the British Anti-Slavery Movement, 1823–1833," *The Journal of Negro History* 46 (July 1961): 154–73.

Furley, Oliver. "Moravian Missionaries and Slaves in the West Indies," *Caribbean Studies* 5 (July 1965): 3–17.

Furness, A. E. "The Maroon War of 1795," *Jamaican Historical Review* 5 (1965): 30–49.

Gocking, C. V. "Early Constitutional History of Jamaica," *Caribbean Quarterly* 6 (May 1960): 114–33.

Goveia, Elsa. "The West Indian Slave Laws of the Eighteenth Century," *Revista de Ciencias Sociales* 4 (1960): 75–105.

Hall, Douglas. "Absentee-Proprietorship in the British West Indies," *Jamaican Historical Review* 4 (1964): 15–35.

———. "The Apprenticeship Period in Jamaica, 1834–1838," *Caribbean Quarterly* 3 (December 1953): 142–66.

———. "The Flight from the Estates Reconsidered: The British West Indies, 1838–1842," *The Journal of Caribbean History* 10 and 11 (1978): 7–24.

———. "Incalculability as a Feature of Sugar Production During the Eighteenth Century," *Social and Economic Studies* 10 (September 1961): 340–52.

———. "Sir Charles Metcalfe," *Caribbean Quarterly* 3 (1953): 90–100.

———. "Slaves and Slavery in the British West Indies," *Social and Economic Studies* 11 (1962): 305–18.

———. "The Social and Economic Background to Sugar in Slave Days (with Special Reference to Jamaica)," *Caribbean Historical Review* 3–4 (December 1954): 149–69.

Heuman, Gad J. "Robert Osborn: Brown Power Leader in Nineteenth Century Jamaica," *Jamaica Journal* 11 (August 1977): 76–81.

Higham, C.S.S. "Sir Henry Taylor and the Establishment of Crown Colony Government in the West Indies," *Scottish Historical Review* 23 (January 1926): 92–97.

Higman, B. W. "The West India 'Interest' in Parliament, 1807–33," *Historical Studies, Australia and New Zealand* 13 (October 1967): 1–19.

Hurwitz, Samuel J. and Hurwitz, Edith. "The New World Sets an Example for the Old: The Jews of Jamaica and Political Rights, 1661–1831," *American Jewish Historical Quarterly* 55 (September 1965): 37–56.

———. "A Token of Freedom: Private Bill Legislation for Free Negroes in Eighteenth-Century Jamaica," *The William and Mary Quarterly* 24 (July 1967): 423–31.

Jones, Wilbur D. "Lord Mulgrave's Administration in Jamaica, 1832–33," *The Journal of Negro History* 48 (January 1963): 44–56.

Jordan, Winthrop D. "American Chiaroscuro: The Status and Definition of Mulattoes in the British Colonies," *The William and Mary Quarterly* 19 (April 1962): 183–200.

Klingberg, F. J. "The Lady Mico Charity Schools in the British West Indies, 1835–42," *The Journal of Negro History* 24 (July 1939): 291–344.

Knaplund, Paul. "Sir James Stephen: The Friend of the Negroes," *The Journal of Negro History* 35 (October 1950): 368–407.

Knox, Graham. "British Colonial Policy and the Problems of Establishing a Free Society in Jamaica, 1838–1865," *Caribbean Studies* 2 (January 1963): 3–13.

Manning, Helen Taft. "Who Ran the British Empire—1830–1850?" *Journal of British Studies* 5 (1965): 88–121.

Mintz, Sidney, W. "Historical Sociology of the Jamaican Church-Founded Free Village System," *West-Indische Gids* 38 (September 1958): 46–70.

Mintz, Sidney W. and Hall, Douglas. "The Origins of the Jamaican Internal Marketing System," in Sidney W. Mintz (comp.), *Papers in Caribbean Anthropology* 57 (New Haven, Conn., 1960): 3–26.

Nossiter, T. J. "Recent Work on English Elections, 1832–1935," *Political Studies* 18 (1970): 525–28.

——. "Voting Behaviour 1832–1872," *Political Studies* 18 (1970): 380–89.

Paget, Hugh. "The Free Village System in Jamaica," *Jamaican Historical Review* 1 (June 1945): 31–48.

Penson, Lillian M. "The London West India Interest in the 18th Century," *English Historical Review* 36 (1921): 373–92.

Phillips, Ulrich B. "A Jamaica Slave Plantation," *American Historical Review* 19 (April 1914): 543–58.

Pitman, F. W. "Slavery on British West India Plantations in the Eighteenth Century," *The Journal of Negro History* 11 (October 1926): 584–668.

Ragatz, Lowell J. "Absentee Landlordism in the British Caribbean, 1750–1833," *Agricultural History* 5 (January 1931): 7–24.

Reckord, Mary. "The Jamaica Slave Rebellion of 1831," *Past and Present* 40 (July 1968): 108–25.

Sheridan Richard B. "The West India Sugar Crisis and British Slave Emancipation, 1830–1833," *Journal of Economic History* 21 (December 1961): 539–51.

Sherlock, Philip. "Jamaica in 1858," *Jamaican Historical Review* 1 (June 1945): 83–91.

Sio, Arnold A. "Race, Colour and Miscegenation: The Free Coloured of Jamaica and Barbados," *Caribbean Studies* 16 (April 1976): 5–21.

Sires, Ronald Vernon. "Constitutional Change in Jamaica, 1834–1860," *Journal of Comparative Legislation and International Law* 22 (November 1940): 178–90.

——. "Governmental Crisis in Jamaica, 1860–1866," *Jamaican Historical Review* 2 (December 1953): 1–26.

——. "Negro Labor in Jamaica in the Years Following Emancipation," *The Journal of Negro History* 25 (October 1940): 484–97.

——. "Sir Barkly and the Labor Problem in Jamaica," *The Journal of Negro History* 25 (April 1940): 216–35.

Smith, M. G. "Some Aspects of Social Structure in the British Caribbean About 1820," *Social and Economic Studies* 1 (August 1953): 55–80.

Speck, W. A., and Gray, W. A. "Computer Analysis of Poll Books: An Initial Report," *Bulletin of the Institute of Historical Research* 43 (May 1970): 105–12.

Wesley, Charles H. "The Emancipation of the Free Colored Population in the British

Empire," *The Journal of Negro History* 19 (April 1934): 137–70.
Williams, E. T. "The Colonial Office in the Thirties," *Historical Studies, Australia and New Zealand* 2 (April 1942): 141–60.

Theses and Unpublished Works

Bailey, Wilma R. "Power Relations in Pre-Emancipation Kingston," Paper presented to the Eighth Conference of Caribbean Historians (1976).
Cox, Edward Locksley. "The Shadow of Freedom: Freedmen in the Slave Societies of Grenada and St. Kitts, 1763–1833" (unpublished Ph.D. thesis, The Johns Hopkins University, 1977).
Duncker, Sheila. "The Free Coloured and Their Fight for Civil Rights in Jamaica, 1800–1830" (unpublished M.A. thesis, University of London, 1960).
Eltis, David. "Dr. Stephen Lushington: Liberal Reformer and Radical Advocate of Negro Rights" (unpublished M.A. thesis, University of Alberta, 1969).
Gocking, C. V. "Constitutional Problems in Jamaica, 1850–1866" (unpublished D. Phil. thesis, Oxford University, 1955).
Hall, Douglas. "Fort George Pen, Jamaica: Slaves, Tenants and Labourers, 1832–1843," Paper presented to the Eleventh Conference of Caribbean Historians (1979).
Knox, A.J.G. "Race Relations in Jamaica, 1833–1958, with Special Reference to British Colonial Policy" (unpublished Ph.D. thesis, University of Florida, 1962).
Kopytoff, Barbara K. "The Maroons of Jamaica: An Ethnohistorical Study of Incomplete Polities, 1655–1905" (unpublished Ph.D. thesis, University of Pennsylvania, 1973).
Manderson-Jones, Marlene. "Richard Hill of Jamaica, His Life and Times, 1795–1872" (unpublished Ph.D. thesis, University of the West Indies, 1973).
Reckord, Mary. "Missionary Activity in Jamaica Before Emancipation" (unpublished Ph.D. thesis, University of London, 1964).
———. "Missions and Slavery, A Study of Protestant Missions in Jamaica, 1815–1834" (unpublished manuscript).
Sipes, Hiram Hill. "The Free Labor Policy of the British Sugar Colonies, 1834–1865" (unpublished Ph.D. thesis, University of Pennsylvania, 1934).
Tikasingh, Gerad. "A Method of Estimating the Free Coloured Population of Jamaica" (unpublished paper, University of the West Indies, Department of History, [1968]).
Williams, H. E. "The Life and Works of Sir Henry Taylor" (unpublished M.A. thesis, University of London, 1949).
Wilmot, Swithin. "Political Developments in Jamaica in the Post-Emancipation Period, 1838–1854" (unpublished D. Phil. thesis, Oxford University, 1977).

Index

absentee proprietors, 3–4, 84, 110, 148; and abolition of the Assembly, 149, 184; attitude toward coloreds, 11; colored assemblymen complain about, 67; in post-emancipation Jamaica, 76; resolving legislative deadlock in 1853, 155; and retrenchment crisis, 142, 144
agriculture, 111, 143, 165
Allen, William, 34–35
American Civil War: effect on clothing, 171; effect on food, 171, 180–81
Anderson, W. W. 145
Anti-Slavery Society: attitude toward apprenticeship 98; establishment of, 33; for immediate emancipation in 1830, 53 n.40; Kingston Branch of, 145; links and correspondence with leading coloreds, 59–60, 105, 112, 160, 164; pressure for amelioration of slaves, 83; as pressure group to defeat 1859 immigration bill, 164; response to Lecesne and Escoffery, 38–39. See also Lushington, Stephen
apprenticeship system, 18 n.39, 63, 74, 100–102, 108, 110–12, 140; abolition of, 106–7; colored assemblymen seeking to abolish, 106; colored assemblymen seeking to protect apprentice, 105–6; examined by representatives of antislavery societies, 60; explained, 97; opposed by colored assemblymen, 94, 97–98

Assembly, House of: legislation (see *individual subjects*); struggles with British Government, 47, 91–92, 97–113, 124, 136–38, 141–46, 148–50, 153–66, 174–85, 191–94; voting patterns in, 57–58, 62, 97, 100, 105, 144–50, 153–66, 172–75, 177–83, 203–4. *See also* Assemblymen; Colonial Office; Constitution; parties; privileges
Assemblymen, black, 72, 78, 130–31, 156, 179, 194; campaigning for election, 121–22; colored fear of uneducated, 102; in Colored party, 153–54; description and occupations of, 62–63; and Edward Jordon, 122, 159–60, 166–67, 172, 175; as Liberals, 157–60, 162–63, 173; and Morant Bay Rebellion, 191; number of, 64–65, 131, 171, 183, 185 n.5; as part of divided minority, 156; as part of opposition to planter executive committee, 1860–63, 171–73; and the small settler vote, 124; threat posed by, 133; vote in the Assembly, 147, 158, 160
Assemblymen, colored: on apprenticeship, 97–98, 106, 108; attitude toward Lionel Smith, 105–6; attitude toward Lord Sligo, 101–2; in Colored party, 154–56; as conservatives, 66; and constitutional crisis, 1838–39, 108–10; as creoles, 64, 97, 110, 122; and crises over retrenchment and revenue bills, 142–47, 149; description and occupation of, 57–63; divisions among, 100,

About the Author

GAD J. HEUMAN teaches in the Department of History and the School of Comparative American Studies at the University of Warwick, Coventry, England. His articles have appeared in the *Jamaica Journal, The Journal of Imperial and Commonwealth History*, and *The Journal of Caribbean History*.

Contributions in Comparative Colonial Studies
Series Editor: Robin W. Winks

Empires in Collision: Anglo-Burmese Relations in the Mid-Nineteenth Century
Oliver B. Pollak

Social Engineering in the Philippines: The Aims, Execution, and Impact of American Colonial Policy, 1900–1913
Glenn Anthony May

The Politics of Dependency: Urban Reform in Istanbul
Stephen T. Rosenthal

Rhodes, the Tswana, and the British: Colonialism, Collaboration, and Conflict in the Bechuanaland Protectorate, 1885–1899
Paul Maylam